BOWEN

An Unfinished Life

BOWEN

An Unfinished Life

Janice Rustad Lininger

Kari Lininger-Downs

Dedication

THIS BOOK IS DEDICATED to Murrel "M. K." Bowen's beloved wife, Maud, and their seven children: Lois, Mary, Evelyn, Bud, Kay, Ada, and Paul. They endured the tragedy of his murder, then had to learn to live without him. Although those responsible were known, no one was convicted of the crime. In their lifetimes Murrel's family never felt justice.

"Justice consists not in being neutral between right and wrong, but in finding out the right and upholding it, wherever found, against the wrong."

Theodore Roosevelt

Contents

Preface   1

We Begin at the Beginning   4

Call of the West   13

An Iowa Bride   26

Their Adventure Begins   31

Life on the Prairie   37

Building a Legacy   55

Rise of the Nonpartisan League   63

Aggression at the Mallet Ranch   86

July 1919   109

August 1919   135

Fall 1919, Winter 1920   179

The (Eventual) Trial   196

Orphaned, then Dismissed   248

Looking Back, Looking Forward   256

Key Influencers   273

Role of the Press   299

Acknowledgements   322

About the Authors   325

Reference Maps   328

Individual Index   332

Bibliography   346

Preface

AT THE ONSET, WRITING THIS BOOK was well out of our comfort zones, and we questioned whether anyone knows another person well enough to document their story. The more we explored and understood the life of Murrel K. Bowen, however, it became apparent that his journey should be shared.

His story brings to life many of the hallmarks of the transition into the 20th century for our still relatively young country. It was a brackish time where the "Wild West" mixed with elements of advancing modernity; the growing pains were often sharp. Progress often brings heightened emotions and anxiety, differing views and fierce debate, and political turmoil. All of which are part of Murrel's story.

While there are different accounts of the details, it is undisputed that Murrel Bowen was shot and killed on his ranch in the Summer of 1919. His wife, Maud, and five of his small children witnessed four armed men descend on the property and the tragedy that followed. Only one of those four men was tried, none were convicted.

Prior to this unimaginable tragedy, the Bowens had built an enviable life; as early homesteaders in Western North Dakota, they did so of their own tenacity, intelligence, and commitment to their community and one another.

For much of her life Maud refrained from recounting that day and the difficult years that followed. In the final chapter of her long life, however, she slowly began to share those memories. Hours of conversation as well as a taped interview with Maud became the outline for much of this book. Many aspects of it stretch our 21st century imaginations – how could these events have actually happened? The quest for verifying and rounding out the details led us to review old family records, visit courthouses and museums, and read scores of old newspapers.

In the end our goal was to portray Maud's account of these events – this is certainly her story as well.

꘎

We Begin at the Beginning

...OR JUST A BIT EARLIER. Before unfolding the story of Murrel K. Bowen, it's worth noting a bit of broader Bowen family history – they were some of the earliest European immigrants to the United States. Murrel's great-grandfather, Thomas Bowen, arrived from Wales in the 1760s. He soon married, and he and his first wife Nancy Agness settled in Greene County, Pennsylvania, near the West Virginia border. They had seven children together, all but one surviving to adulthood. Thomas was part of this country's fight for independence and served two hitches for the Continental Army during the Revolutionary War.

Sadly, Nancy Agness died in 1791. Thomas soon remarried, to a young widow named Elizabeth "Betty" Spicer. Betty was 29 years old when she and Thomas wed, but she'd already led an incredible life.

The Spicer family had been caught up in the conflicts between early settlers and Native Americans, with a dire outcome. Per family history accounts, *"In other localities disturbances had arisen...and when an Indian was killed his friends would start on a raid...to get revenge. Warnings had been sent to [Betty's father, William] Spicer that the Indians were on the war path and that he should flee to the Forte, but he thought they could do the washing and ironing and go the next day..."* On the fateful day of June 4, 1773, as Betty was helping her mother Lydia with the ironing, their farm was raided.

The invaders arrived as William was chopping wood. Thinking it may be a friendly visit, "...*William stuck his ax in the log and started toward the house to get something for them to eat, when suddenly one of the warriors struck him in the head with the ax.*" They killed Betty's mother next. Betty grabbed her younger brother, William Jr., and ran to find help at a neighboring farm. Although they were quickly captured, their speed impressed the group and their lives were spared. While their parents and siblings were all killed, Betty and William Jr. were instead taken captive. Betty was twelve years old; William was ten.

Betty and her brother "...*were soon adopted by their captives and were loved and carefully taken care of.*" Betty lived with the tribe for 18 months, learning their language and many of their customs, including herbal medicine and the enjoyment of smoking a pipe. As part of a treaty signed in November 1774, the following Christmas Day Betty was released by the tribe and returned to friends in Muddy Creek, a settlement near the Spicer farm. Her brother William stayed with the tribe, however, eventually marrying a Native woman. Betty would return to visit him, sometimes bringing her children. She taught William's wife how to prepare a few of his favorite foods, including cookies, doughnuts, and their traditional Christmas meal of roast turkey. She died at the impressive age of 92, regularly smoking a pipe until her final days.[1]

---

[1] *Spicer Massacre, June 4, 1773*, Dr. Clarence C. Wright

Thomas and Betty had six more children together, including Murrel's grandfather, William, born in 1798. William settled in Marshall County, West Virginia, and had seven children with his first wife, Freelove. Like both of his parents, William was widowed and remarried. He and his second wife, Nancy, had nine more children, including Murrel's father, Brice Buel "B. B." Bowen, born in 1844.

B. B. came of age just as the Civil War began, and he fought for the Union as part of the West Virginia Cavalry. After the war ended, he moved west, as did many other veterans, settling in Harlan, Iowa, near the Nebraska border. Roughly a decade later, in October of 1881, he married Mary Prudence Sewell, daughter of Samuel and Sarah Jane Sewell of Polk, Iowa. Mary was 14 years his junior, the second of six children, and displayed perfectionism often characterized by elder siblings. She was known for keeping a fastidious home, being an excellent cook, and as a stickler for proper manners, even requiring children and grandchildren to pen letters to her in black ink.

B. B. and Mary's marriage record cites his occupation at the time as a livestock dealer. Two years later, they purchased a farm near Irwin, Iowa, about sixteen miles northeast of Harlan, and there they built a successful farming and livestock business. For years B. B. raised cattle for himself as well as friends and neighbors; as the county became more settled, he focused on farming and livestock dealing. In addition to the farm operation, they created a lovely home, with fine furnishings and housewares. In 1902 the Bowens retired and moved back to Harlan, where they continued an active social life, often surrounded by family and friends.

This was the home where Murrel K. Bowen was raised. He was born January 31, 1883, and joined by a sister, Hazel, almost five years later. Murrel and Hazel were brought up with strong Midwestern values: hard work, honesty, education, and a love of country, community, and family. Young Murrel worked side-by-side with his father, who taught him the practical knowledge of running a successful farming operation and raising cattle.

B. B. and Mary ensured both children were well-educated. Hazel graduated from Harlan High School, then attended colleges in Iowa, Minneapolis, and Chicago, receiving degrees and certificates typifying a middle-class young woman of her day. She majored in music, including voice and piano, completed a secretarial course, and studied art and millinery. She was remembered in general as excelling in all subjects, and by her brother as being "very spoiled."

Murrel had somewhat humbler academic beginnings. He graduated from Irwin High School in 1899, at just 16, one of three boys comprising its second-ever graduating class. The following year, he attended the Preparatory Academy in Iowa City, over 200 miles from home. After completing his secondary education, he stayed in Iowa City and enrolled at the State University of Iowa, now known as the University of Iowa. He had developed a love for sports and played football on the university's team.

The next chapter in his academic career was pivotal; after three terms at Iowa, at the strong urging of his mother, he enrolled in medical school in Colorado, likely in Denver. His maternal grandparents, the Sewells, had relocated to Alamosa, Colorado, in 1888. While the distance was considerable, the family had remained close, making it a logical location for continuing his studies.[2]

Murrel's journey to the West had begun.

---

[2] Written accounts by eldest daughter Lois Bowen Beach

Murrel's parents, Brice Buel "B. B." and Mary Prudence Sewell Bowen

Murrel K. "M. K." Bowen,
age 5, 1888

Murrel's younger sister,
Hazel Bowen

M. K. Bowen high school graduation, 1899
Murrel seated at far left

B. B., Mary, M. K., and Hazel Bowen

Murrel K. Bowen

M. K.'s sister, Hazel

B. B. and Mary Bowen's home in Harlan, Iowa

"Pet" piglet descending the front steps

Call of the West

ALTHOUGH IT SERVED AS HIS GATEWAY TO THE WEST, Murrel would not be long for Colorado. Per Maud, he felt guilty that he was "wasting his father's tuition money playing poker and football," so began exploring other endeavors to become more productive and purposeful, at least by his own estimation. He and a classmate and friend from Chicago applied for and were hired for summer jobs as cowhands on the sprawling W-Bar Ranch, one of the largest cattle ranches in the nation.

It's not surprising that Murrel knew of cattle baron Pierre Wibaux and his W-Bar Ranch. Located roughly 13 miles north of what is now the town of Wibaux, Montana, it straddled the state line, the majority lying in North Dakota.

Pierre Wibaux

Throughout the range district of the Northwest, no name is more familiar than that of Pierre Wibaux, the millionaire cattle king of eastern Montana.[3] *At its peak in the 1890s…Wibaux's W-Bar ranch probably owned about 65,000 cattle and 300 saddle horses and employed up to 25 men. The spring roundup lasted three months.*[4]

---

[3] *Montana Homeseeker*, Helena, Montana, September 1906
[4] *The Billings Gazette*, Billings, Montana, May 19, 2002

In those days, North Dakota and Montana were considered part of the "Northwest."

Born to a wealthy family in Roubaix, France, Pierre Wibaux became enamored of the fortunes being made raising cattle on the wide prairies of the United States and decided to try his hand.

> When Pierre announced his plans to his family he met with strong opposition on the part of his father who had hoped that Pierre would take his place, along with his brothers, in conducting the textile business which had been in the hands of the family for over seventy years. After persistent and prolonged pleading the father, in a fit of temper, gave him $10,000 and told him that this sum was the last he would get and that henceforth he would have to shift for himself.[5]

In America he became fast friends with another enterprising Frenchman, Antoine Amedee Marie Vincent Amat Manca de Vallombrosa, more commonly known as the Marquis de Morès.[6]

> ...on his arrival in the United States Wibaux went directly to Chicago, where the meat packing industry was then becoming centered...While in Chicago Wibaux met the Marquis de Morès, also a native of France. The Marquis had been working in his father-in-law's bank in New York City until his imagination caught fire as a result of stories

[5] "Pierre Wibaux, cattle king," Welsh, Donald Hugh, 1950
[6] North Dakota Cowboy Hall of Fame

told him by his cousin, Count Fitz-James, who had hunted in the Bad Lands region. De Morès came to Western North Dakota, founded Medora, the future site of his packing plant, and returned to Chicago. Wibaux accompanied de Morès on the Marquis' return to the Bad Lands in either April or May 1883.[7]

Wibaux reminisced:

When I located on Beaver Creek...the cattle business in this state was then in its infancy. Neighbors were few and far between and we had the whole country to range in. ...we had our ups and downs...[but] I must admit that I had had my share of success... I picked out what I considered at that time the finest natural location for a ranch in all of eastern Montana and since then I have travelled over the northwest a good deal and have never seen a better one.[8]

Wibaux also built a ranch house and grounds befitting the natural surroundings.

[Wibaux's home] is called by the people in this section "The White House," both on account of its color and its majestic dimensions...On the first floor alone there are ten rooms, all large ones. The house is equipped with fire places, bathrooms, plumbing and every convenience of a modern establishment.[9]

---

[7] "Pierre Wibaux, cattle king," Welsh, Donald Hugh, 1950
[8] *Montana Homeseeker*, Helena, Montana, September 1906
[9] *Montana Homeseeker*, Helena, Montana, September 1906

The W-Bar was described as a "little colony," with many outbuildings including the bunkhouse where Murrel likely slept.

> *About 200 yards to the rear [of the "White House"] is the superintendent's home, a large and comfortable ranch house that is more typical of the country than the "White House." Adjoining the superintendent's house are the stables built of stone quarried on the place and decorated with buffalo heads picked up on the bench above the valley. In addition to these houses there is a bunk house, wagon shed, blacksmith shop, stables, granaries, root cellar, corrals and all the other improvements that are necessary to a big ranch. Taken altogether, it forms a little colony that is decidedly picturesque.*[10]

BRANDING YEARLINGS ON THE W BAR RANCH.

Cattle branding, a common job for a ranch hand

---

[10] *Montana Homeseeker*, Helena, Montana, September 1906

Wibaux succeeded due to his good business sense and perseverance when things got tough, which they often did.

> ...Wibaux was an astute rancher who studied the market, tried to find the best type of cattle and put up hay at a time when others depended entirely on the open range.[11]

The Marquis did not fare as well.

The Marquis de Morès

> Although both sons of La Belle France, they were unknown to each other until they met in [America]. In the same year (1883) that Mr. Wibaux settled on Beaver Creek, the Marquis located on the Little Missouri – the next stream to the east of Beaver – and began the unfortunate series of investments that in total closely approached the millions...

> De Morès was a singular character. Brave, chivalric, progressive, but alas, in nothing practical. He was a chevalier of the fifteenth century transplanted into this practical age. Fervent in friendship, but quick to take offense, the ambition that would three hundred years ago have made him a champion of high born dames, was misdirected into the sordid channels of business of this day and generation, and there was but one result possible. For the three or four years of his residence at Medora...he and

---

11 *The Billings Gazette*, Billings, Montana, May 19, 2002

Pierre Wibaux were intimate friends. Young, adventurous and voluntary exiles from a common country, they were naturally drawn together, and though their methods of business were as different as well could be, the friendship existing at a time when – with the marquis at least – the few neighbors were anything but friendly, [it] was a boon to each and fondly cherished…[12]

Along with the Marquis, Wibaux was also neighbors and friends with another cattle rancher of the region – Theodore Roosevelt.

Theodore Roosevelt dressed in buckskin

The next man to settle in the neighborhood was Theodore Roosevelt, then an adventurous young man from the east, who came out to the frontier to win his spurs and regain his health. [Roosevelt's Maltese Cross] ranch is just 15 miles east of the Dakota end of the Wibaux ranch and as distances go out west…that means just next door.[13]

Roosevelt had first come to the area in the fall of 1883 to hunt buffalo and other big game.

While utilizing the ranch [of Gregor Lang, at the mouth of the Little Cannonball Creek, near the scoria hills 50 miles south of Medora] as headquarters for his buffalo hunt, Roosevelt spent several evenings with Lang discussing

---

[12] *Montana Homeseeker*, Helena, Montana, September 1906
[13] *Montana Homeseeker*, Helena, Montana, September 1906

politics and prospects for the cattle industry in the Badlands.[14]

He was enticed enough that before he returned East, he made all the necessary arrangements to become a North Dakota cattle rancher.

Roosevelt fully embraced all aspects of his life in the West, although literally and figuratively worlds away from his privileged upbringing and high society circles of New York. In 1886, he even served as co-captain of the spring roundup, spending some of his time writing and hunting game, which presumably became fodder for the chuckwagon. He also commingled his governing and ranching expertise when elected chairman of the newly formed Little Missouri Stockmen's Association, whose constitution and bylaws he authored.[15]

Although a bespectacled East Coaster of privileged birth, Roosevelt was nobody's fool, as evidenced by his account of a lively night out in Wibaux.

> *"A shabby individual in a broad hat with a cocked gun in each hand was walking up and down the floor talking with strident profanity. As soon as he saw me, he hailed me as 'Four Eyes,' in reference to my spectacles, and said, 'Four Eyes is going to treat,'"* the future president wrote. *"...In response to his reiterated command that I should set up the drinks, I rose, and struck him quick and hard with my right*

---

[14] *Theodore Roosevelt and the Dakota Badlands, 1958*
[15] *Theodore Roosevelt and the Dakota Badlands, 1958*

just to one side of the point of his jaw, hitting with my left as I straightened out, and again with my right. When he went down he struck the corner of the bar with his head and was senseless."[16]

This incident aside, Roosevelt had a healthy respect for the hard-working cowboys in the area, stating:

The cowboys are a much misrepresented set of people. It is a popular impression that when one goes among them he must be prepared to shoot. But this is a false idea. I have taken part with them in the rounding up, have eaten, slept, hunted and herded cattle with them, and have never had any difficulty. If you choose to enter rum shops with them or go on drinking sprees with them it is as easy to get into a difficulty out there as it would be in New York, or anywhere else. But if a man minds his own business and at the same time shows that he is fully prepared to assert his rights – if he is neither a bully nor a coward and keeps out of places in which he has no business to be – he will get along as well as in Fifth Avenue.[17]

Wise words indeed.

I have found them a most brave, and hospitable set of men. There is no use in trying to be overbearing with them for they won't stand the least assumption of superiority, yet

[16] *Great Falls Tribune*, Great Falls, Montana, July 7, 2013
[17] *Theodore Roosevelt and the Dakota Badlands*, 1958

there are many places in our cities where I should feel less
safe than I would among the wildest cowboys of the West.[18]

Wibaux, Roosevelt, and de Morès would have made a colorful trio.

With Wibaux, de Morès and Roosevelt on neighboring
ranches, all young men of indomitable spirit, fond of
athletes, the hunting trail and all college bred, what more
natural that a friendship should spring up between these
three that led them into many adventures together and has
lasted all these years. The three used to attend the "stock
meeting" at Miles City [Montana] together and the
autograph of President Roosevelt is still shown in the old
club register... It was here that...Roosevelt wrote some of
his first stories of the west...about the broad prairies of
Medora and Wibaux and further north in the Band Lands
of the Little Missouri.[19]

Alas, the catastrophic winter of 1886-87 devastated the holdings of both Roosevelt and de Morès. De Morès closed his packing plant for good the following summer, and the burg he had built around it nearly became a ghost town. Roosevelt continued to return to North Dakota, endeavoring to recoup his losses, but ultimately sold his cattle interests in 1898 during the Spanish-American War, shortly before going to Cuba with his "Rough Riders" cavalry unit.[20]

---

[18] *Theodore Roosevelt and the Dakota Badlands*, 1958

[19] *Montana Homeseeker*, Helena, Montana, September 1906

[20] *Theodore Roosevelt and the Dakota Badlands*, 1958

Each of these men created lasting legacies. Although Wibaux began leasing his ranch to other stockmen in about 1904,[21] he remained in the area, and would have a Montana town and county named in his honor; de Morès' wife Medora was the namesake for the North Dakota town where he operated, today a thriving tourist destination and gateway to the Theodore Roosevelt National Park and the North Dakota Badlands. Roosevelt of course would become the 26th president of the United States, championing conservation causes that were heavily informed and influenced by his time in the West. Though Roosevelt and de Morès had left the area by the time Murrel came to the W-Bar, according to Maud, the stories of these great men lived on to impress the young medical student-turned-cowhand.

What was possibly meant to be a brief diversion from the regimented path of medicine became his life's work. Murrel quit medical school and followed in his father's footsteps, filing a claim under the Homestead Act to acquire 160 acres of land in what is now Golden Valley County, North Dakota.

> The Homestead Law was a series of enactments beginning with the Act of May 20, 1862 which provided for the disposition of the public lands to settlers without requiring any compensation except the acts of residence, cultivation and improvement... Under the Homestead Law, the applicant was limited to 160 acres and had to reside upon the land and make it his home...for five years.[22]

---

[21] *Montana Homeseeker*, Helena, Montana, September 1906
[22] State Historical Society of North Dakota

He was hardly alone. During those years thousands of homesteaders arrived in the region, hoping to make their fortunes on the rich prairies in the West.

> *The growing of wheat in large quantities demands of the soil certain salts: potash, nitrates, and so on. When the white man came to it the whole Northwestern country beyond the Mississippi and east of the Rockies was a vast, treeless, and almost level plain. For centuries and up to sixty or seventy years ago this plain was swept in the autumn with fires that turned the dried prairie grasses into ashes.*

> *These ashes, accumulating, year after year, made a black loam, thick, rich, and full of the salts required for wheat-raising. The Dakotas...being chiefly prairie, stored the richest of these deposits.*[23]

Murrel's claim was in the northwest corner of Bull Run Township, in Section 8, near the Montana border, roughly 40 miles from the W-Bar. He filed and registered the claim at the land office in Dickinson, North Dakota, for a fee of $14.

His ambition to become a landowner and lead the kind of independent, entrepreneurial, adventurous life epitomized by Wibaux, Roosevelt, and de Morès was becoming a reality. He now had a 160-acre blank canvas of unbroken land on which to build his future.

---

[23] *The Story of the Nonpartisan League*, May 1920

The Chateau de Morès in Medora, North Dakota, along the Little Missouri River in the North Dakota Badlands

～

An Iowa Bride

MURREL RETURNED TO IOWA for a short time to earn seed money and secure the necessary supplies to establish his homestead. It was then that he made another life-changing decision – to marry Maud Plummer.

Born February 18, 1888, five years Murrel's junior, Maud was a pretty, petite young woman with soft features and a "glorious wealth of red gold hair." She was independent, resourceful, courageous, and hard-working, characteristics evident even in her youth.

> In 1863 William Taylor and Harriet Plummer took up a homestead in Shelby County, Iowa. They wanted to make a home for themselves and farm land of their own. I, Maud, was born there on February 18, 1888. I grew up on the farm and attended elementary school near home. After finishing my high school education at Harlan, Iowa, I taught at country school.[24]

Unlike Murrel, she was from a large family, the ninth of eleven children born to William Taylor and Harriet "Hattie" Beems Plummer. Along with their own eleven children, the Plummers raised three grandchildren: Lois, daughter of Maud's sister Jennie, as well as Maxine and Vern, children of her brother Joseph. William Taylor was a successful farmer in Jackson Township, providing a comfortable living for their large family. Land he originally bought for $10 an

---

[24] *O'Fallon Flashbacks*, O'Fallon Historical Society, Baker, Montana, 1975

acre sold for $150 to $200 an acre when he died. He and Hattie were able to retire in 1902, then moved to Harlan.

Maud was very musical; she played the piano by ear and sang for events at church. She enjoyed crocheting, quilting, and sewing; family members still treasure Maud's crocheted afghans and handmade quilts.

With both the Bowens and Plummers then living in Harlan, Murrel and Maud soon became acquainted. He had actually been engaged to another woman he'd met in North Dakota. Either before or after Maud caught his eye, that engagement was broken, and he proposed to his Iowa sweetheart. Maud said she "was sure glad he chose her."

They were married November 28, 1907, by the pastor of the United Brethren Church, at either the United Brethren Parsonage in Irwin (according to their formal invitation), or the home of Maud's brother, Lee Plummer (per their marriage record). Given it was late November in the Midwest, Mother Nature may have changed their plans.

From early photos, Murrel had grown into a handsome young man, with dark hair, a broad face, cleft chin, and lively eyes. He had an earnest, confident look about him. The two made a handsome couple as well as a compatible one.

Soon after their wedding, the newlyweds gathered the necessities for their life as homesteaders and headed for North Dakota.

The Plummer Family
Back: Charles, Joe, Lee
Middle: Jennie, William Taylor, Hattie, Mary
Front: Daisy, Everett, Maud

Maud Plummer Bowen with sister-in-law Hazel Bowen

Maud Plummer Bowen

Their Adventure Begins

IF ANY DOUBT EXISTED THAT MAUD'S COURAGE matched Murrel's, imagine that she was only 19, likely hadn't traveled far from home, and was starting a new life with a new husband as a homesteader in Western North Dakota, nearly 800 miles from her family.

> *In 1907, when I was nineteen years old, I married Murrel Bowen at Irwin, Iowa and in 1908 we came to Beach, North Dakota on the Northern Pacific Railroad. We took up a homestead in the Golden Valley area of North Dakota close to the Montana border.[25]*

> *To the west there is a great expanse of fertile luxuriantly grassed rolling land ideal for cattle raising where the only break is the division line between Montana and North Dakota. Carlyle and Ollie, Mont., Golva and Beach, N. D. have risen from the foundational success of the ranchers. To this land of success came M. K. Bowen from Iowa.[26]*

The newlyweds traveled via an "immigrant train" on the Northern Pacific Railroad, headed for Wibaux, Montana. Homesteading generated multiple revenue streams for railroad companies, and they promoted it vigorously. Settlers shipped their household goods and farm machinery to their new homes in rented box cars, and once they were established, also shipped their grain, cattle, and other products by rail to markets in St. Paul or Chicago.

---

[25] *O'Fallon Flashbacks*, O'Fallon Historical Society, Baker, Montana, 1975
[26] *The Bismarck Tribune*, Bismarck, North Dakota, August 6, 1919

While Murrel and Maud rode in the passenger car, their personal belongings, including Maud's piano, Murrel's horse and saddle, a team of work horses, a wagon and plow, a milk cow, some household items, and a variety of tools, were shipped in a separate rented box car at the cost of $100, roughly $3,400 today.

An immigrant train had both passenger cars and boxcars. The passenger cars were very plain with wooden benches as seats. The cars were crowded, stuffy, and uncomfortable. Coal-burning stoves were used to heat the cars. By the time the passengers reached their destinations, they were covered with soot from the burning coal.

At the railroad yards in St. Paul, hundreds of immigrant cars waited to carry homesteaders to North Dakota. The immigrant trains transported not only immigrants but also people from other states who were headed for North Dakota to file homestead claims or purchase land. The trains filled up quickly, and many of the passengers had to stand or sit on the floor.

Boxcars on the immigrant trains could be rented by families to transport their belongings. Some people brought farm animals, plows and other farm implements, furniture, and household items. Others traveled lightly, intending to buy their materials in a town near their claim.

All food needed on the trip for both the settlers and their animals had to be brought along on the train. Sometimes a family set up a cookstove in their immigrant car so that they could bake bread and prepare meals.

The homesteaders traveled as far as they could on the train and then figured out how to get to their claim from the train stop. If they had wagons and horses with them, they could drive. Some towns had livery stables where horses and carriages could be rented. If settlers had no means of transportation from the train stop to their claim, they had to walk, often many miles.[27]

Upon arriving in Wibaux, the Bowens focused on "proving up" their 160-acre homestead plot, 35 miles to the south-southeast. It was truly au naturel, a swath of prairieland without any semblance of infrastructure. Likely owing to the relationships Murrel had formed before returning to Iowa, he and Maud were offered interim accommodations in a sod house on the property of a neighbor, Mr. William Watson.

This was no doubt a significant benefit, but spending their first months together in a sod home on the windswept North Dakota prairie would have been challenging under the best circumstances. Building a house was a top priority. Using their wagon and team of horses, lumber was hauled from Beach, North Dakota, 21 miles away, a round trip that would have taken at least two days. They procured sufficient supplies to build a house and some outbuildings, including an outdoor privy.

---

[27] State Historical Society of North Dakota

In exchange for land ownership, the basic requirements for homesteading were to build a 12-by-14-foot house, cultivate the land, and live continuously on it for at least five years. By the spring of 1908, within six months of their wedding in Iowa, the Bowens were set up, settled, and ready to embark on their adventure as homesteaders.

It is of note that several of Maud's family members would follow the Bowens to the area, both before and after Murrel's death, including her brothers Lee and Everett, her sister Jennie's daughter Lois, and her sister Mary's sons, William and John Westrope.

BIRD'S EYE VIEW OF BEACH, N. DAK.

× cafe

Beach, ND 1910

The Bowens' original 1908 homestead on Section 8, Bull Run Township
Maud on horseback, Maud's niece Lois Epley, neighbor Charles Woodsend,
and Murrel

The Bowens' original homestead, used to raise winter feed after
their move to the Mallet Ranch
Photo taken in 1917

Life on the Prairie

MURREL AND MAUD BUILT A HAPPY AND PROSPEROUS LIFE for themselves and their growing family. During their ten years on the original homestead land, they had five children – daughter Lois Regene, born March 1, 1909; daughter Mary Elizabeth, born August 17, 1910; daughter Evelyn Maud "Happy," born January 3, 1912; son Bryce Buel "Bud," born June 9, 1913; and son Murrel K. Jr. "Kay," born June 11, 1916. After moving to the Mallet Ranch in 1916, they welcomed another daughter, Ada Jeanette, on February 25, 1918. Their youngest son, Paul Bernard, was born on their land in Montana after Murrel was killed, arriving January 13, 1920.

Life on the prairie was, to say the least, active. The Bowens were committed to developing their new community as well as their own property. When they first arrived, there were no roads, fences, or telephones. As more settlers came, roads –akin to primitive trails – were built. Fences were put up to keep a rancher's cattle on their land, and their neighbors' cattle off of it. A telephone line was extended from Carlyle, Montana. This early telephone was a party line, meaning everyone on the line could hear their neighbors' conversations. Any news spread quickly; listening to one's neighbors over the phone line was called "rubbernecking."

Two early household purchases were an iron cook stove and a treadle sewing machine. The stove heated their home during harsh winters and was well-used for Maud's cooking; one of her specialties was chicken with homemade noodles. The stove also heated the flat irons used for ironing clothes and linens; they had detachable handles and required reheating on the stovetop every ten minutes. To fuel the stove, Murrel mined lignite coal in the badlands or made trips to the Lindstrom mine northeast of Carlyle. Either option required a high degree of effort; the coal needed to be broken up with a pickaxe before it could be transported. In later years, it could be purchased from local businesses, such as Logan's Garage in Beach, or from J. P. Grimm, proprietor of the Sentinel Butte Coal Mine, who would even deliver it.

> We used lignite coal for most of our fuel. Beach, North Dakota was our shopping center as the towns of Carlyle and Ollie, Montana hadn't been started yet. In the fall we would go 21 miles to Beach and get a supply of things to do us through the winter. Some of the winters were good, some long and some bad.[28]

The foot pedal-operated treadle sewing machine was another necessity, as Maud made most of the children's clothing. Commercial patterns were a luxury, but she adeptly made her own patterns out of newspapers. Electricity was a pipe dream, as it did not reach rural North Dakota until the late 1930s; kerosene lamps and lanterns were used to light their home.

The Bowens produced most of their own food; purchased groceries were limited to staples such as sugar and flour.

---

[28] *O'Fallon Flashbacks*, O'Fallon Historical Society, Baker, Montana, 1975

Their dairy cows provided milk, cream, and butter; they raised meat to can or cure; their chickens provided eggs. They planted a large garden and grew a good quantity and variety of vegetables, including carrots, green beans, peas, tomatoes, cabbage, onions, potatoes, and turnips. Strawberries were planted to be eaten fresh during the season and made into jam to enjoy the rest of the year. They dug their own root cellar to store hearty vegetables and canned preserves.

Maud and Murrel equally shared child rearing as well as farming and ranching duties, although both preferred working outdoors. They often played cards to determine who would work outside. Maud said she once caught Murrel cheating, and in jest declared a forfeiture and burned the cards. That only put a short stay on the games, however; soon there was another deck.

As both their family and farming operation grew, they were able to hire outside help. Murrel thought a "hired girl" was necessary to help with cooking and cleaning; while Maud was considerably less fastidious, Murrel ...*couldn't stand things dirty...Mother always had a hired girl to do the housework and cooking.*[29]

The job of a "hired girl" in the early 1900s was much like an apprenticeship and provided practical experience in managing a home. Duties included cooking, washing dishes, caring for young children, carrying water from the well, and

---

[29] Written accounts by eldest daughter Lois Bowen Beach

washing clothes. Most girls "hired out" at the age of 16; they received room, board, and a modest salary. The Bowens also employed farm hands to assist with planting, tending, and harvesting crops and caring for the cattle herd.

These individuals were often like extended family – one of the young women, Ada Olreigh, may have been the namesake for the Bowens' youngest daughter. One of the ranch hands, Carl Thompson, became a great friend and stayed with the Bowens for many years. Not everyone was so loyal, however.

> *M. K. Bowen was among the business visitors in the city during the week. On coming to the city he stationed his car in front of Frank Essene's cafe. While at dinner a thief made away with his coat. It is thought that one of the farm hands who came in with him waited until Bowen went to dinner and then made away with the valuable garment, afterward catching a passing freight train that was leaving the city.*[30]

Their activities didn't revolve solely around the farm; the Bowens also had an active social life. They regularly attended community events in the nearby town of Ollie, Montana, and further afield in Beach. A family favorite was going to the circus. The Bowens' eldest daughter Lois fondly recalled…

> *…her father taking the family to Beach to see the Barnum and Bailey Circus. "We would get up real early in the*

---

[30] *Golden Valley Chronicle*, Beach, North Dakota, October 22, 1915

morning and mother would dress us in fancy, lacy, white dresses. Of course, girls never wore slacks at that time. It was 20 miles or more to Beach with a team and buggy and by the time we arrived, we would be all gritty and dirty. There would be buggies and wagon loads of people coming to the circus. Dust would be flying." Lois paused to laugh as she recalled this vision. "When we got to the circus, it was really a thrill. Then the families would get rooms at the Lewis Rooming House and stay one night and sometimes two."[31]

Murrel would surprise the family and announce they were going to the circus just a day before the event, giving Maud short notice to get the children ready, which often included sewing new garments. She didn't seem to mind, though, and worked best at the last minute.

Odd Fellows emblem, signifying Friendship, Love, Truth; Murrel often wore his Odd Fellows badge

The Odd Fellows Lodge in Ollie, of which Murrel was an active member, sponsored a host of social activities, including picnics, card parties, dances, and "moving pictures." They also organized a baseball team.

One of the primary purposes of [the Odd Fellows] is to develop life-lasting friendships among people. In connection to this, many lodges also organize social activities where members can enjoy each other's company. The first [Odd Fellows] lodges were set up to protect and care for their members and communities at a time when

---

[31] *Fallon County Times*, Baker, Montana, May 19, 1994

there was still no welfare state, trade unions or national health insurance. The aim was and still is to provide help to people and communities in times of need.[32]

Some of the Odd Fellows' most memorable events were "jackrabbit roundups." Rabbits bred in vast numbers on the prairie, running in packs of up to twenty, and were a nuisance to homesteaders – and their gardens. To control the population, and for entertainment, the Lodge sponsored regular roundups. The event started at daylight and lasted until about nine o'clock in the evening. Participants were divided into two teams; the team that nabbed the most rabbits was treated to an oyster supper by the losers. The rabbit hides were sold in Beach.

The Bowens loved dancing and regularly attended community dances; popular moves of the day included the two-step, schottische, polka, and waltz. Dances were held in schoolhouses, barns, the Odd Fellows Lodge, or private homes. Both young and old attended; babysitters were not part of homesteading life, so children went along. This was a special treat for the Bowen girls, as Murrel often danced with his daughters. During community dances, the women prepared and served a midnight supper, after which children bedded down, but many adults danced long into the night.

Rodeos and basket socials were also held in Ollie. Wild horses were rounded up in the badlands and sold to rodeo

---

[32] International Order of Odd Fellows

organizers; fresh wild horses drew large crowds and provided plenty of excitement. During basket socials, participating ladies brought a "basket" made from a shoe box decorated with tissue or crepe paper, filled with a picnic lunch. Men bid on the baskets, with proceeds donated to community projects, then share its contents with the basket maker. While that lady's identity was intended to be a secret, it was often a badly kept one.

Murrel was a lifelong sports fan; while there were no local football teams, he enjoyed the rodeos and took the family to many baseball games in Beach. Ever an avid card-player, he continued playing poker long past his medical school days.[33]

Christmas was a special time for the Bowens. Murrel cut their Christmas tree in the badlands, which Maud and the children strung with popcorn and cranberry garland. Some of the presents under the tree were homemade, while others were ordered from the Sears, Roebuck, and Co. catalog. Maud made dolls from purchased porcelain heads and handmade cloth bodies, a craft she had learned from her mother.

Mary Sewell Bowen's appreciation for "fine things" was apparently inherited by her son.

> *Dad loved the west, his favorite pictures were "Charlie Russell" paintings, of which he had several. He liked nice things and always bought Mother and us kids nice gifts*

---

[33] Written accounts by eldest daughter Lois Bowen Beach

when he'd go to St. Paul or Chicago with a shipment of cattle.[34]

He once brought home a new Victrola phonograph, record stand, and several records. The whole family stayed up most of the night dancing and listening to the records. One might say Murrel was a romantic.

> *He loved music, and always was bringing home new records for the Victrola phonograph. Some of his most favorite songs were by Harry Lauder, the [Scottish] tenor. Some of them were: "Let's Go Out to the Ball Game," "Coon Hunting," and "Let Me Call You Sweetheart."*[35]

During another trip he bought Maud a china cabinet and new set of dishes; while Maud loved cooking and entertaining, a biproduct she didn't care for was dishwashing. That was a chore the children learned early.

When Murrel was away on his business trips, he often wrote letters home; daughter Lois treasured this note from 1917:

---

[34] Written accounts by eldest daughter Lois Bowen Beach
[35] Written accounts by eldest daughter Lois Bowen Beach

Harlan, Iowa
Nov. 19, 1917
Miss Lois Bowen
Ollie, Mont.

Dear Daughter — Pa has
arrived at grandpas and am
sure tired have been on the go
steady since I left home. How
are you getting along at
school and how about that
arithmetic. Has Mary passed
you yet I think she will before
I get back. Glad you had a
good social and did well with
your speaking. Be good and
I'll see maybe I can find some
furs. I saw some dandy ones
in St. Paul last night.

From Dad

During their first years in North Dakota, the Bowens relied on horses for transportation. A team pulled their buggy in warm weather, in winter, they were hitched to a sled. The gumbo roads of the area could be problematic for both wagon wheels and horse hooves; gumbo is a dense, clay-like soil that becomes very slippery when wet.

Maud said she first rode in an automobile in 1908, during a Fourth of July celebration with friends, but the Bowens didn't purchase their own until several years later. North Dakota had passed the first state traffic in 1905; the speed limit was set at 8 miles per hour in towns, 25 miles per hour in the country. With gumbo roads making driving difficult, the horse and buggy may have been just as fast.[36] Gasoline for the car was purchased at grocery stores for twelve cents a gallon; there were no standalone gas stations.

> *I remember when he came home in the first car, a second hand Buick, bought from Olie Attleweed, Beach, and had Mother and the hired girl, Ada Olreigh, learn to drive it. Later years he was a Ford man (Model Ts and As).*[37]

It's questionable whether Maud succeeded with her driving lessons. She drove many miles during her lifetime and never had an accident, but not because she was considered by her family to be a good driver.

Murrel and Maud were active in nearby communities. Murrel served on school and township boards, and they were both involved in building schools in Bull Run Township. Maud served as the township clerk and managed contractor bids for schoolhouse construction[38]; Murrel hauled the lumber from Beach.[39] They were members of the United Brethren Church in Ollie; Maud formed a ladies' quartet and sang for church events.

By all accounts, Murrel and Maud were true partners in life, complementing and contrasting one another. Murrel was raised in a small family, Maud in a more raucous home alongside ten siblings and three nieces and nephews. Murrel

---

[36] State Historical Society of North Dakota

[37] Written accounts by eldest daughter Lois Bowen Beach

[38] *Golden Valley Chronicle*, Beach, North Dakota, August 14, 1914

[39] *Golden Valley Chronicle*, Beach, North Dakota, August 21, 1914

put a greater value on "refinement" and had more formal education, Maud was not materialistic and preferred informality. Both were fun-loving, adventuresome, intelligent individuals who agreed on the most important things in life: love of family, the value of good friends, hard work, fair play, being active in the community, and being true to their beliefs.

The Bowen family circa 1910
M. K., Maud, Lois, and baby Mary

The Bowen family circa 1914-15 — M. K., Maud, Lois (standing in back), Mary (sitting in front), Evelyn (standing on chair), and Bryce Buel "Bud" Bowen, born June 9, 1913 (seated at center)

Lois Regene Bowen, born March 1, 1909

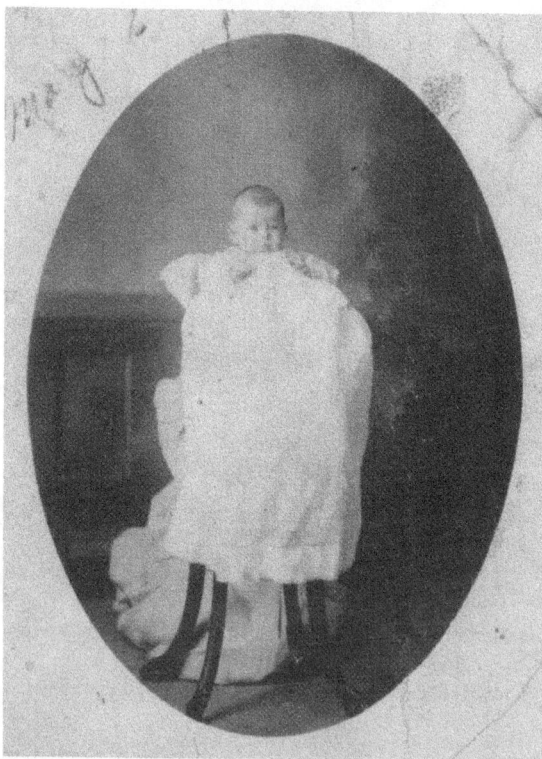

Mary Elizabeth Bowen, born August 17, 1910

Evelyn Maud "Happy" Bowen, born January 3, 1912

The Bowen family on a bright winter's day — M. K., Maud, Lois, Mary, Evelyn, Bud

Murrel K. "Kay" Bowen, Jr., born June 11, 1916
Playing with the well at the Mallet Ranch, with the "big barn" in the distance

Lois and Bud Bowen playing at the Mallet Ranch, 1918

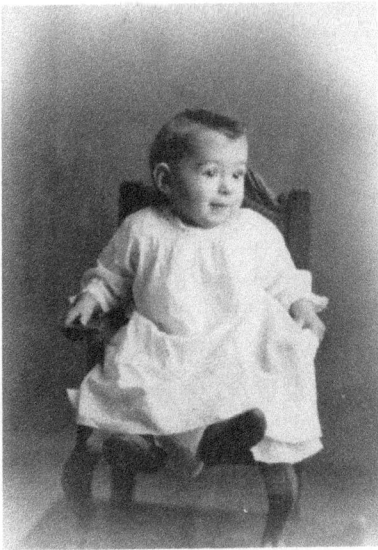

Ada Jeanette Bowen, born February 25, 1918, at the Mallet Ranch

Paul Bernard Bowen, born January 13, 1920, in Montana

Building a Legacy

WHILE THE BOWENS BEGAN with a standard 160-acre homestead claim in 1908, their holdings and fortunes soon grew. Murrel was ambitious, and expanded their property to several thousand acres, making the Bowens the largest landowners in Bull Run Township at the time. Like Pierre Wibaux, Murrel purchased livestock best suited for the prairie grassland and harsh winter conditions, resulting in fewer losses. He eventually amassed a herd of over 300 prime grade cattle.

As written by his good friend Martin Blank, editor of the *Golden Valley Progress*:

> *He was an industrious man and by dint of hard labor was not long in enlarging, taking over a ranch in the community, stocking it with cattle and as his herd grew later leased some school sections. In less than ten years after he had come to the valley, MK Bowen commanded thousands of acres of the best pasture land in the county and owned three hundred head of good grade cattle.[40]*

Per accounts in the *Golden Valley Chronicle*, by 1916 Murrel was regarded as a "big" and "prosperous" farmer:

> *M. K. Bowen, the big farmer of the Ollie country, was transacting business in the city Wednesday of this week.[41]*

---

[40] *Golden Valley Progress*, Beach, North Dakota, August 8, 1919
[41] *Golden Valley Chronicle*, Beach, North Dakota, February 18, 1916

M. K. Bowen, a prosperous farmer of the Ollie neighborhood, was a Beach visitor during the week. He shipped in a car of additional stock for his farm. Mr. Bowen is some stock farmer.[42]

Murrel also raised both wheat and flax, but he favored flax, which garnered the highest price among typical crops by a wide margin. Per Maud, it was one of the first crops they planted, although that very first crop was short-lived.

We broke the sod and planted our first crop of flax. It was doing fine until a hailstorm took it.[43]

In addition to his farming and ranching business, Murrel purchased a grain threshing machine and a steam engine and did custom threshing and sod-breaking work for friends and neighbors.

Instead of investing in their own equipment for threshing, a process that also required as many as ten extra workers, most farmers hired threshing crews. Before threshing began, grain had to be cut, bundled, and shocked, then stacked in hayracks which were transported to the threshing machine. The machine separated grain kernels from the stalks. Grain was put into wagons and hauled to market, and stalks were saved for bedding down cattle the following winter. This process usually took two days per farm and could continue as late as November.

---

[42] *Golden Valley Chronicle*, Beach, North Dakota, March 31, 1916
[43] *O'Fallon Flashbacks*, O'Fallon Historical Society, Baker, Montana, 1975

Men may have worked hard in the field, but women had to feed the ravenous threshing crew. That meant five meals every day: 5:00 a.m. breakfast, including bacon, potatoes, pancakes, bread, butter, and coffee; morning lunch at 9:30 a.m., with coffee, meat sandwiches, and a dessert of cake or cookies; main lunch at noon, with meat, potatoes, vegetables, dessert, and coffee; afternoon lunch at 3:30 p.m., with sandwiches and coffee; and evening supper at 7:00 p.m., with a similar menu as the main lunch. The three main meals were served in the farmhouse, but morning and afternoon lunches were taken to the field. Threshing crew fare was somewhat of a competition; if meals were skimpy, the crew gossiped about it to the next farmer's wife.

Sod-breaking was another successful venture for the Bowens, and their rig broke up many acres in the neighborhood. During early homesteading years, breaking the sod was a vital first step, enabling the claimant to start improving the land as soon as possible. Breaking sod with a horse-drawn plow was long and tedious work, but Murrel's steam engine pulled an eight-bottom plow, able to break up to 15 acres a day, at a charge of $3 an acre.

The Bowens had enjoyed nearly ten happy years on their original homestead land, but in the summer of 1916, they bought another large parcel in Golden Valley County, known as the Mallet Ranch, and relocated the family there. Previously owned by Dr. O. A. Niece, a dentist from Beach, the ranch was located on Section 10, two miles east of their original homestead.

The ranch contained a valuable spring-fed lake known as "Teddy's Lake," one of several reasons it was ideal for raising cattle. Per Maud, the lake was named after Theodore Roosevelt, who had visited the Mallets on numerous occasions when they owned the ranch in the late 1800s. Its buildings were also strategically situated.

> The hilly road to the ranch, which lies 22 miles south of Beach, emerges on the top of a butte. There in the valley, sheltered on the north by the high rim of a semicircular butte, lies his ranch house, barn and out buildings. It nestles in the coulee, a perfect picture of all that a farm home should be.[44]

Murrel also leased several school sections; with the expanded land holdings, he did not delay in similarly growing his herd.

> M.K. Bowen returned the first of the week from a several week's business trip through South Dakota, Minnesota, and Iowa. While away he purchased three carloads of cattle with which he will stock the Mallet ranch near Carlyle which he purchased last summer. Mr. Bowen is one of the most enterprising farmers of the Carlyle country and realizes the expediency of going into diversified farming.[45]

While the Bowen family's move to the Mallet Ranch appeared to be a hallmark of their success, it brought about

---

[44] *Golden Valley Progress*, Beach, North Dakota, August 8, 1919
[45] *Golden Valley Chronicle*, Beach, North Dakota, December 1, 1916

a series of tragic events that forever changed their livelihood – and lives.

The Mallet Ranch

M. K. Bowen's threshing crew

M. K. Bowen sod breaking crew
Murrel is likely in the brimmed hat, which he often wore

Murrel holding daughter Lois on his steam engine

Harvesting west of Hartse School, north of Hammervolds, Carlyle

Rise of the Nonpartisan League

IN ORDER TO CONVEY THE EVENTS surrounding Murrel Bowen's death, describing the political climate and social tensions underway, particularly the rise of the Nonpartisan League, is fundamental.

Murrel's formative and adult years largely overlap with the Progressive Era – a period from the 1890s to the late 1910s characterized by widespread social activism and political reform, focused on defeating corruption and monopoly. Rebellion and revolution were rife. Labor strikes, often resulting in loss of life, were on the rise, from miners and factory workers to railroad workers and police officers.

A long list of seminal events in American and world history transpired during these decades. Reformer Jane Addams established Hull House in Chicago in 1889 to provide social services to immigrants and other disenfranchised groups. Upon the assassination of President McKinley in 1901, Vice President Theodore Roosevelt took office with hopes to reform several arenas of society. In 1904, "muckraker" Ida Tarbell published her collection of articles describing corruption of the Standard Oil Company. In 1906, Upton Sinclair published *The Jungle*, based on his investigation into the labor conditions of Chicago's meat slaughterhouses and packaging plants. In 1911, the tragic Triangle Shirtwaist Factory fire in New York City took 146 lives, mostly young immigrant women. The Bolshevik Revolution in 1917 led to the assassination of the last imperial tsars of Russia the following year.

Pushes for reform were not limited to urban centers. They also extended into rural America, and North Dakota was at the epicenter of reforms to address the hardships of homesteaders, farmers, and ranchers.

Although land procured under the Homestead Act was effectively free, establishing an operation to make a living on it was quite the opposite. What little money homesteaders may have had upon arrival in the West was quickly depleted by purchasing horses, equipment, and other necessities to produce and sell their first harvest. They also had to buy materials to build a home and a barn, as well as any food not grown themselves. Loans to cover those expenses were commonplace – loans that carried a minimum legal interest rate of 10 percent, often higher.

> ...in 1913 a bill was introduced...to bring down the legal rate of interest... [to] 10 per cent, but the law was so adroitly worded that loans were still made at 12, 14, and even higher rates. The redress of a borrower [was] a suit to recover. But the suit must be brought usually against the local bank to whose favor the farmer must look for his other money advances and to which he must go to get his cash when he had sold his wheat.

> ...[the] National Comptroller of the Currency...reported that he found 69 of the 150 national banks in North Dakota to be charging 12 per cent or more on their farm loans. "About a dozen banks in North Dakota," he said, "reported loans aggregating from $1,000 to $8,000 at rates

ranging from 15 to 24 per cent," and…in some instances from 28 to 48 per cent was charged for small loans.[46]

Once they put blood, sweat, and toil into producing a successful harvest, a complex and often corrupt value chain sought to extract as much monetary benefit as possible, a fraction going back into the hands of the farmer.

> *…the plain straight road from farmside to dinner-plate [was lined] with strange devices for taking toll as the wheat went along. Commission men in the market centers juggled it back and forth; "mixing houses" played tricks with it; upon vast complicated machines like gigantic wheels of fortune men gambled in it; railroads levied on it excessive charges for transporting it; a line of middlemen passed it superfluously one to another, each taking a heaping handful as it pursued the tortuous path prepared for it – until at last, a mere spector of the portly bushel it had started, it came to table. "The farmer raised a bushel and got paid for a peck; the consumer received a peck and paid for a bushel."*[47]

Some of the primary culprits were grain elevators, which often assigned a lower grade to grain when it was purchased compared to when the same grain was sold to mills.

> *…the wheat that comes out of the terminal elevator, that goes from the terminal elevator to the miller down the*

---

[46] *The Story of the Nonpartisan League*, Charles Edward Russell, May 1920
[47] *The Story of the Nonpartisan League*, Charles Edward Russell, May 1920

river, is not the kind of wheat that goes into the elevator from North Dakota. It is depreciated and doctored wheat.

...we turn to the records of the terminal elevators or "mixing-houses" of Minneapolis in search of possible information and this is what we find:

In two years these elevators received 15,571,575 bushels of No. 1 Northern wheat, and shipped out in the same two years 19,978,777 bushels of that same grade. That is to say, they shipped 4,407,202 bushels more of No. 1 Northern than they received. At the beginning of the two years they had no No. 1 Northern, so the excess cannot be accounted for on the theory that it was wheat left over. Where did it come from? Wheat is not ordinarily planted and reaped in elevator bins.

"Of course, it isn't exactly on the square," grain-dealers have said to me... "but that is what everybody does and always has done, and you couldn't change it."

If the farmer could have had this value it would have changed for him the raising of wheat from an unprofitable to a profitable business. But the farmer did not get this value. The owners of the elevators got it and the spreading knowledge of that fact could result only in added bitterness in the farmer's mind. For he had raised that wheat, it was the product of his toil and his hard-won acres; and no sophistries could obscure the fact that if it was No. 1 when it came out of the elevator, it was No. 1 when it went in. Yet he had not been paid for No. 1; he had been paid for

Rejected or No Grade, away down at the foot of the market list.[48]

In bitter irony, the seed a farmer purchased to plant the following spring's crop often had to be procured from the same large grain companies.

But this was only the beginning of the Northwestern farmer's evil lot. It must be apparent from what has gone before that this farmer must sell his product to a great and wonderful organization designed to make his selling price low and equipped with almost unlimited power to that end; and he must buy whatever he bought from great and wonderful organizations designed to make his buying price high and equipped with almost unlimited power to that end. A farmer confronted with these vast forces was in a state so utterly impotent that he seemed like a figure of fun. A straw in a cyclone, a cockle-shell in a tidal wave, a leaf tossed over Niagara would have as much chance.

To think of combating this condition by forming a third party was idle dreaming...it was a fiction that North Dakota or any other state or the United States was governed by a party. The party was only a name. State and country were governed by influences that combined back of the parties, so that no matter which party might win at the polls the real power lay in that party control. In North

---

[48] *The Story of the Nonpartisan League,* Charles Edward Russell, May 1920

Dakota the railroads, the elevator companies, the millers, and the banks had exercised that control...[49]

It was against these forces that A. C. Townley, a bankrupt flax farmer from Golden Valley County by way of Minnesota, aimed to rally the farmers of North Dakota.

A. C. Townley

...Arthur C. Townley was born and raised on a farm in Minnesota and was a voracious reader on topics like politics and economics.

After teaching, Townley began a thriving farming operation in Golden Valley County, North Dakota, in 1907. He soon switched to flax and borrowed heavily for farm equipment. Unfortunately, an early frost in 1912 wiped out his business, sending him into bankruptcy.

In part, the experience caused Townley to turn to socialism. In November 1913, the Socialist party of North Dakota recognized his talents and hired him as an organizer in the western counties.

The Socialist party began in North Dakota in 1900, and many Norwegian immigrants leaned toward it...Townley began organizing [for the Socialist party] in late 1913. Recognizing that farmers liked the platform but not the

---

[49] *The Story of the Nonpartisan League,* Charles Edward Russell, May 1920

party, he realized that the organizers needed to place less emphasis on the party and more on reforms.[50]

For more than a year the bankrupted Townley moved about North Dakota, turning these things over in his mind and talking with farmers about them…Much of his traveling was done on foot, he being too poor to proceed otherwise. On some days he walked thirty miles, for he is a lithe, spare man, all muscle and endurance. As he walked and talked a new agrarian movement took shape in his mind.

The state is in area one of the largest in the Union, and compared with some others is sparsely settled. To attempt to organize it was appalling. The farmers had been approached (and stung) by so many plausible and talented persons with grand schemes…that they had come to look upon every stranger that came into the barnyard as a probably bunco man.[51]

That same year, frustrated that a long promised state owned elevator had yet to be established, a group of farmers came to Bismarck, the state capital, and began to discuss the idea of a nonpartisan party focused on their interests.

…Governor [Louis] Hanna had campaigned on the promise of a state-owned elevator, but once elected, Hanna took no action to fulfill that promise. Farmers were tired of waiting. They believed the time was right for action. In 1915, when the North Dakota chapter of the American

---

[50] Prairie Public Newsroom, May 17, 2022
[51] *The Story of the Nonpartisan League,* Charles Edward Russell, May 1920

Society of Equity held its state convention in Bismarck, a new idea began to surface. The plan was to organize farmers into a nonpartisan political party. Republican legislator Treadwell Twichell learned of the plan and addressed the farmers. It was reported that he said the farmers should go home and slop the hogs and leave governing of the state to the politicians. Twichell later denied making that statement, but Society members believed he did and their anger grew.

Townley then went to Bismarck to observe the 1915 Legislative session. The Legislature killed a proposal for a state-owned terminal elevator, previously passed by the 1913 Legislature and approved by the voters.

Seeing the farmers' anger, Townley decided to form a new farmers' organization. With his Socialist party experience, he developed a platform of state ownership and used his own organizing techniques.[52]

Possibly during this same event in Bismarck, Townley met a farmer from the north central part of the state, Frank Wood. Wood would become the co-author and first enlistee in the Nonpartisan League.

The Nonpartisan League was born on a farm near Deering, North Dakota. In February 1915, A.C. Townley appeared at the farm of Frank B. Wood to pitch the idea of a new political movement that would not be tied to the Democratic, Republican or Socialist parties. Wood and

---

[52] Prairie Public Newsroom, May 17, 2022

Townley had met earlier in Bismarck. At that time Wood invited Townley to come to his farm in the spring after the snow melted. The always-restless Townley did not wait for spring.[53]

Townley [telephoned Wood], seven miles away, asking for an interview...[Wood] expected Townley would appear the next day. Instead, as quickly as a thin, active man could walk the seven miles over the snow the visitor shoved into Mr. Wood's house and held out a sinewy hand. "What the devil are you doing here at this time of the year?" was the greeting he got.[54]

The two men talked deep into the night. Wood was at first skeptical, but Townley's unrelenting enthusiasm finally convinced him. After several days of passionate talk, the two men scribbled out a League platform on a scrap of wrapping paper by the light of a kerosene lamp. The next morning, they steered a bobsled to neighboring farms. Frank Wood performed the introductions, Townley made the pitch. The combination was extremely effective.[55]

By less colorful accounts, they made those first neighborhood campaigns in the Woods' family Ford.

The first day, thanks to the Ford, they were able to see nine men, and got them all. In six days they got seventy-nine, and had not a refusal...They went on thus until they had three townships in that county organized. Every man that

---

[53] The Bank of North Dakota Story
[54] *The Story of the Nonpartisan League*, Charles Edward Russell, May 1920
[55] The Bank of North Dakota Story

signed had to contribute his dues, and I give it as an illustration of the financial condition of the region that with all these signatures they had not collected a cent of money. Every farmer had paid in a post-dated check; that is, a check dated the following October. It was February or March, and the farmers had little money, and would have little until they should sell the next wheat crop.

The Farmers' Nonpartisan League was the name he had chosen for his organization. He had conceived another idea that I submit only a born leader would have thought of or dared to carry out. It was to fight money with money; to raise a fund large enough to make an effective campaign against the unlimited resources of the other side, and to get this from one of the poorest communities in the North. He had the audacity to make the annual dues six dollars – at a time when nine-tenths of those to whom he must appeal were poverty-stricken strugglers...[this] plainly shows to what desperation the farmers had been driven.

In a short time Townley had 10 automobiles rolling through the state...then 20, then 40, then 60. He bought [the vehicles], ran into debt for them, chartered them, borrowed them. Steadily the figures of membership went up. By July he had 10,000, and when in September the League's newspaper, The Nonpartisan Leader, made its first appearance, it had 22,000 subscribers, every one of them a member of the League.[56]

---

[56] *The Story of the Nonpartisan League*, Charles Edward Russell, May 1920

Amassing 22,000 members in just seven months across a geographically large and sparsely populated state, in Model Ts traveling on mostly primitive roads, was a phenomenal accomplishment. In later years, at its peak, the NPL had tenfold that number.

> ...by 1919 the NPL operated in 13 states and two Canadian provinces. Before the party's collapse in the 1920s, there were over 250,000 paying members.[57]

> "[Townley] is rather slow in action and exceedingly deliberate in the use of words. As he commences to talk he appears to be about five foot ten; when he finishes he seems to be about ten foot five. Rather thin in appearance, he is yet strong in physical make-up. His eyes are set deep, but they match his sarcastic drawl. His hair is dark, and his nose is rather prominent. He speaks slowly and enunciates clearly; his gestures go out after you, reaching out to tear down your refusals to agree with his ideals. His voice is expressive, strong, and resonant. As irony, sarcasm or sympathy is hurled at his crowd, his voice betrays his mood before his words articulate the thought. He is one of the great native orators of America."[58]

Townley and Wood kickstarted their efforts at an opportune time. Frustration over inaction to establish a state-owned elevator was felt far and wide. And whether or not he said

---

[57] *High Plains Reader*, Fargo, North Dakota, November 28, 2015
[58] The Bank of North Dakota Story

it, Twichell's "go home and slop the hogs" insult became a rallying cry that incensed farmers across the state to action.

The NPL also capitalized on less formal but strongly felt divisions in many communities. In Beach, the local *Golden Valley Chronicle* newspaper characterized the two sides as "silk stocking, sort of aristocratic fellows" vs. "laboring men who wear overalls and Rockford socks, occasionally."[59] "Rockford socks" are the red-heeled variety sometimes used to make sock monkey toys.

NPL badge, similar to the one Murrel frequently wore

Maud states in her taped interview that Murrel joined the League early on, sometime in 1915; she joined the Nonpartisan League Ladies Auxiliary in both Beach and Sentinel Butte. Murrel approached his involvement with typical fervor and campaigned vigorously for their platform.

Murrel and other NPL members believed the League was the path to a more just – and profitable – future. The excessive cost of capital, deceptive grain grading, false scales, unfair dockage fees, and high shipping costs were a few of the conditions the NPL fought to correct. Murrel was soon selected as an NPL delegate and became a high-profile "Leaguer" in Golden Valley County.

---

[59] *Golden Valley Chronicle*, Beach, North Dakota, April 24, 1914

M. K. Bowen, the big Ollie farmer, attended the mass meeting of the Non-Partisan league in this city Monday.[60]

In early April 1916, Murrel was one of three representatives chosen from Golden Valley County to attend the NPL convention held in Fargo, where its candidates would be chosen for the following statewide election.

The Farmers' Nonpartisan League convention held in Fargo last Friday and Saturday was the most successful and enthusiastic political gathering ever held in that city or elsewhere in the state. A full state ticket was placed in the field, Lynn J. Frazier, of Hoople, near Grand Forks, for governor.

Two Beach people were on the program, Mayor Brinton and Beach's cartoonist, J. M. Baer. J. D. Halstead, Geo. F. Hunt of Beach, and M. K. Bowen, of Ollie, were Golden Valley representatives who also attended.

…"There have been some great days in the history of this nation – some very great days – but there never was as great a one for the people of any section as today is for the people in the state of N. Dakota." This statement was made by A. C. Townley, president of the Nonpartisan league…

Ray McKaig…one of the members of a lobby…sent to the last legislative assembly, told of some of the things that he had seen at Bismarck during the session. "There is a vast difference between statesmen and politicians," said the

---

[60] *Golden Valley Chronicle,* Beach, North Dakota, April 14, 1916

speaker. "A little boy once asked his father what the difference was between toad stools and mushrooms. The father replied that mushrooms were good while toad stools were poisonous fungi, but that it was hard to tell the difference between them. It is the same with politicians and statesmen, they look much alike often, but one is an insidious poison while the other represents constructive policies."[61]

The NPL's core platform aimed to address the corruption and unfair practices that shifted the value of grain and livestock further and further away from farmers and ranchers. They sought to establish:

- State owned terminal elevators, flour mills, stock yards, packing houses, and cold storage plants
- State administered hail insurance
- Exemption of farm improvements from taxation
- State inspection of dockage and grading
- Rural credit banks operated at cost[62]

Although Townley had been an active member of the Socialist party, most NPL members, including Murrel, did not identify as "Socialist" or "radical," rather, as ambitious entrepreneurs who aimed to see the full fruits of their labor.

…most of the farmer members of the League showed little interest in socialism. …Leaguers were committed to

---

[61] *Golden Valley Chronicle*, Beach, North Dakota, April 7, 1916
[62] *The Story of the Nonpartisan League*, Charles Edward Russell, May 1920

capitalism, though, as small property owners, they opposed corporate capitalism.[63]

The NPL adopted the goat as its mascot. "Getting someone's goat" means to irritate them – something the NPL aimed to do to the political and corporate establishment, but good.

In 1916, when Governor Hanna was running for re-election against the NPL-sponsored candidate Lynn Frazier, two children came to an NPL picnic with a goat wearing a sign that said "We have got Hanna's goat." The goat appeared on the speaker's platform and the NPL crowd had fun watching the goat in his special outfit.

"The goat that can't be got" became the official symbol of the NPL in October 1919. Members wore goat pins and the goat appeared in photographs and even Christmas cards. The goat could "butt" its opponents, it could "kick" against wrong-doing. Governor Lynn Frazier said that the goat was an animal "that works with its head when attacked."[64]

In their first bid for state offices, the NPL fared amazingly well. That fall Frazier was elected governor, and the NPL also captured the State House of Representatives. By 1919 they controlled both houses of the legislature. In just four years, the platform had effectively taken over North Dakota politics. Although achieving results akin to those of political masterminds, they strove to remain the party of the people.

---

[63] *High Plains Reader*, Fargo, North Dakota, November 28, 2015
[64] State Historical Society of North Dakota

The League wanted to present itself as the pure expression of discontent among North Dakota's 80,000 farmers. It did not want to be seen as a politically sophisticated protest movement. Frazier, therefore, was the ideal embodiment of the League's "innocence."

Frazier's fundamental decency and personal conservativeness – he was a teetotaler and a prohibitionist who regarded dancing as sinful – made farmers skeptical of the charge that the League consisted of "a bunch of radicals," Bolshevists, and free lovers. Frazier was the least "Bolshevist" farmer in America.[65]

Under Governor Frazier's leadership, a slate of acts aligned to the party platform was signed into law in the Spring of 1919, each designed to lower the cost of producing and marketing grain and livestock and bring fairness to the process.

A definite turning point in the history of North Dakota and perhaps the United States—was reached when Governor Lynn J. Frazier...signed the bills creating the Industrial Commission, the Bank of North Dakota, the Home Savings Association, the Hail Insurance Department, the Terminal Elevator and the Flour Mill Association, the acts providing for Workmen's Compensation and for the inspection of mines, and the three bonding acts which provide a fund of $17,000,000 these state owned industries.

---

[65] The Bank of North Dakota Story

It was a gala day for the Nonpartisan Legislatures who form a majority of both houses and their supporters who packed the galleries and floor of the Representatives chamber. Some of the gray haired farmers...had been fighting for 26 years to enact these measures into law and as Governor Frazier signed each bill, the announcement was a signal for a burst of applause.

Probably in the entire history of the United States so many measures of equal importance have ever before been enacted into law in a single day... Moving picture cameras were set up in the chamber and every detail of the session will be embodied in the film that will be circulated throughout the United States to show how democracy appears in the making in North Dakota.[66]

This was an era when North Dakota was at the forefront of progress; it is bittersweet that Murrel did not live to see his ambitions for reform come fully to fruition, many of which are still in existence today.

[Frazier] was quoted in the May 16, 1920 issue of New York Times Magazine, "In my estimation, that which we have started in North Dakota is the one hope of putting the government...into the hands of the people ... This change can be brought about in a true American manner by the use of the Non-Partisan ballot."[67]

---

[66] *Golden Valley Progress*, Beach, North Dakota, August 8, 1919
[67] The Bank of North Dakota Story

The NPL's heyday was a brief one, however. While Townley was a force of nature in creating the NPL, he was also highly controversial, cited as prioritizing his personal success over broader moral victories. Opposition to Townley and his tactics soon led to infighting and factions within the party.

> The anti-NPL movement gained strength during and after World War I. Charging that the NPL's leaders, many of whom were former Socialists, were opponents of American participation in World War I, the anti-NPL forces coalesced in late 1918 into the Independent Voter's Association. Vitriolic political infighting followed. The IVA attacked on many fronts, rapidly sowing disunity within the NPL and splitting the coalition of cooperative groups that had helped support the League.[68]

Opposing views within the NPL and IVA were not contained to fierce intellectual debates; angry and even violent conflicts occurred between their supporters. One such incident from October 1919:

> A yelling mob of University of North Dakota students composed of sons of I.V.A. leaders, sons of bankers, politicians and merchants, threw Maurice Smith, a reporter for the Grand Forks American, and a student of the university, into a stream of water running through the state university, kept him in the stream with paddles, pelted him with mud, and forced him to duck his head in

---

[68] State Historical Society of North Dakota

the mud, because he is a supporter of the Nonpartisan League.

"It isn't because we have anything against you," the mob leader said to the student who was thrown into the icy water. "It's because you believe in the Nonpartisan League, which isn't right. You are about the only one in the school who does and we don't want you around. You're working for the wrong gang and the wrong paper."[69]

Those who dared to express a favorable view to the Nonpartisan league have been branded as free lovers, Bolshevists, atheists and, more mildly perhaps, breeders of community strife.[70]

Big business, the IVA, and the anti-NPL/"anti-Townley" factions were collectively referred to in the press as "the gang." Newspapers and their editors on either side were often lightning rods:

The editor of the McHenry Tribune, a Nonpartisan paper at McHenry, Foster county, has been engaged for several days trying to remove yellow paint, applied liberally to the front of his place of business by townsmen.[71]

As sentiment against Townley and the NPL grew, the IVA gained favor.

In 1920, the IVA took control of one legislative house and in 1921 forced a recall election that deposed Governor

---

[69] *The Bottineau Courant*, Bottineau, North Dakota, October 2, 1919
[70] *Golden Valley Progress*, Beach, North Dakota, August 8, 1919
[71] *The Fargo Forum*, Fargo, North Dakota, May 8, 1918

Frazier... The NPL era, one that significantly altered North Dakota government, had ended.[72]

...the League organization was quickly falling to pieces by March 1921. Membership drives were failing, bills went unpaid and revenues fell.[73]

While the NPL era was short lived, effectively from 1915 to 1921, it engrained principles and institutions that have endured to this day.

The NPL left an indelible mark on the state. The Bank of North Dakota at Bismarck, opened in 1919, has become a large and powerful economic force; the State Mill and Elevator at Grand Forks, completed in 1922, provided a market for grain and a source of feed and seed; the state hail insurance program benefited many farmers until its elimination in the 1960s. Perhaps most importantly, the NPL established an insurgent tradition in the state that blurred party lines for four decades, and both the League and the IVA elevated a generation of leaders to power. Each official recalled in 1921, for example, later regained public office.[74]

...its principles continued as part of the Republican Party for a time and then in its merger with the Democratic Party in the late 1950s.[75]

---

[72] State Historical Society of North Dakota
[73] Prairie Public Newsroom, May 17, 2022
[74] State Historical Society of North Dakota
[75] Prairie Public Newsroom, May 17, 2022

...the NPL was the most significant challenge to party politics-as-usual in American history...[and] the most successful agrarian movement in American history. ...the state bank, state mill and state elevator in North Dakota all stand as a living testament to the NPL and the aspirations of its members. Almost 100 years later, all three are a great success. Few American political movements can point to such institutional longevity. ...it's important for...other parts of the country to recognize that one of the most innovative political movements the nation has ever seen was invented by farmers in North Dakota.[76]

---

[76] *High Plans Reader*, Fargo, North Dakota, November 28, 2015

THE FARMER'S BURDEN

The Nonpartisan Leader, June 24, 1918

Aggression at the Mallet Ranch

MURREL AND MAUD COULD NOT HAVE ANTICIPATED the strife, conflict, and eventual tragedy that moving to that part of the township, on that land, would bring. Not long after the Bowens relocated to the Mallet Ranch, Murrel was at odds with their adjacent neighbor, Delbert Offley.

The specific underlying reasons for this conflict remain murky, outside of some references to "jealousy" and "differences over the range and stock." Not knowing for certain what drove such hatred and deadly animosity is one of the most unsatisfying elements of this story.

> To tell a concrete story, it may be said that bad blood has been brewing in the Bowen neighborhood for a number of years and fears of bloodshed have often been expressed by the people there.[77]

> Differences arose over the range and stock which soon developed into a feud between Bowen and Offley.[78]

> [Murrel] was a logical thinker and decision maker, very, very good in mathematics. He was honest, but quick-tempered, had no liking for people who were dishonest, deceiving, underhanded, or liars.[79]

---

[77] *The Beach Advance*, Beach, North Dakota, August 1, 1919
[78] *The Bismarck Tribune*, Bismarck, North Dakota, August 6, 1919
[79] Written accounts by eldest daughter Lois Bowen Beach

There is great feeling around the Bowen home and likelihood between Offley and Bowen adherents of an old-fashioned Kentucky feud.[80]

An "old-fashioned Kentucky feud" referred to a series of neighborhood conflicts in the late 1800s and early 1900s, most notably between the Hatfields and the McCoys.

The trouble with Offley was much more than a war of words. Soon large numbers of the Bowens' cattle began to mysteriously die or go missing altogether. Per Murrel's accounts, Offley made frequent threats to put him out of business, or worse.

During the next months many of Mr. Bowen's cattle were either stolen or poisoned, living conditions were almost unbearable for the Bowen family with the war, drought, and hard times...[81]

The cattle did not have a merciful end, either. They foamed at the mouth and writhed in pain, left in twisted positions. Even the mare they brought from Iowa fell victim. The value of the lost livestock was estimated to be as high as $30,000, over $500,000 today.[82]

Long before the [Bowens'] house is in sight, one sees from the road the gleaming white bones of cattle that were poisoned and died on the range. Sometimes it is only a hoof, or a leg bone, sometimes the bones are still covered with a

[80] *The Bismarck Tribune*, Bismarck, North Dakota, August 2, 1919
[81] *The Fallon County Times*, Baker, Montana, May 19, 1994
[82] *The Nonpartisan Leader*, Fargo, North Dakota, September 22, 1919

weatherbeaten hide. These latter are the cattle and horses that were poisoned this spring.

Here is the carcass of the mare with which Bowen courted his wife in Iowa twelve years ago. When they came to North Dakota in the following year, the mare was brought along.

Hans, the hired man, tells of the morning of the last light snow of this spring when he went out and found the barn open, the stock loose and poisoned. The mare had strength enough to walk outside, and died in the coulee. Near its body lie the glistening bones of two cows, one a thoroughbred, and with calf. They found the poison over on the west end of the range, and came this mile before dying.

Down in a clump of trees where still a little water runs is the place where the bones of more than a hundred head of stock are piled. They…were hauled here after each outbreak of the poisoner. Some of the later victims are intact enough to show the tortured way in which their heads were twisted back in their last agony.[83]

Murrel sought assistance from all levels of law enforcement, including the United States Department of Justice at Fargo. They interestingly hypothesized that the poisoning may have been the work of German operatives.

---

[83] *Golden Valley Progress*, Beach, North Dakota, August 8, 1919

"The fall of 1917, Offley made threats to put Bowen out of business. In the spring of 1918, Bowen lost 112 head of cattle through poisoning. He notified the United States department of justice at Fargo, and an investigation was started which resulted in no poisoning evidence. The United States officials believed it possible that German agents were endeavoring to embarrass the government and diminish the food supply during war time.[84]

Back in 1917, when his cattle first began to foam at the mouth and die in tortures, the federal secret service sent out an investigator, who was baffled and withdrew from the case, saying that he did not believe that the cattle were killed by pro-Germans.[85]

"Mr. Bowen...had examined the stomachs of various animals and found they were completely burned away. In some cases the second stomach was hard and crisp and the inner walls of the intestines and the mucous membrane so decomposed by the particular form of poisoning used that it peeled off in shreds similar to noodles.[86]

While financially and emotionally devastating, this was not the only aggression towards the Bowens. Some of their cattle went missing altogether; Murrel suspected Offley and even one of the Bowens' own ranch hands, Ennis Taylor, who lived with his wife in a small apartment on the ranch.

---

[84] *The Bismarck Tribune*, Bismarck, North Dakota, August 6, 1919
[85] *Fargo Courier-News*, Fargo, North Dakota, August 1, 1919
[86] *The Bismarck Tribune*, Bismarck, North Dakota, August 6, 1919

"Bowen declared that during this time (the spring of 1918)...Taylor was working for him. Taylor and D. R. Offley had many conferences together of a secret nature and it was at this time that Bowen, so he said, began to suspect Taylor of being in conspiracy with Offley to assist the latter in carrying out his threat to kill Bowen. There was also one Jenson who rented a place just a short distance away and east of Bowen's, who was implicated, so Bowen alleged.[87]

That spring, the Bowens reportedly lost another three dozen head of cattle to theft.

Cattle rustlers are active in the vicinity of Golva and Alpha, [North Dakota], and Ollie, Montana...Over 175 head of cattle have been run off the range this spring and summer and the efforts of the local sheriffs and police have resulted in no clues being obtained...

The losses which have been reported...are as follows: Strom Brothers, Ollie, Mont., 30 head; A. A. Vinclatte, Ollie, Mont., 50 head, Henry Funk, Alpha, N. D., 35 head; M. K. Bowen, Ollie, Mont., 35 head and John Tyler, Alpha, N. D., 25 head.[88]

"About two months after calving time in 1918, thirty-six head of Bowen's cows and their calves disappeared. These were branded with Bowen's mark and the tips of one ear

---

[87] *The Bismarck Tribune,* Bismarck, North Dakota, August 6, 1919
[88] *The Weekly Times-Record,* Valley City, North Dakota, August 8, 1918

were cut off. Bowen and his man rode the range for days in the attempt to locate these cattle but were unsuccessful.

"It was after this search that a boy named Stupps reported to Bowen that he had seen Offley and…Taylor driving off these cattle and that Offley had told him that he had the right to drive them.[89]

Murrel's suspicion of Offley and Taylor being behind the death and theft of his herd continued to grow.

"During all this time Taylor was working for Bowen. Bowen…had permitted the calves to run with the cows longer than usual so that when the thirty-six head, which he suspected would return some day without their calves, should come back, he would better be able to pick them out.

"During all this time, so Bowen alleged, Taylor and Offley were having secret little talks together, and now and then (more particularly after the department of justice agents had made investigations) Taylor made remarks to Bowen as though seeking information as to what was going to happen."[90]

Murrel also tried to enlist county officials to hold accountable those responsible for his cattle disappearing and dying.

Bowen and State's Attorney R. F. Gallagher have been at enmity for months. Attempts to secure warrants for arrest

---

[89] *The Bismarck Tribune*, Bismarck, North Dakota, August 6, 1919
[90] *The Bismarck Tribune*, Bismarck, North Dakota, August 6, 1919

of parties believed responsible for the death of cattle and stealing calves had failed. The state's attorney refused to issue warrants.[91]

The Bowens' land was also being vandalized. A herd of cattle belonging to Offley was repeatedly found in their winter pasture. According to Maud, they came onto the property only during the night through a cut fence.

By December of 1918, the situation had become severe enough to force Murrel to put the Mallet Ranch up for sale. From the *Chicago Tribune*:

> *3,500 a. ranch; 400 a. farm, well improved, with or without herd and machinery; also newly broken, otherwise unimproved 320 a.; always plenty water, fertile, friable chocolate loam soil; close towns, advantages, good roads; Golden Valley county, North Dakota, extraordinarily successful county; exceptionally good, seasonable rainfall. Many photographs properties. Owners, H. G. GARBER, Majestic Hotel, Chicago, and M. K. BOWEN, Carlyle, Montana.*[92]

Hugh Goode "H. G." Garber, listed as co-owner of the ranch, was an attorney and special agent of the United States Department of Justice. He and Murrel met when Garber was sent to investigate the cattle poisoning[93], and they became business partners in growing flax on some of the idle parcels

---

[91] *Golden Valley Progress*, Beach, North Dakota, August 8, 1919
[92] *Chicago Tribune*, Chicago, Illinois, December 15, 1918
[93] *Mandan Pioneer*, Mandan, North Dakota, January 23, 1920

in the area.[94] As the Bowens' financial situation deteriorated, it appears they also sold a stake in the ranch to him.

One night later that winter, Murrel came upon two suspicious men on horseback.

> "...about January 15...Bowen was met by two night riders who suddenly appeared from a bunch of horses on the ranch. He had seen night riders many times before but in view of the threat to kill him, as soon as he was able to make out the figures in the moonlight, Bowen began to shoot with his rifle which he carried constantly. The two men on horseback immediately disappeared, and no complaint about shooting was heard in the neighborhood, nor did Bowen report the affair to the authorities. Bowen told me that Offley rode a pacing horse and that he was able to tell at the distance of 200 yards from the swing of the animal that one rode a pacer.
>
> "Recently (about Feb. 10) Bowen noticed brown spots about the size of a bushel basket covering an area of several acres. On these spots the snow was melted and there was a peculiar odor. Then a young bull took sick and died and appeared to have the same trouble which affected the other cattle."[95]

That spring, Murrel turned to the state level, hoping to enlist the assistance of North Dakota Governor Lynn Frazier and

[94] *Grand Forks Herald*, Grand Forks, North Dakota, May 24, 1918
[95] *The Bismarck Tribune*, Bismarck, North Dakota August 6, 1919

Attorney General William Langer, both of whom he'd campaigned for vigorously.

> Bowen applied to the Attorney General's office. Others in the same community, friendly to Bowen, have lost cattle and other animals and have applied to the state's attorney for a warrant only to be denied. Attorney General Langer was fully advised as to the situation, but absolutely ignored appeals for protection.[96]

> In the spring of 1919, Bowen came to Bismarck. He charged that Offley was trying to put him out of business. He related various incidents to the attorney general. Then he returned home and shortly afterwards he reported the death of another cow, presumably by poisoning.[97]

In response, Langer sent Assistant Attorney General Albert Sheets to investigate. According to Sheets' account:

> "Bowen gave me what he declared to be one of the best samples he could find of the grass and dirt from one of these poisoned patches, and stated that in it we would surely find poison... Bowen is of the opinion that the poison is either Lewis Lye, of which the cattle are very fond, or else fly poison mixed with salt.

> The attorney general's department sent the sample to...the North Dakota agricultural college... There is a letter on file...stating: "Following is an analysis of the sample of stomach and contents, said sample being submitted by Mr.

---

[96] *Golden Valley Progress*, Beach, North Dakota, August 8, 1919
[97] *The Bismarck Tribune*, Bismarck, North Dakota August 6, 1919

> Bowen of Beach. This analysis...shows, Alkaloids – none.
> Metallic poison – none. Cyanides – none. No poisons were
> detected in the sample..."[98]

The *Golden Valley Progress* reported this account of Sheets'
investigation:

> ...at the request of Governor Frazier, Attorney General
> Langer sent one of his assistants out to the Bowen ranch.
> This youthful lawyer pooh-poohed the idea of cattle
> poisoning, and gave his opinion that the cattle had died
> from eating fermented grain, "as the lining of their
> stomachs were all eaten out."[99]

Governor Frazier continued to be engaged, and enlisted the
U. S. Department of Animal Husbandry, who found an
unidentifiable substance in the sample of the cattle sent to
them.

> Governor Frazier then interested Dr. J. B. Hollenbeck of
> the United States Department of Animal Husbandry. The
> doctor made a thorough examination and failed to find any
> traces of disease. Part of the carcasses were sent to the
> Agricultural College chemists. They could find none of the
> known poisons. The federal experts found a quantity of
> mysterious powdered substance, which baffled the
> analysts.[100]

---

[98] *The Bismarck Tribune*, Bismarck, North Dakota August 6, 1919
[99] *Fargo Courier-News*, Fargo, North Dakota, August 1, 1919
[100] *Fargo Courier-News*, Fargo, North Dakota, August 1, 1919

Next, an investigator from the Montana Stock Growers' Association, Frank Evans, was brought in by the attorney general's office.

> *...not content with this report, Attorney General Langer secured the services of Frank Evans, a law enforcing officer of the Montana Stock Growers' association, and a man with many years' experience in ferreting out cattle mysteries. He went to Beach and spent considerable time there with Bowen. His investigations lasted until April 10, when he returned to Bismarck and made an affidavit of his findings...[101]*

> *Then the state hired a detective [Frank Evans], who made a report urging that the authorities take action. Neither Attorney General Langer nor the state's attorney of Golden Valley county made a move. The cattle on the Bowen ranch continued to die by the dozen. Bowen wrote to the authorities, telling of threats that had been made to kill him...It is claimed that bitter League enemies occupy the county offices and would not give Bowen justice.[102]*

Maud held Evans in high esteem and trusted his commitment to finding the cause of the poisoning. She said Evans was similarly unsatisfied with the outcome of the investigations; however, her accounts of those conversations are starkly different from his published affidavit in the case. From *The Bismarck Tribune*:

---

[101] *The Bismarck Tribune*, Bismarck, North Dakota August 6, 1919
[102] *Fargo Courier-News*, Fargo, North Dakota, August 1, 1919

...at the request of Attorney General Langer I spent 26 days at and around Beach North Dakota as an investigator in the M. K. Bowen cattle poisoning case, I did everything that I thought could possibly be done during that time and at all times had the complete cooperation of Mr. Langer and his whole office force; in the time I spent in the employment of Mr. Langer on the M. K. Bowen case I thoroughly satisfied myself that further investigation would be useless expenditure of money; no crime had been disclosed by the evidence; and so far as I could learn no crime had been committed; I so reported to the office of the Attorney General's office and about the 10th day of April 1919, I left Bismarck for my ranch on the Powder River in Montana intending to stop at Beach...; on arriving in Beach I found M. K. Bowen, and Geo. Beauchams and they were anxious to find out the result of my trip to Bismarck; we talked over the affair together and I told him that nothing further could be done in the face of the fact that no poison had been found or could be found and then...Bowen told me that he thought that politics had interfered and that he was going down to see the Governor. I left the next day for Miles City... The day after I arrived in Miles City I received a telegram from M. K. Bowen, which said "Meet Governor Frazier on No. 3 tonight and be prepared to go to Billings if possible." ...On the night of the 14th of April or thereabouts Governor Frazier got off the train at Miles City and met me on the platform of the depot and had the following conversation with me, in part as follows:

Gov. Frazier – Mr. Evans?

Mr. Evans – Yes.

Gov. Frazier – Mr. Bowen has been to Bismarck to see me about his cattle that are being poisoned, what do you think about it?

Mr. Evans – I have looked the situation over carefully, don't see what can be done, as the analysis showed no trace of poison either in the stomach or in the stuff we gathered up where the cattle had been eating.

Gov. Frazier – Do you think that Mr. Langer is on the square in this deal?

Mr. Evans – As far as my connection has been with Mr. Langer, I am satisfied that he is.

Gov. Frazier – I think so too, but there are some who don't. If I should want you to go back on the case would you be willing to do it?

Mr. Evans – Yes, I would.

Gov. Frazier – I am going on to the Springs and will let you know what I decide to do.

Gov. Frazier was badly crippled with rheumatism and I helped him on the train and I have never seen or heard from him since. I then returned to my ranch...

As far as my report was concerned, Langer could do nothing else but drop the case. Personally I was not satisfied with the case but I felt that Langer had done everything he possibly could.

...I found what I thought was poison but the chemical analysis showed that it was not poison.[103]

Frustratingly, the investigations again failed to bring about further action. News accounts after Murrel's death conquer with Maud's feeling that Evans had found credible evidence, but it was somehow obfuscated or suppressed.

Neither Attorney General Langer nor the state's attorney of Golden Valley county made a move. At least three citizens of Golden Valley county have declared that this detective unearthed sufficient evidence to warrant the arrest of two persons [who would later be] connected with the shooting of Bowen.[104]

The detective presented evidence at the Attorney General's office to show that not only had Bowen's cattle been killed in some mysterious manner, but also reported the location of a number of head of cattle stolen from the Bowen ranch and their brands burned out. The detective was dismissed. Attorney General Langer declared, paid up, and told he could go back to Montana, that no traces of poison had been found and stealing of cattle was purely a local matter for county authorities. The detective on his return, came through Beach to get a saddle and told what had happened at the Attorney General's office. It is understood some very damaging affidavits are available. If county authorities

[103] *The Bismarck Tribune*, Bismarck, North Dakota, August 8, 1919
[104] *The Producers News*, Plentywood, Montana, August 8, 1919

were ever notified, no action resulted, although several months have passed since that time.[105]

According to Maud, Frank Evans told her that the powder found on the carcasses was the powder used to keep flies off cattle. Her conclusion was that the poison had been placed in this powder, aligned with Murrel's hypothesis as told to Sheets. Evans also told her that they found a horse's hoof print with a missing front horseshoe at the scene of the poisoning; Maud said that a neighbor in Bull Run Township, Ira "Jay" Stark, rode such a horse.

The Bowens' friend Martin Blank also took up the cause that spring, visiting Bismarck to solicit help from the attorney general's office.

> *Martin Blank...had called at the attorney general's office and made insinuations that the department was ignoring the cattle poisoning condition... He threatened to "show up Langer" if something was not done. His visit was early in May and was made after M. K. Bowen...had made charges that politics had entered into the affair.*[106]

A hundred years later, the reasons for these aggressions can only be gleaned through speculation. While he had many close, devoted friends in the area, to some Murrel also had the reputation of being arrogant. Years after his death, two of Murrel's grandchildren happened to meet one of the Bowens' former ranch hands, who thought highly of him

---

[105] *Golden Valley Progress*, Beach, North Dakota, August 8, 1919
[106] *The Bismarck Tribune*, Bismarck, North Dakota, August 6, 1919

and confirmed his many positive attributes, but also this one. His daughter Lois described him as *"...always ready to help a friend or neighbor...but quick tempered, [and] had no liking for people who were dishonest, deceiving, underhanded, or liars."*[107] Thus, perhaps the perpetrators simply didn't like him. As the largest landowners in the township, there may have also been a degree of envy towards the Bowens. As Blank wrote:

> *Whether the jealousy of his neighbors as a result of his success had anything to do with it or not or whether there were some who wanted his range, the writer would not attempt to say, but it is a fact that over 200 head of cattle were poisoned in the course of a year. The poisoning baffled both government and state experts, all of whom agreed that the cattle were being killed by some substance maliciously placed.*[108]

If jealousy or sheer dislike of Murrel were the drivers, the resulting actions seem, to put it mildly, extreme. What may be closer to the truth is what some still living in the area have heard over the years. As this story goes, Murrel came upon one or more of the men smuggling stolen cattle in the badlands, and these aggressions were effectively threats to remain silent. Murrel's account of regularly happening upon "night riders" may support this theory. If true, it seems he kept this dangerous information even from Maud, which would have been out of character. It was not raised during the subsequent investigation and prosecution of his killing,

---

[107] Written accounts by eldest daughter Lois Bowen Beach
[108] *Golden Valley Progress*, Beach, North Dakota, August 8, 1919

nor throughout the years of Maud's conversations with family.

It is not disputed that hundreds of their cattle mysteriously died, some were stolen, some were recovered with burned-out brands, and Delbert Offley's cattle were frequently found on their land. Regardless, no charges were raised in response to any of these events, and the Bowens had no recourse for the devastating financial losses or invasion of their property. This is where broader political conflict may have met local action, or inaction.

Murrel had long been involved in local concerns, spurring several high-profile challenges of what he perceived as injustice and dirty local politics involving Golden Valley County Sheriff John Pierzina and State's Attorney Richard Gallagher. Murrel made clear his opinion that Pierzina and Gallagher were intentionally ignoring their duties, and this did not go unnoticed.

> The Golden Valley county officials are hostile to the Nonpartisan League and Bowen frequently asserted that it was politics that held them from running down the cattle poisoners. He had made a number of efforts to interest the attorney general in the case. Failing to secure aid from Langer, he and many of his friends believed that the attorney general was more interested in preserving his own friendly relations with the anti-League county

officials than in hunting down and prosecuting the men who ruined him.[109]

The conflict with Pierzina and Gallagher may have started as a result of the general election in November of 1918, through which Pierzina became sheriff. In February of 1919, Murrel was one of several citizens who voiced concern over perceived election fraud committed by County Auditor M. C. McCarthy regarding the contest between Pierzina and his opponent, Warren Woodward.

> *...[about the middle of February 1919] Tom Kroma...in company with M. K. Bowen, Ernest Johnston, Charles Slocum, and Walter Haun called on Gallagher and demanded McCarthy's arrest in connection with the handling of the ballots at the last general election, on facts produced at the election contest of Woodward vs. Pierzina, and that Gallagher refused...*[110]

Per Maud, McCarthy and Pierzina were aligned with the IVA Democrat party, Woodward with the Nonpartisan League. Murrel and the others started a petition to recall McCarthy, but when they presented it and related evidence to Gallagher, he dismissed them and refused to act. Murrel's challenge of Pierzina's election and vocalizing his feelings about Gallagher's lack of diligence may ultimately have had dire consequences, but not before they would tangle again.

---

[109] *Fargo Courier-News*, Fargo, North Dakota, August 1, 1919
[110] *The Bismarck Tribune*, Bismarck, North Dakota, September 20, 1919

Another conflict between Murrel and Gallagher was over, of all things, a stolen pig. The pig belonged to a neighbor and friend of the Bowens, Mike Rataezyk; the Rataezyks were employed on the Jensen farm in Section 9, which bordered the land of Charles Woodsend.

According to Rataezyk, Woodsend, with the help of Ira "Jay" Stark, captured his pig and held it in Woodsend's chicken coop. According to Maud, Rataezyk went to Gallagher's office multiple times asking for help; Gallagher's response each time was that more evidence was needed. Rataezyk enlisted several neighbors and witnesses, including Murrel, to accompany him and help plead his case.

> *M. A. Rataezyk...said that in December, 1918 he lost a hog and that certain parties told him Charles Woodsend and Jay Stark had caught the hog and shut it up; that he had told State's Attorney Gallagher these facts and was informed they were not sufficient on which to issue a warrant for the arrest of the accused parties... About two weeks later he again called on Gallagher in company with Bowen, Miegs, and Rathje when a complaint was sworn out before Judge Plumason and left with Gallagher to be served in case enough evidence was secured to warrant an arrest.*[111]

There were several additional witnesses to "the hog affair."

---

[111] *The Bismarck Tribune,* Bismarck, North Dakota, September 20, 1919

C. A. Glazier...was present when the hog was caught and Woodsend had told Rataezyk two or three days later that his hog was in his, Woodsend's, chicken coop...

John Boegli [the Bowens' ranch hand]...was present with several others at the time the hog was caught by Woodsend and Stark and his description of the manner in which it was accomplished caused some considerable amusement...

Samuel Fisher...had been called to Gallagher's office and questioned regarding the hog affair...[Fisher] had questioned Woodsend, who admitted shutting the animal up because Rataezyk's hogs had been running loose all fall and that he had to keep his animals shut up and that this would teach Rataezyk a lesson. He did not know what had become of the hog.[112]

The pig was never recovered. Despite numerous witnesses saying that Woodsend had taken the hog and penned it on his property, Gallagher did not move against Woodsend or Stark. This incident may have also soured Murrel's friendship with Charles Woodsend; per Maud, they had previously been good friends with the Woodsends and played cards with them frequently while living on their homestead land.

A more serious conflict arose when Rataezyk and his wife, Mary, accused Stark and Ennis Taylor of attempting to shoot

---

[112] *The Bismarck Tribune*, Bismarck, North Dakota, September 20, 1919

them. Again they went to Gallagher's office for recourse, again they received no response.

> *[Gallagher] is also said to have refused to take action against Ennis W. Taylor and Ira J. Stark when they are alleged to have attempted three times to shoot...Rataezyk and his wife...*[113]

As the pattern of inaction on the part of local authorities continued, those responsible for the crimes against the Bowens may have become more brazen, ultimately leading to Murrel's death. In Maud and Murrel's minds, those individuals were Offley and Taylor. While politics may not have been a driver of the initial neighborhood aggressions, the fervent opposition and negative feelings between IVA and NPL supporters at all levels very likely hindered Murrel's ability to obtain justice for them.

---

[113] *The Bowbells Tribune*, Bowbells, North Dakota, September 5, 1919

Last photo of Murrel K. Bowen, April 20, 1919, Easter Sunday,
taking the Rataezyks to Easter services at St. Phillips

Rataezyks on horseback, Lois, Maud holding baby Ada, M. K.
leaning on the Bowens' Ford

July 1919

AFTER NEARLY TWO YEARS OF THEFT AND SABOTAGE, the Bowens were in a dire financial position.

> *The poisoning of the cattle had ruined him. His wife a few months ago wrote a brief letter to an old friend in Golden Valley asking him to pay up her husband's life insurance policy, as owing to his losses he would have to drop it. She wrote that he would be killed.*[114]

> *He was reduced to straightened circumstances as a consequence of the poisoning and finally forced to give up his herd. Ten carloads of cattle were shipped from here to a South Dakota range in May.*[115]

> *June 6, 1919 – M.K. Bowen, who lives east of Ollie, shipped 10 cars of cattle to Ortley, S. Dak. last week.*[116]

Murrel had concluded that Bull Run Township was no longer a viable place to prosper, nor a safe place for the family. He had already put his hard-earned Mallet Ranch up for sale; he now began to explore potential locations to resettle and begin again.

> *...before his death he announced to friends that he was giving up, and was going to move away.*[117]

---

[114] *Fargo Courier-News*, Fargo, North Dakota, August 1, 1919
[115] *Golden Valley Progress*, Beach, North Dakota, August 8, 1919
[116] Handwritten note by youngest daughter Ada Bowen Rustad
[117] *Golden Valley Progress*, Beach, North Dakota, August 8, 1919

He initially targeted Saskatchewan, Canada, knowing some friends who had relocated there from North Dakota.

Saturday, July 12, 1919

Just before leaving on a trip to investigate Canada, he penned his final plea to Governor Frazier, postmarked from Beach on July 12.

> *One of the last acts of MK Bowen…was to send a letter to Governor Frazier accusing Attorney General Langer and State's Attorney Gallagher…for failing to protect him. The letter…reads like a dying accusation of Attorney General Langer. The rancher, driven desperate by the mysterious killing of his cattle, wrote in part as follows:*

> *"I shall always think I deserved more of an investigation than I have had. Everything that was found out was treated as nothing, instead of trying out and running down each circumstance, as is done where there is money and consideration behind the deal.*

> *"I have got tired doing this and that, and every time I get a piece of evidence, have the whole thing thrown into the waste basket. Whether intentionally or not, I am treated as though I was some detestable crook or outlaw who was getting his just dues.*

> *"I have a family of small babies, and but for them I know what I would have done before now; and if something isn't done to stop this slander and damnable persecution, I intend to place all claim on my American rights. Not*

wishing to be disrespectful or not trying to infer that you or anyone else, except the attorney general and the state's attorney, have not done their duty, I think that you do not understand all the circumstances.

"Respectfully yours,

MK Bowen"[118]

Governor Frazier's response:

"Your letter at hand. The fact that the attorney general's office is not cooperating with this office, makes it hard for me to take any legal action in a case of this kind. I expect Attorney Lemke up from Fargo in a few days, and will take this matter up with him and see if something cannot be done independent of the attorney general's office."

Before action could be taken to start this unofficial proceeding…Bowen was killed.[119]

On or about Sunday, July 13, 1919

…in early July of 1919 Mr. Bowen and some relatives and friends took two Model Ts and went to Canada looking for a new location.[120]

Tuesday, July 15, 1919: Moose Jaw, Saskatchewan

By July 15, the party had reached Moose Jaw, Saskatchewan, roughly 350 miles from home. From there he mailed a

---

[118] *Fargo Courier-News*, Fargo, North Dakota, August 1, 1919
[119] *Fargo Courier-News*, Fargo, North Dakota, August 1, 1919
[120] *The Fallon County Times*, Baker, Montana, May 9, 1994

greeting card to eldest daughter Lois, including a cheeky note. Lois was then visiting Maud's niece, Lois Epley, in Willard, Montana, to assist the young family while Charles Epley was traveling with Murrel in Canada.

To Lois Bowen Willard, MT USA, C/O Mrs. C. B. Epley

Moose Jaw, Canada, Sask., July 15, 1919

Pa is in Canada and don't you and Auntie go to any dances without asking me. We left Ep on the reservation.

M. K. B.

The Epleys and Bowens had a close relationship, and the Epleys were known to the Bowen children as "Uncle and Auntie Ep."

Lois and Charles Epley ("Uncle and Auntie Ep")
Lois was the daughter of Maud's sister, Jennie

Wednesday, July 16, 1919: Saskatoon, Saskatchewan

The following day, Murrel wrote to his friend Martin Blank, editor of the *Golden Valley Progress*. The letter was sent from Saskatoon, a further 140 miles from Moose Jaw, and Blank published it in the paper. In it, Murrel notes several progressive actions of the Canadian government that matched the goals of the Nonpartisan League, namely state owned grain elevators and hail insurance. He also relayed that he had decided to stay in the United States.

M. K. Bowen of the South country, with a party of neighbors drove thru to Canada several weeks ago writes the Golden Valley Progress that he is not ready to give up his home in the Dear old U. S. A. The men are making the trip in a Ford and expect to cover extensive area of the dominion. The letter from Mr. Bowen is dated July 16th at Saskatoon and follows in full:

Friend Blank,

Well, we got here in time for the provincial fair and, believe me, it is some fair. These Canadians have good horses and sheep – better considerable than their cattle and hogs. We have just seen two sections of country in a five hundred mile area that have any crops. One is under the Yellowstone ditch, which is excellent, and then North of Moose Jaw for 35 or 40 miles. The rest does not look any better than at home and I will say right now that I HAVE NOT BEEN CONVINCED THAT I CARE TO LEAVE THE GOOD OLD U. S. A.

We heard tonight that there had been today a big cyclone northwest of here that did much damage and there was considerable loss of life. We leave here in the morning for Lashburn which is about 150 miles northwest of here where Frank Milne is located – an old Golden Valley county resident and a neighbor of mine.

We have had a good trip so far. Old Henry Ford just travels fine. We expect to eat supper at Lashburn tomorrow night.

Land is not easy to get here now as there is a new law just in force which partially holds up filing to give the returned soldiers the preference until they are satisfied. Canada has so far appreciated their soldiers and showed it more than has the U. S. Congress – I say CONGRESS, not the rank and file of the people.

I have been considerably interested in the government owned elevators and the hail insurance operated here by the provinces and find them a thoro success. Will write more about them next time.

They told us in Montana before we crossed the line that they would charge us to change our money and American bankers wanted 1½ percent. But we just kept it and came across and they grab our money here just like a cat does a mouse, usually with the expression – if he's from the states – "well thank goodness here is some honest to God money again."

Respectfully yours,

M. K. BOWEN[121]

Monday, July 21, 1919: Leaving Lashburn, Saskatchewan

As mentioned in the letter to Blank, the plan was to travel from Saskatoon to Lashburn, a further 150 miles northwest,

---

[121] *Golden Valley Progress*, Beach, North Dakota, undated, approximately July 1919

near the Alberta border. The Bowens' friends and former neighbors, the Milnes, had relocated there. Per a postcard from Grace Milne written to Maud on July 22, the party had left Lashburn and started for home the previous evening, a 650-mile journey.

July 22, 1919 – Dear Maud, Just a few lines to let you know the boys started home last night. We sure were glad to see them. Wish you and the kids could have come too, but M. K. likes this country fine. We are all fine, but have very poor look out for a crop. You certainly have had fierce luck. Write soon. Love to all, Grace

Fierce luck indeed. Altogether, the party traveled almost 1,300 miles, bumping along in Model Ts, to assess the prospect of moving to Canada.

Roughly Saturday, July 12 through Saturday, July 26, 1919

While Murrel was investigating Saskatchewan, trouble at home continued. Offley's cattle were repeatedly found on the Bowens' winter pasture, which Maud and the children were left to address alone.

> *Two weeks ago Bowen resolved to leave his 3,000 acre ranch and move to Canada. While he was on a home-seeking tour a herd of cattle was turned in his pasture. Mrs. Bowen and the children drove them out repeatedly, but at night they were mysteriously driven on the ranch again.*[122]

> *...John Boegli, Bowen's ranch foreman, and Mrs. M. K. Bowen, [said that] cattle belonging to D. R. Offley, had gone over into Bowen's land and were driven off several times during the past three weeks Bowen had been in Canada.*[123]

Maud was by then expecting their seventh child. With eldest daughter Lois visiting the Epleys, the five children at home with Maud ranged from just under nine years to 17 months old.

Sunday, July 27, 1919: Murrel Arrives Home

> *...Bowen returned Sunday and was told that it appeared cattle were purposely driven onto his land.*[124]

---

[122] *Fargo Courier-News*, Fargo, North Dakota, August 1, 1919
[123] *Golden Valley Progress*, Beach, North Dakota, August 8, 1919
[124] *Golden Valley Progress*, Beach, North Dakota, August 8, 1919

...Bowen returned from Canada, unable to secure a suitable farm. His first act was to try to drive the strange cattle from his land.[125]

Monday, July 28, 1919: Murrel Corrals Offley's Cattle

Exasperated and angered at learning of the continued harassment while he was away, leaving Maud to manage it alone, Murrel escalated his response. Rather than driving the cattle back onto Offley's property, as they had always done, he decided to hold the cattle in the Bowens' corral. He would release them for compensation of damages in the amount of $5 per head.

> *In the morning he found them grazing in his pastures as before. He then left them there.*[126]

> *Monday Bowen had the cattle driven into a corral at his home.*[127]

Tuesday, July 29, 1919

Offley's nephew and ranch hand, George Tubbs, was first to come after the cattle.

> *A ranch hand from Offley's came over Tuesday and asked for the cattle... Bowen told him to tell Offley not to be afraid to come over, they could settle for the damages without any trouble.*[128]

---

[125] *Fargo Courier-News*, Fargo, North Dakota, August 1, 1919
[126] *Fargo Courier-News*, Fargo, North Dakota, August 1, 1919
[127] *Golden Valley Progress*, Beach, North Dakota, August 8, 1919
[128] *Golden Valley Progress*, Beach, North Dakota, August 8, 1919

Tuesday or Wednesday, July 29 or 30, 1919

> *D. R. Offley, who owned the cattle, came later and demanded them... Bowen is said to have refused to give them up, until he had been paid for the damage done.*[129]

Another card stacked against the Bowens involved an old friend, former ranch hand, and fellow homesteader Carl Thompson. He had fought in WWI and returned home from the war just a day before Murrel's murder. That fateful morning, he left the Mallet Ranch to retrieve his horse, which he'd boarded with a neighbor while away.

Carl often said in the years that followed that if he had been at the ranch the day Murrel was killed, it would not have happened.

The Bowens' loyal friend
Carl Thompson in his WWI uniform

---

[129] *Fargo Courier-News*, Fargo, North Dakota, August 1, 1919

Thursday, July 31, 1919

Murrel's counter movement, while given the circumstances may have seemed reasonable, created a powder keg.

Outside of the situation with Offley's cattle, which may have become almost routine, Maud recalls the day as starting out quite normal. She and Murrel had been busy with ranch chores and tending to the children. Toward evening they returned to the house and were in the kitchen discussing the day's activities. Eldest daughter Lois was still with the Epleys, about 50 miles away. Mary, Evelyn, Bud, and Kay were outside playing in the yard. Murrel was making a sandwich for toddler Ada. Their last, fleeting, peaceful moments together.

> *The evening that was his last he sat on the porch there, by his wife, playing with their youngest child.*[130]

While the family went about their day, Offley traveled to Beach to obtain replevin papers – court orders granting the right to retrieve personal property claimed to be wrongfully taken or detained. The property was to be seized by designated officers; Ennis Taylor and Ira "Jay" Stark were enlisted by Offley to serve in that capacity. Taylor had until recently been employed by the Bowens as a ranch hand; Stark lived in the neighborhood. Both had been involved in the trouble with the Rataezyks. The orders were signed by

---

[130] *Golden Valley Progress*, Beach, North Dakota, August 8, 1919

Judge A. M. Stoddard, and State's Attorney Gallagher deputized Taylor and Stark.

> *Offley applied for replevin although it was known in the state's attorney's office of a bitter feeling between Taylor and Bowen. He was given constable powers and told to go and get the cattle.*[131]

> *...when [they] went to his office to secure replevin papers for the purpose of going to Mr. Bowen's ranch to take possession of cattle under his control, the state's attorney knew they were armed with "rifles, shotguns and revolvers, and he had reason to believe they intended to kill M. K. Bowen, but he took no action to prevent the murder."*[132]

It is curious how easily Offley was able to gain support from authorities, but after many months and many attempts, Murrel could not.

The parallel series of events would merge at dusk, approximately 8 o'clock that evening.[133] The subsequent chaotic minutes and hours are described next, from multiple – and often inconsistent – accounts.

According to Maud, Murrel looked out the window and saw four men, Offley, Taylor, Stark, plus Offley's brother-in-law, George Jeffrey, coming over the crest of the butte overlooking the ranch.

---

[131] *Golden Valley Progress,* Beach, North Dakota, August 8, 1919
[132] *The Bowbells Tribune,* Bowbells, North Dakota, September 5, 1919
[133] *Jamestown Weekly Alert,* Jamestown, North Dakota, August 7, 1919

Thursday Taylor, with Jay Stark, George Jeffrey and Bert Offley, all armed with revolvers and rifles, rode up to the Bowen home, two in an auto, two on horseback.

The four men, [Maud] says, came up to the corral just at dusk.[134]

Per Maud, Taylor and Stark were the two on horseback, and Offley and Jeffrey were in the car. Murrel could see Taylor and Stark were heavily armed. With four of his children still playing outside in the yard, he ran for the barn unarmed, in just overalls and short sleeves, aiming to keep the situation as calm as possible.

He saw his four neighbors ride over the crest of the butte and went down to the corral to deliver the cattle.[135]

Taylor handed a replevin paper for the cattle to him and he swung open the gate to let them out. From the porch Mrs. Bowen and her children watched the scene.[136]

The porch was roughly sixty yards from the barn and corral.[137] Per Maud:

...while Mr. Bowen was reading the paper the four men nodded at each other; while Bowen was returning from letting the cattle out Taylor pulled a gun that looked like a nickel plated or white. He held it in his hands. Mr. Stark was partly back and Mr. Taylor was going toward my

[134] *Golden Valley Progress*, Beach, North Dakota, August 8, 1919
[135] *Golden Valley Progress*, Beach, North Dakota, August 8, 1919
[136] *Golden Valley Progress*, Beach, North Dakota, August 8, 1919
[137] *Golden Valley Progress*, Beach, North Dakota, August 8, 1919

husband. Mr. Stark called, "get him" and the next thing I saw my husband was right in front of him and I heard two shots. Mr. Taylor fired the first two shots...two small cartridges were picked at the spot where Taylor fired first...I distinctly heard Stark say "get him"...Offley was at the corral when this occurred and that was the last she saw of him, and did not observe if he had a weapon. Jeffrey was on the outside of the corral with Stark...she did not see Jeffrey with a gun...Stark had a rifle in hand and a pistol strapped on his waist...[138]

Three of the men drove the cattle down the road, while Taylor remained by the gate. It is alleged that someone shouted to Taylor, "Get him," and that Taylor drew a revolver and shot Bowen twice.[139]

From her chair Mrs. Bowen watched them, saw Taylor draw his shiny white handled revolver and heard the shots..."I saw Taylor draw a revolver and said, "They're going to shoot Murrel"...[140]

Mrs. Bowen was sitting on the porch. Taylor is said to have continued after the fleeing rancher, and to have fired at him repeatedly. It is claimed that he cornered the wounded man in the barn and killed him. A bullet was found in one of the barn timbers, a horse was shot in the hip.[141]

[138] *The Beach Advance*, Beach, North Dakota, August 8, 1919
[139] *Fargo Courier-News*, Fargo, North Dakota, August 1, 1919
[140] *Golden Valley Progress*, Beach, North Dakota, August 8, 1919
[141] *Fargo Courier-News*, Fargo, North Dakota, August 1, 1919

Accounts from the four men tell a different story; they claim Murrel was "in a high rage" and threatened to shoot them first, although he'd already complied with the replevin papers and released Offley's cattle.

> *There were some words, it is said, over the condition of the cattle. Bowen, it is alleged, started for the barn in a high rage, in spite of efforts of Taylor and Stark to detain him. When he reappeared he was, it is alleged, pumping shells into a Winchester.*

> *...Taylor swears that Bowen was aiming at him when he (Taylor) whipped out an automatic and fired two shots at Bowen. This failed to stop Bowen, and, as he came on, Taylor, it is alleged, fired a third time. All of the shots, it was later discovered, took effect, but the third shot evidently was the one which caused Bowen's death.*[142]

Per Offley:

> *"Bowen has tried to get me on his place for a year, and although some of my property was over there, I feared to go after it, having heard he was 'laying for me,' but I thought I would be safe if accompanied by the officers.*

> *"When we first drove up Bowen saw a gun sticking out of Taylor's pocket and said, 'Don't come around here showing off your authority to me,' but I did not think he*

---

[142] *The Bismarck Tribune*, Bismarck, North Dakota, August 1, 1919

would attempt to shoot anybody until he came out of the barn with the gun and aimed it at Taylor."[143]

Per Taylor:

> *"We met Bowen near his barn," said Taylor, "and he asked: 'What are you – – doing here?' I served the papers on him. Bowen said we could have the cattle. Offley asked if the animals had been fed, and Bowen said they had at which Offley said they did not look like it. Bowen flew into a rage and said: 'I ain't going to take any more – – off you s – – b's' and started for the barn.*
>
> *"I told him to stay where he was but he continued on, so I caught hold of him and said he mustn't go into the barn, fearing he had a gun there, but he broke away, rushed into the barn and came out with a repeating gun in his hands, pumping a load into it. I then shot twice as he was raising the gun to shoot, but although both shots struck him in the left side, he was in the act of taking aim at me when I fired the shot that killed him, and he dropped in his tracks."*[144]

As soon as Maud heard the shots, she hurried into the house to get a shot gun they kept there.

> *When she heard the shots and saw her husband run toward the barn, she went into the house for a gun.*[145]

---

[143] *The Beach Advance*, Beach, North Dakota, August 1, 1919
[144] *The Beach Advance*, Beach, North Dakota, August 1, 1919
[145] *Fargo Courier-News*, Fargo, North Dakota, August 1, 1919

> *"…I hurried into the house to get a shot gun."*[146]

> *Mrs. Bowen…said that there was a sawed off shotgun in the residence…*[147]

Mary, who would turn nine in a few weeks' time, went into the house with Maud. Seven-year-old Evelyn gathered up her two younger brothers and, horrifyingly, headed for the barn.

> *While Mrs. Bowen was in the house, her children ran down to the barn.*[148]

Shot gun in hand, Maud then also headed for the barn with Mary. Maud kept trying to fire the gun at Taylor. She could not get it to work.

> *She reappeared with a shot gun, which she tried to fire repeatedly, but it would not work and she afterwards discovered that it was not loaded.*[149]

> *…it refused to operate. Then, she says, she ran to the barn to obtain a rifle, after her husband had been killed. Mrs. Bowen charged that the whole affair was a frameup, and that all of the posse were armed, while her husband neither had a gun nor attempted to shoot.*[150]

> *…she then got a shot gun from inside the house while Taylor was shooting; that she did not hear any shots after*

---

[146] *Golden Valley Progress*, Beach, North Dakota, August 8, 1919
[147] *The Fargo Forum*, Fargo, North Dakota, August 2, 1919
[148] *Golden Valley Progress*, Beach, North Dakota, August 8, 1919
[149] *Golden Valley Progress*, Beach, North Dakota, August 8, 1919
[150] *The Fargo Forum*, Fargo, North Dakota, August 2, 1919

the first two; that she started for the barn, when she saw Stark standing by a separator with a rifle on her...she could not operate the shot gun so ran to the barn to ask Mr. Bowen how to do it, and saw him lying there like he had fallen over...[151]

...She states that Stark leveled his rifle at her. She went on to the barn. Stark let her pass. She went into the barn intending to ask her husband how to handle the gun. She found him dead on a pile of manure, with her children clustered about him.[152]

...by the time she had ran to the barn, defying the threats of death, she was a widow.[153]

A sensational feature of the shooting was the part Mrs. Bowen took in the affair, she...fired at least eight shots at Offley and the constables as soon as the shooting at the barn began, but fortunately missed her marks.[154]

Per Taylor:

"...firing began from another source and we discovered Mrs. Bowen at the house, about 15 rods away, firing at us with a rifle. We all ducked, but she fired at least eight shots, when Constable Stark got the drop on her with his rifle and

---

[151] *The Beach Advance*, Beach, North Dakota, August 8, 1919
[152] *Golden Valley Progress*, Beach, North Dakota, August 8, 1919
[153] *Golden Valley Progress*, Beach, North Dakota, August 8, 1919
[154] *The Beach Advance*, Beach, North Dakota, August 1, 1919

she put down her gun, which I understand was found empty."[155]

Per Offley:

> *"About the same time the firing began at the barn Mrs. Bowen opened up from the house and bullets whizzed all around us, and we all sought cover."*

> *"When Mrs. Bowen began to shoot I jumped into a little creek but the bank was so low it gave little protection, and that Mrs. Bowen saw me there was plain from the fact that two or three bullets whizzed over me."*[156]

What happens next would be pivotal. Maud stated consistently that it was she who then placed the shotgun by Murrel's body, and Murrel had not handled a gun.

> *...she did not know what had become of the shot gun, but thought she dropped it by his side...*[157]

> *She had personally secured a shot gun during the fracas and later placed it near her husband's body.*[158]

She grabbed another gun, a rifle, hanging in the barn.

> *...when she could not operate the shot gun she asked one of her children where the rifle was and being informed, took it from a place on the wall...and went outside to try and operate it, when Stark said, "Stop, or I will kill you,"...she*

[155] *The Beach Advance*, Beach, North Dakota, August 1, 1919
[156] *The Beach Advance*, Beach, North Dakota, August 1, 1919
[157] *The Beach Advance*, Beach, North Dakota, August 8, 1919
[158] *The Bismarck Tribune*, Bismarck, North Dakota, July 6, 1921

had shot the rifle as the posse fled, aiming three times at Taylor...[159]

Then she rushed over to the range rider's horse and seized the rifle which he used on his trips about the ranch ever since the cattle poisoning began. Hans, the Bowen's farm hand, having heard the shots, came into the barn. He testified that he saw Offley in the dark corner, with a gun leveled at Mrs. Bowen, who did not know [Offley] was there. The hired man says he begged Offley not to shoot her. At this moment Mrs. Bowen went out of the barn and began firing at Taylor, who ran away over a hill. She then confronted Stark, who stood near a threshing separator with a gun leveled at her...

...Stark said "Stop or I will kill you."..."You get out of here you dirty dogs," she answered gathering her children about her, the widow returned to the house[160]*...then phoned for the sheriff and to other parties for help...*[161]

Per Maud, Evelyn had taken the younger children into the bedroom and locked the door. When Maud and Mary returned to the house to call for help, they coaxed them to come out. Evelyn eventually emerged with a white streak in her hair, a mark of fright she would wear for the rest of her life.

One of her six children, a girl of eight [this would have been Mary], telephoned to the nearest town, Ollie, Mont.,

---

[159] *The Beach Advance*, Beach, North Dakota, August 8, 1919
[160] *Golden Valley Progress*, Beach, North Dakota, August 8, 1919
[161] *The Beach Advance*, Beach, North Dakota, August 8, 1919

that "papa has been killed and we need help." Mrs. Bowen then called her relatives and the sheriff.

One of the children [according to Maud, 7-year-old Evelyn] then looked out of the window. "Oh, mama, we're all going to be killed," she sobbed. "There are men hovering all around." Mrs. Bowen saw Stark and Taylor on the hillside and she then determined to prevent their escape in the motor car which had been abandoned at the corral. She went out and fired a shot thru the hood and then got a hammer from the barn and smashed the spark plugs...She then returned to the telephone and finished her calls...[162]

...the four men...hovered around so she wrecked their auto so they could not take it...[163]

Given the party line telephone, the Bowen home was soon filled with friends and neighbors. Per Taylor, he also telephoned the sheriff, but it's unclear where he would have done so – he would have had to ride to another home, make the call, then return to the Mallet Ranch.

"I then telephoned the sheriff that I had shot Bowen and asked him to come down to the scene at once which he did, taking us all into custody pending the coroner's inquest. The shooting by me was done in self defense, as I was confident Bowen would shoot me if I did not get him first."[164]

[162] *Golden Valley Progress*, Beach, North Dakota, August 8, 1919
[163] *The Beach Advance*, Beach, North Dakota, August 8, 1919
[164] *The Beach Advance*, Beach, North Dakota, August 1, 1919

About 10 o'clock...Sheriff Pierzina, Coroner Rice and Dr. Maercklein drove down to the Bowen home and held an investigation...[165]

About 11 o'clock at night, Sheriff Pierzina arrived with the coroner, H. L. Rice. They went directly to the barn, without calling on Mrs. Bowen.[166]

Dr. C. J. Maercklein...[went] to the Bowen place on the night of the killing with the coroner, sheriff and Dr. Niece, and [examined] the body as best he could in the poor light...[167]

Dr. Niece was the dentist from Beach that had sold the Mallet Ranch to the Bowens. As the neighbors continued to arrive...

...One of the men from Ollie came in and told [Maud] Stark was on the place again. She went out to the barn and ordered him off. The sheriff stepped up and wanted to have [the] car removed, saying it would cause further trouble.

"Search it," said Mrs. Bowen. The sheriff looked in the back seat and found a rifle. He left it, but when the crowd of men yelled for him to look further, he found a box of cartridges. He asked for someone to take the car away, but no one volunteered. He and the coroner went away, telling the widow she could move the body anywhere she wished. Mrs. Bowen demanded that Stark be arrested, and the sheriff merely replied that Stark was "under subpoena."

165 *The Beach Advance*, Beach, North Dakota, August 1, 1919
166 *Golden Valley Progress*, Beach, North Dakota, August 8, 1919
167 *The Bismarck Tribune*, Bismarck, North Dakota, September 19, 1919

Taylor had given himself up shortly after Mrs. Bowen had telephoned the sheriff. At midnight the states attorney, after Mrs. Bowen had telephoned that others were at large and that the sheriff had not taken them in custody, drove out and arrested them himself.[168]

Although demanded to do so by Mrs. Bowen, Sheriff John Pierzina...refused to arrest parties in the shooting although they were present and Mrs. Bowen pointed them out and called attention to guns they had strapped on them. Stark and Offley were later arrested by the state's attorney and a deputy sheriff...[169]

Such was the last day of Murrel's life, a day of terror. How could the family have slept that night, deeply grieving and traumatized: Maud, now a 31-year-old widow with six children, expecting her seventh; Mary, who might have otherwise been thinking of her imminent ninth birthday; 7-year-old Evelyn who bravely ran into the fray and protected her younger siblings; confused and helpless 6-year-old Bud, 3-year-old Kay, and little Ada, just 17 months. And Lois, while the eldest, was just ten years old, hopefully spending a final peaceful night with the Epleys not yet knowing her father was gone.

---

[168] *Golden Valley Progress*, Beach, North Dakota, August 8, 1919
[169] *Golden Valley Progress*, Beach, North Dakota, August 8, 1919

CERTIFICATE OF DEATH.

State of North Dakota
Bureau of Vital Statistics

1 Place of Death
County Gol Valley State N Dak Registered No. 228
Township Bull Bury or Village or
City No. St., Ward
(If death occurred in a hospital or institution, give its name instead of street and number.)

2 Full Name Murrel K Bowen

(a) Residence. No. St., Ward. 1448
(Usual place of abode) (If nonresident give city or town and State.)

Length of residence in city or town where death occurred years, months, days
How long in United States, if of foreign birth years, months, days

PERSONAL AND STATISTICAL PARTICULARS

3 Sex Male
4 Color or Race White
5 Single, Married, Widowed, or Divorced (write the word) Married
5a If Married, Widowed, or Divorced HUSBAND of (or) WIFE of
6 Date of Birth (month, day, and year) Jan 31-1883
7 Age Years Months Days If less than 1 day, ...hrs or ...min.
8 Occupation of Deceased
(a) Trade, profession, or particular kind of work Farming & Ranching
(b) General nature of industry, business, or establishment in which employed (or employer)
(c) Name of employer
9 Birthplace (city or town)
(State or country) Iowa.

PARENTS

10 Name of Father Bruce B Bowen
11 Birthplace of Father (city or town)
(State or country) Virginia
12 Maiden Name of Mother Mary P. Sewell
13 Birthplace of Mother (city or town)
(State or country) U S A.
14 Informant Mrs M K Bowen
(Address) Carlyle Mont
15 Filed Aug 3 1919 C O Halvorson Registrar

MEDICAL CERTIFICATE OF DEATH

16 Date of Death (month, day, and year) July 31 1919
17 I HEREBY CERTIFY, That I attended deceased from 19..., to 19...
that I last saw h... alive on 19...
and that death occurred, on the date stated, at m.
The CAUSE OF DEATH* was as follows:
Gunshot Wounds
(duration) yrs. mos. ds.
CONTRIBUTORY
(Secondary)
(duration) yrs. mos. ds.
18 Where was disease contracted if not at place of death?
Did an operation precede death. Date of
Was there an autopsy?
What test confirmed diagnosis?
(Signed) H L Rice Coroner
(Address)
*State the Disease Causing Death, or in deaths from Violent Causes, state (1) Means and Nature of Injury, and (2) whether Accidental or Homicidal. (See reverse side for Add. space.)
19 Place of Burial, Cremation or Removal Beach N D
Date of Burial Aug 3 1919
20 Undertaker H A Bertrand Beach ND
Address

M. K. Bowen death certificate

August 1919

AN UNEXPECTED, VIOLENT DEATH OF A LOVED ONE is devastating; funeral arrangements to make, children to console, finances to settle, future plans to reconstruct. The same death caused by a criminal act, to which the widow served as the sole adult witness outside of the accused, would be unimaginable.

> *The killing of M. K. Bowen, a rancher, last night, has revealed a story of official incompetence and negligence that will assume state-wide importance. The slaying comes as the climax of more than a year of mysterious cattle poisoning, in which Bowen lost between 200 and 300 head. Mixed in the case is a political feud, and bitter animosity stirred by the war. Bowen was an active member of the Nonpartisan League, and was on the county loyalty committee, which circulated cards of allegiance.*

> *The tragedy is heightened by the fact that Bowen leaves his wife and six small children penniless.*[170]

Friday, August 1, 1919: Coroner's Inquest, Threats of a "Neck-Tie Party," Daughter Lois and the Epleys Arrive

News of Murrel's death stirred intense reactions across Golden Valley County, including speculation that his activism with the Nonpartisan League was a factor.

> *There had been bad blood for some time, it is said, between Bowen and Offley and other of his neighbors. The affair has*

---

[170] *Fargo Courier-News*, Fargo, North Dakota, August 1, 1919

created intense excitement here, and the killing is fast developing into a bitter partisan issue, although friends of Taylor insist that he fired only in self-defense and that his act had no political significance.

Beach is much incensed today over alleged efforts to make political capital from the killing of M. K. Bowen...Bowen was a prominent leaguer in the southern part of Golden Valley county, and socialist agitators here are alleged to be endeavoring to make it appear that Bowen was murdered because of his politics. There are open threats of a neck-tie party, in which Taylor, who is confined in the county jail here, will feature, and promises of what Governor Frazier will do.[171]

"Neck-tie party" is slang for a hanging or lynching by mobs taking punishment into their own hands.

Maud and her brother Lee drove into Beach the morning after the shooting, where she was approached by one of the editors of *The Beach Advance*.

Mrs. Bowen, with her brother, Lee Plummer, came to town the morning after the tragedy to attend to several very important matters. She did not arrive until near 10 o'clock. The coroner's inquest was set for 2 p.m. She was kept busy arranging her affairs.

The frantic woman had no more than alighted from the automobile until the gang editor began hounding her. She

---

[171] *The Bismarck Tribune,* Bismarck, North Dakota, August 1, 1919

asked him to wait until later as she had to look after some matters and hurry back home for the inquest. She went on her way only to be stopped a few minutes later by the gang editor. She appealed to him to not bother her as she was all wrought up and had more than she could attend to as it was before the inquest. She was approached the third time by this overzealous news hound and on this occasion her brother happened to be present.

"I don't want to talk about the horrible affair now. The inquest will be in a few hours and then you can get the testimony."

"Yes, but I want it right now," he insisted.

At this juncture Mr. Plummer stepped up and told him that he had better be on his way and not annoy Mrs. Bowen.[172]

They returned to the ranch, where the coroner's inquest was held that afternoon. Eldest daughter Lois had also returned home after news of Murrel's death reached the Epleys.

Little Lois Bowen...received the sad news of the death of her father last Thursday evening and started for her home near Beach, N. D., and was accompanied by her aunt, Mrs. Epley.[173]

...an inquest was held at the home of the deceased Friday afternoon by Coroner H. L. Rice, who made his selection of

[172] *Golden Valley Progress*, Beach, North Dakota, August 8, 1919
[173] *Fallon County Times*, Baker, Montana, August 7, 1919

the jury on the scene, and after the jury had been approved by Mrs. Bowen, proceeded with the inquest, State's Attorney R. F. Gallagher conducting the examination.[174]

Per a handwritten note by daughter Ada Bowen Rustad, we infer those present were Coroner Rice, Sheriff Pierzina, Dr. Maercklein; the jurors, Philipp Blancher, Carl Thompson, and Peter Palmer; as well as several family, friends, and neighbors, many of whom testified: Ed Honnold, W. D. Bundren, Charles McClure, Maud's brother Lee Plummer, Martin Fleet, Henry Alvin Hoverson, Mike Rataezyk, Maud's nephew William Westrope, her niece Lois Epley, and the Bowens' ranch hand John "Hans" Boegli.

Newspaper accounts also cite Gallagher, Dr. Niece, and one Dr. Thomas Templeton, from Carlyle, as being part of the proceedings.

Dr. Niece...guarded Taylor in the automobile some distance from the house while the officers were conducting their inquiry, as the crowd at the house was hostile and it was thought best to keep Taylor away from there.[175]

Gallagher was responsible for conducting the examination of the witnesses, but Lee Plummer later testified that Gallagher was not active at the inquest.

---

[174] *The Beach Advance*, Beach, North Dakota, August 8, 1919
[175] *The Bismarck Tribune*, Bismarck, North Dakota, September 19, 1919

[Plummer] said Gallagher neglected his duty at the inquest and that most of the questions were asked by Mrs. Bowen and others in the crowd. . .[176]

At the inquest large numbers of the neighbors testified as to [the Bowens'] high standing in the community. No one appeared to testify for the accused man.[177]

The more important evidence was given by Martin W. Fleet, John Boegli, Ed Honnold, and Mrs. Bowen, essentially as follows:

Fleet testified…that he arrived soon after the shooting and… saw [the] deceased lying dead in the barn; that Jay Stark came up, armed with rifle and pistol and was ordered off the place by Mrs. Bowen; that three weeks or a month before he had heard George Jeffrey say that he…would "get" Bowen, or that if he did not get him, Taylor would, and that he, Jeffrey, had it in for Bowen and was "sure going to finish him."

Boegli, hired man for Bowen, testified in effect that he was milking in another part of the barn when shooting occurred; that after the shooting Taylor ran into the barn where he was; he heard a number of shots; the first two not very loud and the others very loud, and after the first two shots heard Mr. Bowen say, "Get out of here you dirty dogs," and the louder shots followed; that he saw Offley with a gun; that Offley held up the gun at him; that Offley

[176] The Bismarck Tribune, Bismarck, North Dakota, September 20, 1919
[177] Golden Valley Progress, Beach, North Dakota, August 8, 1919

showed him the body of Bowen that was lying about ten feet within the barn. That Offley kept coming in and out of the barn. Then Mrs. Bowen came into the barn to get a rifle that was kept in the barn and loaded it.

That Offley raised his gun as if to shoot Mrs. Bowen, when he (Boegli) told him that was enough and about that time Stark came back to the place and asked, "Is Bert Offley here?" Boegli said no and Stark asked, "Is he shot?" and Boegli replied no one got shot except Bowen.

Ed Honnold testified that Taylor had told him in a Carlyle pool hall that he had some trouble with Bowen and that he was going to get the s—of a b—. He said he was going to get him if he had to get him with a rifle in the Badlands.[178]

Mrs. Bowen asserts that the husband neither had a gun nor attempted to shoot.[179]

As part of the inquest, Drs. Templeton and Maercklein, the latter having come to the Mallet Ranch with Sheriff Pierzina the night before, examined Murrel's body. Per Maud, he was still covered with dirt and manure, and the lighting in the barn where he lay was poor. There was also testimony regarding the gun shells that were found on the ground and in the barn, including in the body of one of the Bowens' horses.

---

[178] *The Beach Advance*, Beach, North Dakota, August 8, 1919
[179] *The Bismarck Tribune*, Bismarck, North Dakota, August 2, 1919

Several different...shells were found on the ground this morning where the shooting took place.[180]

At the inquest Friday afternoon a large number of witnesses testified to finding empty shells at the scene...and Drs. Templeton and Maercklein testified as to the location and character of the wounds...[and] that Mr. Bowen had been shot three times in the left side with a 45 caliber pistol.

There were five empty 45 caliber and two 32 caliber shells found on the ground at the point where the shooting took place, which indicates two pistols were used, and it is upon this and other evidence that the claim is made by friends of the deceased that the whole truth of the shooting has not yet been disclosed. A 32 caliber bullet was taken from the body of the horse which stood in the Bowen stable and its source has not yet been determined.[181]

...where Taylor stood when he fired the fatal shots, five empty 45-caliber shells were found. Taylor used an automatic, and while he said on the morning after the shooting that he shot three times, he indicated [later] that he wasn't quite certain as to the actual number of bullets "fired." At another point, near where Taylor stood, two empty 32-caliber shells were found.

Their presence there can't be explained.[182]

---

[180] *Golden Valley Progress*, Beach, North Dakota, August 8, 1919
[181] *The Beach Advance*, Beach, North Dakota, August 8, 1919
[182] *The Fargo Forum*, Fargo, North Dakota, August 4, 1919

At the close of testimony, the case was given to the jury, which brought the following verdict:

> *...we find that M. K. Bowen came to his death by shots fired from a large caliber revolver feloniously by the hands of W. E. Taylor. We also implicate Ira J. Stark, Bert Offley, and George Jeffrey to be accessories to the fact.*[183]

Inquest jurors Blancher, Thompson, and Palmer, as well as Rice, signed the Coroner's Warrant.

> *The four men who came armed to the Bowen ranch to take home the cattle of D. B. Offley were ordered held without bond by the coroner's jury. E. W. Taylor, the farm hand who had been deputized as constable, admitted the shooting.*[184]

During and after the inquest, however, there appeared to be a lack of urgency to arrest the four men.

> *[Mrs. Bowen] asked that he be arrested at once. The state's attorney said that he would attend to it. Jeffrey was at the Bowen place during the progress of the inquest. After two hours had passed and no arrest had been made Martin Blank...asked Mrs. Bowen...if she had demanded arrest of Jeffrey an hour or two before. She said she had but that he was still free. Blank started from the scene, the sheriff followed him to his automobile, and told him that he had better keep his mouth shut or he would "get his."*[185]

---

[183] Coroner's Warrant, Inquest Conclusion, August 1, 1919
[184] *Golden Valley Progress*, Beach, North Dakota, August 8, 1919
[185] *Golden Valley Progress*, Beach, North Dakota, August 8, 1919

The four men were afterward placed under arrest, but were allowed to be at large later without bail. They were also allowed to associate together and agree if they wished, on a story of murder. Taylor had previously claimed self-defense.[186]

Despite the lackadaisical attitude about detaining the accused, the outcome of the coroner's inquest gave initial hope that they would be punished.

When M. K. Bowen, the Golden Valley rancher was slain, his enemies and a number of the county officials thought nothing would be heard of it, and that his assailants would go free. The testimony at the coroner's inquest held in the ranch house was such that the four men could not be turned loose immediately. Officials that went out there light heartedly, sure that everything would be smoothed over, came back with more sober thoughts. The friends of Bowen thronged the rooms, determined to see fair play. Not a witness appeared in favor of the accused men. Not one neighbor had a word of criticism for the dead man, who, according to the view spread over the county by the gang paper [The Beach Advance], deserved all he got.

This matter is too serious to be concealed. The eyes of the entire state are on the city of Beach and this county. Many dark deeds have here gone unpunished. It is imperative that justice should be done at last.[187]

---

[186] *The Producers News*, Plentywood, North Dakota, August 8, 1919
[187] *Golden Valley Progress*, Beach, North Dakota, August 8, 1919

Saturday, August 2, 1919: Additional Wounds Discovered, the Accused Walk Freely, Langer Reacts in Shock

The determination of the jury at the coroner's inquest was that Taylor killed Murrel, and Offley, Stark, and Jeffrey were accessories to the crime. However, even more compelling evidence was discovered the following morning. While examining Murrel's clothing, Maud discovered two additional bullet holes in the back of his shirt. She traveled to Beach to present her findings and request another examination of his body.

> *Mrs. Maud Bowen, widow of the rancher who was slain...drove into Beach today with new evidence against the men held for the shooting. In gathering up the clothing of her dead husband, she discovered two small bullet holes in the back. These were not discovered at the coroner's inquest yesterday. Re-examination of the body was demanded by Mrs. Bowen...*[188]

> *Saturday morning a statement was made to Coroner Rice that it was believed that Mr. Bowen had been shot in the back twice in addition to the three shots in the left side, and upon looking over the two shirts of deceased...the coroner found two holes in the back of the shirts, which seemed to bear out the charge that two shots had been fired from a 32 caliber revolver in addition to those fired from the 45 automatic of Taylor.*

---

[188] *Golden Valley Progress*, Beach, North Dakota, August 8, 1919

> *Coroner Rice at once called upon Drs. Maercklein, Stough, and Museus to make a thorough examination of the body at the morgue, but Dr. Museus not being found, the other two made the examination.*[189]

In addition to being a respected physician with a large practice in Beach, Dr. Raymond Stough had served several terms as the county coroner.

> *Two wounds in the back were overlooked by physicians at the time of the inquest as Bowen's body was lying on a board, and his back was massed with blood and dirt, covering the wounds.*[190]

> *...two wounds were revealed in the back. This appears effectually to destroy the claims of the defendants that only one of them, E. W. Taylor, did any shooting. The three bullets in the side of M. K. Bowen were 45 calibre. Those in the back apparently are 32 caliber. A 32 caliber bullet was also found in the rancher's saddle horse, in whose stall he crouched in vain effort to escape death.*[191]

Along with Boegli's testimony that he saw Offley in the barn with a gun, the discovery of additional wounds in Murrel's back corroborates Maud's account throughout the rest of her life – that Offley also shot Murrel in the back, delivering the fatal wounds.

---

[189] *The Beach Advance*, Beach, North Dakota, August 8, 1919
[190] *The Fargo Forum*, Fargo, North Dakota, August 4, 1919
[191] *Golden Valley Progress*, Beach, North Dakota, August 8, 1919

Meanwhile, the four men accused were seen walking freely on the streets of Beach.

> Although technically under arrest, the four men appeared twice today on the street without guards. They lounged about and entered stores while the deputy sheriff was across the street a block away. Instead of being separated so that they could not get together on the story of the happening on the night of the killing, they spent the day chatting together in the office of Sheriff John Pierzina.
>
> Those few citizens of Beach who are in sympathy with the Nonpartisan League are uneasy. The feeling is often expressed that they fear they have no protection from the law and that the "prisoners" could easily obtain a revolver and kill someone on the streets of the city. The fact that Attorney General Langer is politically allied with the anti league officeholders of Golden Valley county also arouses considerable consternation. Without any intention of mixing politics in the case, it is felt that it is much safer to appear to be an IVA.
>
> The "prisoners" today all asserted that Taylor was the only one who shot Bowen, and that he did it in self defense.
>
> Offley, when seen by a reporter this morning, said that Bowen was a "Loud Talking Nonpartisan" and was always making trouble.[192]

---

[192] *Golden Valley Progress*, Beach, North Dakota, August 8, 1919

Martin Blank reported that he and Pierzina tussled over the accused men not being in custody.

> *"You've been disturbing the peace around here all day. Don't you get too gay OR I'LL GET YOU!" – sheriff of Golden Valley county to [Blank, after he asked Maud] if she had asked for the arrest of one of the party of murders.*

> *"I'll make you prove some of the d———n lying reports you've been sending to the governor about me, you "'**'/…'*"!!"** liar." – the sheriff with a big automatic sticking out of his hip pocket and a shining official star on the front of his vest. Gee but this country is full of brave birds.* [193]

> *Farmers are preparing new petitions to Governor Frazier to remove both the sheriff and States Attorney R. F. Gallagher. A few months ago the slain man circulated petitions asking [for] their removal on the ground of fraud in the election.* [194]

When Attorney General Langer heard of Murrel's death, it was reported he was shocked by the news.

> *Attorney General Langer was notified by the representative of The Courier-News of the Bowen slaying. "My God!" he exclaimed. "What, is that true?"*

> *"I didn't know anything about this," Mr. Langer went on, "save that Bowen is the fellow who has been complaining*

---

[193] *Golden Valley Progress*, Beach, North Dakota, August 8, 1919
[194] *Golden Valley Progress*, Beach, North Dakota, August 8, 1919

to me about some of his cattle having been poisoned. That isn't true, for I had one of my assistants and a detective working on the case some time, and they reported that there was nothing to the charge made repeatedly by Bowen. It's too bad he was killed."

"You had a detective on the case?" the reporter asked.

"Yes, the state had one and the federal government had one. Both made reports to me."

"Mr. Langer, friends of Bowen have said that one of the detectives had stated in his report that there was enough evidence to convict someone of the killing of Mr. Bowen's cattle. Is that true?" again asked the newspaper man.

"That is not true. Both detectives reported that there was no poisoning, no plot to poison Bowen's cattle and that there was no evidence of any. In fact the report of one of the men was very uncomplimentary to the rancher, for Bowen was thought of as a disturber. Both men have about the same opinion of the case," answered Langer.[195]

When asked by the reporter for the formal records from the cattle poisoning investigation, however, Langer refused to share them.

Mr. Langer, when asked for the detective's report, said that one of them was in the desk of an assistant who was out of

[195] *Fargo Courier-News*, Fargo, North Dakota, August 1, 1919

*town, and that he could not let the reporter see the other
one.*

*"It is too important to the case; come back some other time,
after this affair is over," he said.*[196]

After another emotionally grueling day, Maud returned
home, still feeling under threat.

*Mrs. Bowen was calm today after her exciting tragedy. She
wore the red and blue button of the Nonpartisan League
which Bowen had on his overalls when he died.*

*Mrs. Bowen drove back to her ranch home tonight, feeling
that she was still in danger of being attacked. The county
officers took every firearm from the ranch house. Her
parents will arrive from Iowa for the funeral tomorrow.*

*The widow… is well educated, and formerly a school
teacher in her home in Iowa. She and Mr. Bowen have lived
22 miles south of Beach for 11 years.*[197]

Sunday, August 3, 1919: Murrel's Funeral, State Investigator Arrives

Three days after Murrel's death, Maud, their families, and
their many friends bid their goodbyes; Murrel and Maud's
parents had made the trip from Iowa to attend.

*The funeral of Mr. Bowen was held in Beach, Sunday
afternoon, from the Methodist church and was very largely*

---

[196] *Fargo Courier-News*, Fargo, North Dakota, August 1, 1919
[197] *Golden Valley Progress*, Beach, North Dakota, August 8, 1919

attended by friends of deceased, many coming from a distance and from other parts of the state to attend it. The services were conducted by Rev. Thatcher, who spoke of the worth of deceased and his good characteristics and qualities that made him many friends.[198]

Farmers and their wives drove for 60 miles from Montana and North Dakota to attend the funeral of M. K. Bowen, the ranchman who was slain... Few, if any, of the residents of Beach attended. Their sympathy lies with the men who lolled on the green lawn of the jail as the mourners came to the morgue nearby.

The Methodist church...was filled with the friends of the family. Both Mr. and Mrs. Bowen spent their youth in Iowa and there is a large community of farmers nearabout from the same state. [Murrel's] father, B. B. Bowen, a retired farmer of Harlan, Iowa, was there, as was Mrs. Bowen's father, W. T. Plummer, also a retired farmer of the same place.

The services were in [the] charge of the Odd Fellows Lodge. Besides Mr. Bowen's fraternal emblem his widow had pinned on his breast the red, white, and blue badge of the Nonpartisan League.

"Murrel was so proud of this button," she sobbed, "and he shall wear it to his grave."[199]

---

[198] *The Beach Advance*, Beach, North Dakota, August 8, 1919
[199] *Fargo Courier-News*, Fargo, North Dakota, August 4, 1919

CARD OF THANKS

We wish to take this means of expressing our thanks and appreciation to our friends and neighbors and our friends from Ollie who assisted us so kindly during the trying hours following the murder of our beloved. Our heartfelt thanks go out to the Odd Fellows who assisted at the funeral and for the beautiful flowers they gave. We also wish to thank the able pastor who spoke such cheering words of comfort. May God Bless all who administered to us is our wish.

Mrs. M. K. Bowen and family[200]

He was buried in the Beach cemetery.

Given the escalating concern, and among some, outrage, that the four suspects were effectively walking the streets as free men, reports arose that a group of farmers had stockpiled weapons on the edge of Beach. It was speculated they may have been plotting a "neck-tie party" for fear the four men might otherwise go unpunished.

When the law breaks down, justice of a more primitive sort rises to take its place. Such was the secret danger that D. R. Offley, E. W. Taylor, George Jeffrey and Ira J. Stark were in immediately following the slaying of M. K. Bowen.

The farmers of Golden Valley county have always been suspicious of the county officials here. Rightly or wrongly, they felt that even Attorney General William Langer had

---

[200] *Golden Valley Progress*, Beach, North Dakota, August 8, 1919

been delinquent in his duties. And when there was delay in the arrest of some of the men...and later, when the men...were allowed more liberty than is customary in the case of men about to be charged with murder in the first degree, the friends of Bowen who are numerous...felt that it was up to them to step in.

The prisoners may have known how near they were to be lynched. ...with the coming of night, all the blinds of the jail were pulled tight, and the men no longer ventured outside on the lawn...

Long before the details of the slaying reached the outside world, the facts were known in every farm home in the county. Even in McKenzie county the farmers were talking of the danger of the four men escaping trial. They were ready at a moment's notice to come to Beach and prevent any miscarriage of the process of the law.

It is said that in a coulee on the edge of town Golden Valley farmers had secreted rifles, prepared to pick up the punishment of the accused slayers the minute the county officials laid it down.[201]

In response, Governor Frazier assigned an investigator to travel to Beach and restore order. Inspector Seaman Smith, former sheriff of Golden Valley County, arrived the same day as the funeral. His presence went a long way toward

---

[201] *Golden Valley Progress*, Beach, North Dakota, August 8, 1919

diffusing tensions and creating confidence that justice would be seen.

S. A. Smith

Governor Frazier himself was forced by circumstances to take a hand in this crisis. His special investigator, Seaman Smith, former sheriff of Golden Valley county, was rushed here with full authority to make arrests and to preserve order.[202] After calling at the jail, he drove out to the Bowen ranch to begin his inquiry.[203]

Messages from several were sent from Beach to the effect that the four men held for the murder of Bowen were running at large, that they appeared on the streets, in buildings and went about without the usual escort assigned to prisoners held for murder. The sheriff has accused the editor of the Progress with circulating lies and various sundry other things for the purpose of discrediting him. The sheriff accosted the editor on the street Monday morning and in vile language denounced the editor "for having spread the — lies." Mr. Smith was present and in prompt order cooled the sheriff down and advised him that time would tell whether the editor had lied or not.

The presence of Mr. Smith has meant a great deal to the citizens of Beach – it is possible that he has averted further

---

[202] *Golden Valley Progress*, Beach, North Dakota, August 8, 1919
[203] *Fargo Courier-News*, Fargo, North Dakota, August 4, 1919

trouble as it is known that the sheriff and many of his followers…are bitter against those friends of Bowen who are afraid to assert their opinions.[204]

He is a big man, and a determined one, and all alone he swung affairs back into their accustomed channels.

The last threat of lynching died down with his appearance. Likewise, those who had been talking of violence against the editor of the farmer paper in Beach also quieted. The town people suddenly discovered the danger of civil strife, and were glad to have it ended.

There are hotbeds in Beach and…many crimes that have gone unpunished.[205]

Monday, August 4, 1919: Suspects Held, Attorney Simpson Arrives

The charge of slaying M. K. Bowen…ceased to be a joke today. Upon receipt of a telegram from Governor Frazier, John Pierzina, sheriff, locked E. W. Taylor, D. R. Offley, J. Stark, and George Jeffrey in separate cells.

Today they did not lounge about on the grassy lawn or walk the streets on their way to meals.[206]

Maud had input into naming the prosecuting attorney in the case. She agreed upon Leslie Simpson from Dickinson, who

---

[204] *Golden Valley Progress*, Beach, North Dakota, August 8, 1919
[205] *Golden Valley Progress*, Beach, North Dakota, August 8, 1919
[206] *Fargo Courier-News*, Fargo, North Dakota, August 4, 1919

was well-known across the state and had a solid reputation. He arrived in Beach on August 4.

> *Hon. L. A. Simpson, one of the best known and most successful criminal lawyers in the Northwest, has been retained by Mrs. M. K. Bowen to aid in the prosecution of the men held for the murder of her husband.*[207] *"I do not know of another lawyer in the state whom I would rather have aid in the prosecution."*[208]

> *Mrs. Bowen, accompanied by Mr. Simpson, drove into Beach today to swear out a formal complaint charging the four men with murder in the first degree. The hearing will be held this week.*[209]

> *The state's attorney stated that he was very glad to have Mr. Simpson's aid in the prosecution and that he would render every assistance possible to see that justice is done…[however] it is known that he and Bowen were on bad terms and that he was friendly with some of the parties accused…*[210]

Tuesday, August 5, 1919: Arrest Warrants Issued, Frank Evans Returns

After Simpson made the formal complaint, signed by Maud, warrants of arrest were issued with charges of murder in the

[207] *Golden Valley Progress*, Beach, North Dakota, August 8, 1919
[208] *The Bismarck Tribune*, Bismarck, North Dakota, August 8, 1919
[209] *Fargo Courier-News*, Fargo, North Dakota, August 4, 1919
[210] *Golden Valley Progress*, Beach, North Dakota, August 8, 1919

first degree, which were signed by Judge Stoddard and Sheriff Pierzina.[211]

That afternoon at 4:30 p.m., Pierzina brought the four defendants before Judge Stoddard. They were informed of their right to a preliminary examination hearing, which they requested. The hearing was set for August 8th at 9:30 a.m. in Beach.[212]

Maud had requested that Frank Evans, the most recent investigator of the cattle poisoning, return to Beach immediately. He arrived on August 5th.

> *Evans, whom Mrs. Bowen regards with utmost confidence, was summoned to Beach by Mrs. Bowen, following the shooting as one of the men who could bring about justice.*

Per Evans:

> *I left the next day for Beach and arrived there on Tuesday the 5th of August, 1919. Mrs. Bowen introduced me to Mr. Simpson, a lawyer she had called in on the case and he said he wanted to have a talk with me. I told him, "...I will do everything I can to help you to bring to justice the men who killed Bowen."*[213]

---

[211] Warrant of Arrest, August 5, 1919
[212] Justice's Return to District Court, August 5, 1919
[213] *The Bismarck Tribune*, Bismarck, North Dakota, August 8, 1919

Wednesday, August 6, 1919: Subpoenas Issued

Subpoenas were sent to witnesses for the prosecution, including many who had testified at the coroner's inquest.[214]

Given his close relationship with the Bowens, and as one called to testify in the formal hearings, Martin Blank recused himself of writing further pieces related to the details of Murrel's murder. Thereafter, "...*Paul Greer, daily newspaper representative [from Grand Forks], a stranger in the community and not long in the state, who is absolutely unbiased or prejudiced in any way...*" wrote several of the related stories in the *Progress* thereafter.[215]

One of Greer's poignant articles infers he made a visit to the Mallet Ranch during the week after Murrel's killing.

> *It is easy to understand Bowen's regret over being driven to give up this pleasant home. But in this cattle country, when a man has a hidden enemy who is determined to drive him out, it is the part of discretion to leave before actual violence is done.*
>
> *Driving down the [illegible] sees in the yard. The youngest is just old enough to call out the word "papa" in an innocent way that is heartbreaking.*
>
> *The car is driven up to the corral where Taylor, Offley, Jeffrey and Stark accosted Bowen on the night he was shot. Taylor, who was known as an enemy of the rancher, had*

---

214 Subpoenas for Preliminary Hearing, August 6, 1919
215 *Golden Valley Progress*, Beach, North Dakota, August 8, 1919

deputized as a constable by some unknown means for the purpose of serving a replevin paper for Offley's cattle. He claims that he was the only one that shot Bowen, and the others tell the same story. This will perhaps be determined at the preliminary hearing which may be held Wednesday. There is the pile of refuse in the stall where Bowen was found dead. His favorite mare, who stood there also was shot and lies outside where it was taken for the extraction of a bullet that may establish that two or more men fired their shots. There is a bullet hole through the posts and another that extends through four of the studdings.

…One who views this ruin of Bowen's life work, and who understands the love a man has for his stock, wonders if he is not happier now that he is dead. Then the thought comes to the young widow and her six children, and one knows that Murrel Bowen would have willingly borne a thousand times more agony than to have left them without his support.[216]

Although by most accounts, their financial prospects were still extremely precarious, one last article from Martin Blank described the recovery Murrel had been making, suggesting that had he lived, the Bowens' fortunes might have started to turn.

Although suffering great financial losses as a consequence of the loss of his cattle, Mr. Bowen, with a good crop of flax on his school sections, a fair stand of wheat on several tracts and a herd of pure bred shorthorns with a fine

---

[216] *Golden Valley Progress*, Beach, North Dakota, August 8, 1919

*increase last spring, was about to emerge from his
difficulties and his circumstances, as the truth now reveals
itself, would have placed him on a solid financial footing
this fall. Providence was kind to Bowen this year – until
his tragical end – rain fell on his sections and good crops
of grass, wheat and flax are everywhere evident.*[217]

Friday, August 8, 1919: *Golden Valley Progress* **Published**

A substantial portion of the August 8th publication of the
local *Golden Valley Progress* newspaper was dedicated to
Murrel's murder, including re-publication of pieces from the
Fargo Courier-News, accounts by correspondent Paul Greer,
and several fiery opinion pieces by Martin Blank. Blank
would soon face libel charges as a result.

> *"The Golden Valley Progress will perhaps touch the match
> to the powder this week and start stirring up community
> strife just like the other league papers in the state. I've
> always had a lot of consideration for the editor of the
> Progress because he has kept down community fusses and
> avoided saying things that might stir up a feeling of hatred
> in the community – I hope that he behaves himself on this
> murder proposition."*

> *That was the statement of a well-known businessman,
> usually quiet but decidedly opposed to the Nonpartisan
> league.*

[217] *Golden Valley Progress*, Beach, North Dakota, August 8, 1919

And right here is where we want to let that bird know that the gauntlet has been laid down to us and we will stir this community as she has never been stirred before. But our activities will not be confined to the slinging mud at the defenders of the murderers of M. K. Bowen, but we are going to exert our every effort to see that they will be understood when all is over that the people of this community want law and order and will not tolerate the classes that now uphold those responsible for M. K. Bowen's death and were just as ardent in support of other murderers who have been given immunity baths in this community.

When the sheriff of Golden Valley county refused to arrest the parties connected with the shooting when demanded to do so by the only eye witness; when the sheriff of Golden Valley county was more interested in getting the automobile away from the scene of the murder than he was in getting the dead body of Murrel K. Bowen removed from the manure pile upon which it was resting; when the sheriff of Golden Valley county showed up at the coroner's inquest without all of the guns that were on the scene at the shooting; when the sheriff of Golden Valley county gave the prisoners privilege to walk around on the streets of Beach as tho they had done nothing – both before and after the inquest which ordered them held without bail for first degree murder – when the sheriff did all of this, the editor of the Golden Valley Progress decided then and there – regardless of the threats to "get him" made by the sheriff at the inquest – the editor then made up his mind that the time had come when the rottenness of the county should be bared – and by the eternal Gods he's going to bare it, unless the dirty cowards resort to the same tactics to "get him" that they did Murrel Bowen.[218]

It is possible that the sheriff and his friends may accuse the Golden Valley Progress of lying about his conduct in regard to handling the Bowen murder case. If he does or they do, just remind them that the Golden Valley Progress is liable if we have lied and that the editor be "pinched" for slander. And then ask whosoever say that we lie why they do not take action against the paper and the editor. The sheriff has made the crack that he would show that Nonpartisan paper that there was law in the county, so if we have lied, let him make good.[219]

Blank also published his sentiments about Attorney General Langer.

We wonder if Bill Langer's heart throbbed just a little – or more when word came to him that M. K. Bowen, the man whom he turned so coldly down when asked for help, was foully murdered – and by a man whom Langer should have had sent to prison months ago. God may forgive Bill Langer for his stupid political trickery but the good people of Golden Valley county never will.[220]

The fact that Attorney General William Langer had failed in his duty to protect Bowen adds to the uneasy feeling

---

[218] *Golden Valley Progress*, Beach, North Dakota, August 8, 1919
[219] *Golden Valley Progress*, Beach, North Dakota, August 8, 1919
[220] *Golden Valley Progress*, Beach, North Dakota, August 8, 1919

over the whole state. When the machinery of justice is clogged by political entanglements, no man can feel that his life is safe. With Langer in the attorney generalship, and working at odds with the administration, seeking to block many of the laws enacted by the last legislature and endorsed by the people at the referendum election, the condition approaches that of anarchy.

There is a feeling that if the men who were in the party that slew the Golden Valley rancher had felt that they would be prosecuted for their crime, Murrel Bowen would have been alive today. The fact that for many months he had suffered persecution and injury at the hands of cattle thieves and poisoners would have led anyone to believe that he was without any defense, a man that could be shot down without fear of consequences.

With Attorney General Langer hand-in-hand with the corrupt ring in Golden Valley county, law and order was practically dead and buried.

The efforts of the gang editor of Beach to make it appear that Taylor, Offley, Jeffrey and Stark had committed no crime is the most dastardly part of the events following the shooting. It is notorious that his paper is controlled by at least two of our county officers. That their parrot should take it upon himself to defend the prisoners and defame the widow is an indication of the disgraceful situation in this county. It is such papers as that one that are sowing seeds of anarchy. The bitter attacks on the Nonpartisan league, on Governor Frazier and everyone connected with the *farmer administration are direct incitement to weak minds to perform deeds of murder.*

Many people in this state are worried for the governor. Defeated in the democratic contest by ballot the old gang is desperate enough to attempt any crime to recover its power.

That is why the case in Golden Valley has aroused the indignation of the whole state. That is why the farmers want to see our corrupt county officers removed from office.

The law is supreme in North Dakota, and will be upheld. That is the fight in which the Golden Valley Progress is enlisted.[221]

---

[221] *Golden Valley Progress*, Beach, North Dakota, August 8, 1919

Friday, August 8 through Tuesday, August 12, 1919: Preliminary Hearing

The preliminary examination hearing to determine whether formal charges against the four men were warranted began August 8th. The hearing was overseen by Judge Stoddard, who had also signed Offley's replevin papers on July 31st.

> *The preliminary hearing has been set for today. The prisoners are confident they will be released, either free men, or on bonds, at this time.*[222]

> *The preliminary hearing of E. W. Taylor, Ira J. Stark, Bert Offley and George Jeffrey...was begun...at the junior high school auditorium.*

> *A large crowd gathered Friday morning in anticipation of hearing the evidence, but on motion of the defendant's counsel, the hearing was held behind closed doors, even the witnesses being separated and not allowed to hear the testimony of others, a proceeding conceded to be wise on all sides.*

> *The prosecution was conducted by Judge S. L. Nuchols, of Mandan, appointed special representative of the attorney general's office, he having been nominated for this duty on the request of Attorney General Langer, by Mrs. Bowen's counsel, Hon. L. A. Simpson of Dickinson...who, with State's Attorney R. F. Gallagher, joined Judge Nuchols in prosecuting the case.*

---

[222] *Fargo Courier-News,* Fargo, North Dakota, August 4, 1919

The defendants were represented by Attorney Mark F. Jones, of the firm of Keohane & Jones, Beach, who conducted a very vigorous cross examination of witnesses.[223]

In addition to Jones, court records show that the defendants were also represented by John Keohane and R. M. Andrews.[224]

The defendants by their counsel demanded that the testimony in the case be reduced to writing. It was so ordered. It was stipulated in open court...that Mrs. M. [Loebe] be appointed...to take the testimony in shorthand notes and to transcribe the same into longhand and that the reading and signing by each witness of the testimony given by such witness be waived.[225]

The defense requested that only Judge Stoddard, Mrs. Loebe, Maud, Simpson, Nuchols, Gallagher, the defendants and their counsel, Coroner Rice, Sheriff Pierzina, and his deputies be present. Witnesses would only be admitted for their own testimony, and any thereafter. Although the defense protested S. A. Smith's presence, Judge Stoddard allowed him to stay given his role as a special investigator for the state. These questions being addressed, the hearing began at 2 o'clock that afternoon, with the state calling Maud as its first witness.[226]

---

[223] *The Beach Advance*, Beach, North Dakota, August 15, 1919
[224] Preliminary Hearing Record, August 12, 1919
[225] Preliminary Hearing Record, August 12, 1919
[226] Preliminary Hearing Record, August 12, 1919

By 6 o'clock that evening, her testimony had not concluded, thus she was on the stand again when the hearing resumed at 9 o'clock the following morning. Coroner Rice and Drs. Maercklein and Stough followed. That afternoon, C. A. McClure, Henry Hoverson, Lee Plummer, and Ed Honnold testified on behalf of the state.

After taking Sunday off, the hearing was reconvened on Monday, August 11th, with testimony from William Westrope, W. A. Cooper, John Boegli, Martin Fleet, Sheriff Pierzina, Martin Blank, and Emil Rustad.

> The hearing of E. W. Taylor...continued today behind closed doors, [August 11] being the third day of the hearing.
>
> It is understood that the defendant will offer no testimony, but will rest his case when the state completes the introduction of testimony.[227]

During the course of the testimony, the exhibits A to Z were offered and received as evidence:

> A – Notice to present bond and copy of Bond.
>
> B – Bowen's shot gun – 12 gauge – Serial # E-487789 – Model 1897 – Winchester.
>
> C – White handled revolver (Pearl) – Automatic Colt – Caliber 32 – Rimless – smokeless – Serial #107142 (Taylor's gun).

---

[227] *Grand Forks Herald*, Grand Forks, North Dakota, August 11, 1919

D – Union suit.

E – Over shirt.

F – Colt 45 – Government Model C – 19683.

G – Colt's Automatic – Caliber 32 – Rimless – smokeless – Serial #279409.

H – Rifle – 30 W. C. F. Serial #659350 – Winchester – Model 1894.

I – Rifle – Model 1892 – Winchester – No. 418924 – A. D. 13.

J – Holster – Leather automatic – Stamped – Al. Furstnow – Miles City, Mont.

K – One 45 Caliber bullet with Bar x (⚹) also Five Rem. U.M.C. empty 45 caliber shells – Two 32 A.C.W.R.A. Co. empty shells.

L – Three 45 caliber bullets taken out of body of Bowen.

M – Eight Rem. U.M.C. Large caliber bullets with figures 18 on end, of each.

N – Two 32 W.C.F. & W.R.A. Co. bullets.

O – Horse bullet in envelope.

P – Nine revolver bullets 32 A.C.P. Rem. U.M.C. U in center of cap.

Q – 32 loaded bullet – W.R.A. Co. A.C.

R – *Diagram produced by Dr. Stough.*

S – *Diagram produced by Dr. Stough.*

T – *Rem. U.M.C. 32 A.C. P. x mark on outside of shell – empty shell*

U – *30-30 Savage Rifle – 78.659*

V – *Order to release cattle signed by A. M. Stoddard Justice of the Peace, dated July 31, 1919.*

W – *Black clasp pocket book, containing coins, charm (Swift Premium Ham) and papers as follows: ticket for flax issued 12-27-'18; M. K. Bowen; receipt for registered article from M. K. Bowen to Governor Frazier; issued from Beach P. O. July 12, 1919; piece of letter from Carl Thompson, Co.M, 333 Inf. 84th Div. A.E.F.; protested check from First National Bank of Carlyle, Mont., dated Nov. 19, 1918, to the order of Woodward Bros., for $1.00, signed by M. F. Meigs, and notice of protest also with it.*

X – *Leather pocket book with stamp of First National Bank of Beach, North Dakota, containing M.O. Receipt for $10.95, from Beach P.O. No. 80000 and business card from Sunnybrook Stock Farm, containing name on back written in pencil.*

Y – *Pocket knife, tire gauge, and lead pencil enclosed in metal case.*

Z – *30-30 Peters loaded shell with mark in part of loaded bullet protruding.*

AA – Box of 19 loaded bullets – 30-30 Peters.[228]

On the afternoon of August 11th, the state rested its case. The defense then motioned the court to dismiss the complaint on the grounds that there was not enough evidence to show that a crime had been committed. As there was a desire to argue this motion, the hearing was adjourned until the following day. Defense attorney Mark Jones and prosecutor Nuchols made the final arguments.[229]

> *No witnesses were put on for the defense and at the conclusion of the testimony the motion of defense for dismissal of accused was denied by the court...after exhaustive arguments by counsel.*[230]

It is unclear why no witnesses were called for the defense. Judge Stoddard overruled the motion for dismissal and ordered the defendants to be charged with first degree murder and held in the custody of the sheriff. His statement after the examination:

> *...it appearing to the court that the crime of Murder in the First Degree... has been committed and that there was probable cause to believe that the defendants committed said crime...I ordered that each of said defendants...be committed to the custody of the sheriff of said county...*[231]

> *All four accused men were held...without bail, there being no other course open to the court in view of the one-sided*

---

[228] Preliminary Hearing Record, August 12, 1919

[229] Preliminary Hearing Record, August 12, 1919

[230] *The Beach Advance*, Beach, North Dakota, August 15, 1919

[231] Preliminary Hearing Record, August 12, 1919

evidence, and it not being in the power of a justice in such case to grant bond. The defense is preparing an application to the district court for freedom of all the prisoners on bond awaiting the term of the district court next December. Judge Nuchols and Attorney Simpson departed for their homes Tuesday noon, and all excitement over the case has subsided so far as the general public is concerned.[232]

This was the outcome that Maud and the Bowens' friends had hoped for and expected. It likely gave them initial hope that justice would be done. The detailed written testimony of the preliminary hearing as taken by Mrs. Loebe is unfortunately not part of the formal court records on file at the Golden Valley County courthouse, thus we are unable to include it here. More importantly and unfortunately, it would also not be fully leveraged during subsequent proceedings related to the murder.

The Defendants[233] [234]

Outside of what has been described thus far, following is additional information about the four defendants and their relationships to the Bowens, gathered from conversations with Maud and publicly available sources.

---

[232] *The Beach Advance*, Beach, North Dakota, August 15, 1919
[233] United States Federal Census 1920
[234] Plat map of Bull Run Township

Delbert "Bert" Rufus Offley was born in December 1882 in Codington County, South Dakota; he was just a month older than Murrel.[235] Outside of the decade he farmed in Golden Valley County, he spent much of his professional life as a merchant.[236]

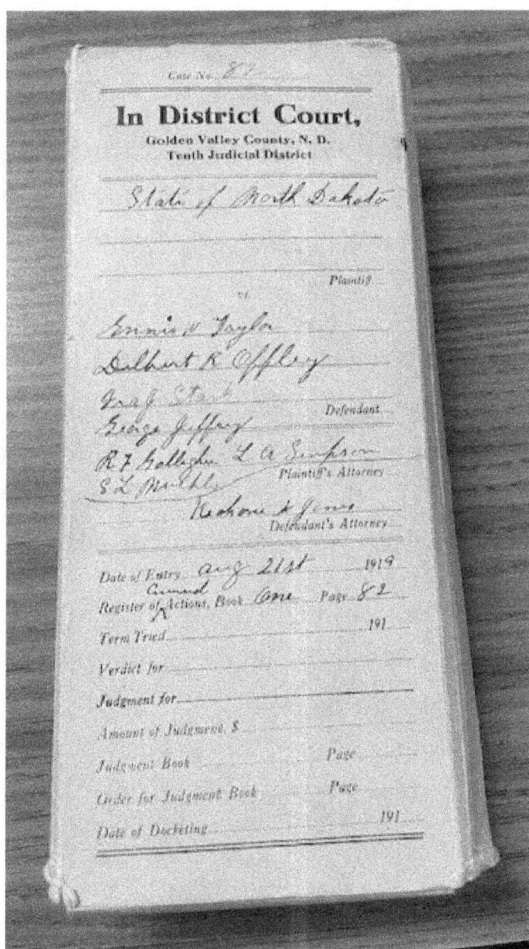

Preliminary hearing court records,
Golden Valley County Courthouse

---

[235] *Sioux County Pioneer*, Fort Yates, North Dakota, March 2, 1922
[236] *Union County Courier*, Elk Point, South Dakota, May 7, 1903

He and his wife Emma married in 1908 in Minneapolis, and by 1910 were living in Golden Valley County. The Offleys owned a half section of land on Section 14, part of which bordered the Mallet Ranch, and another 160 acres nearby on Section 12. They had four children close in age to the Bowen children; they may have attended school together. His brother Ray had 160 acres that abutted both Delbert's land and the Mallet Ranch.

George Robert Jeffrey was born in Wisconsin in 1884. He was the brother of Offley's wife, Emma. He owned a quarter of land bordering Ray Offley's property in Section 14, close to the Bowens.

Ennis Walter Taylor was born in 1880 in Upshur County, Texas, age 39 at the time of Murrel's shooting. He came to North Dakota helping drive 1,000 Texas cattle to *"the fertile ranges of western North Dakota."*[237] He was described as *"...nearly six feet tall, dark and weighs 150 pounds."*[238]

Taylor worked on threshing crews in the area, including Murrel's, and was also employed by the Bowens during much of their time on the Mallet Ranch. He and his wife Mary lived in an apartment on the ranch when Taylor worked for the Bowens. They seemed to live largely hand to mouth.

> *[Taylor] has no...means of paying counsel...no means, money or property, except his wearing apparel, a few*

---

[237] *Grand Forks Herald*, Grand Forks, North Dakota, May 19, 1926
[238] *Jamestown Weekly Alert*, Jamestown, North Dakota, August 7, 1919

dishes and some bedding, all of which does not exceed in value the sum of $25.00.[239]

Murrel had become suspicious of Taylor after seeing him in "secret conferences" with Offley. Taylor was also cited as being involved in the attempted shootings of the Rataezyks.

Ira J. "Jay" Stark was born in 1896 in Minnesota. The second eldest of seven children, he moved with his parents to Ollie, Montana in the spring of 1908.[240]

At 23 years old, he was the youngest of the four men at the time of Murrel's murder. He owned a quarter of land in the southeast corner of Section 1 in Bull Run Township.[241] He was named by the Rataezyks as being involved in the aggressions against them.

Some sources cited that the four defendants were members of the Nonpartisan League, thereby negating any potential political motivations in the killing. Per the *Golden Valley Progress*, however:

> *Examination of the records of the Nonpartisan league state headquarters in Fargo show that none of the four men...are members of the league. The dead man was a member in good standing.*
>
> *The editor of the local gang sheet wired to the gang dailies of the state that the accused men were members of the league. Where he got his information or whether he*

---

[239] Court Records, June 14, 1921
[240] *The Fallon County Times*, Baker, Montana, October 18, 1934
[241] Plat map of Bull Run Township

deliberately lied to save somebody's scalp will perhaps be revealed as the case progresses.[242]

Friday, August 15, 1919: Bail Is Set

On August 15, Sixth Judicial District Judge W. C. Crawford ordered bail for the prisoners set at $10,000 each,[243] over $150,000 today.

Saturday, August 16, 1919: Three Defendants Free on Bond; Martin Blank Charged with Criminal Libel

The following day, Jeffrey, Stark, and Offley had bond posted,[244] allowing them to be free pending the trial – a trial that would not occur for nearly two more years.

Jeffrey's bail was posted by a combination of three people: Fred Kragbak, a farmer from Golva, Offley's mother Sarah Jane, and Samuel Fisher, a neighbor from Bull Run Township who put up a sizable $8,000.

Stark's bail was put up by a combination of four people: again Sam Fisher, Fisher's daughter Ettie Erickson, Charles Woodsend, and Loren Bearfield, another neighbor in Bull Run Township. Woodsend, who had been a friend of the Bowens, pledged $5,000.

Offley's bail money was put up by three people: George Christensen, a storekeeper and farmer from Golva and former Golden Valley clerk of district court who ran on the

---

[242] *Golden Valley Progress*, Beach, North Dakota, August 8, 1919
[243] Order Fixing Amount of Bail, August 12, 1919
[244] Bail Bond, August 16, 1919

IVA ticket[245], and two farmers from Golva – Claud Schouboe and J. H. Sifert. Christenson put up $7,000, the others covered the balance.

Fisher, Christensen, and Woodsend must have had strong feelings to put up these considerable sums. Fisher, Christensen, and Bearfield would later be called by the defense as character witnesses at the murder trial, to help prove that Murrel *"...had the general reputation of being a bullying bad man and...habitually carried a gun."*[246]

Taylor was without any bondsmen and remained in jail from 1919 until 1921.

Also on August 16th, Sheriff Pierzina began a pursuit of Martin Blank, whose opinion pieces against Gallagher, Pierzina, and Langer in the August 8th edition of the *Golden Valley Progress* brought about criminal libel charges.

> *John Pierzina...left this morning for Fargo with a warrant for the arrest of Martin Blank...who is charged by State's Attorney Gallagher with criminal libel.*
>
> *Blank, who has been conducting an active propaganda in connection with the recent killing of M. K. Bowen, is alleged to have charged Gallagher editorially in this week's edition with conniving with Offley to shoot Bowen.*[247]

---

[245] *Adams County Record*, Hettinger, North Dakota, July 14, 1921
[246] *Adams County Record*, Hettinger, North Dakota, July 14, 1921
[247] *The Bismarck Tribune*, Bismarck, North Dakota, August 16, 1919

Tuesday, August 19, 1919: Martin Blank Leaves the State

Martin F. Blank...is a fugitive from justice today, according to information received by Cass county authorities this afternoon, he is in hiding in Moorhead or nearby.

Blank, whose interests are being looked after by William Lemke, vice president of the Nonpartisan league, eluded arrest by driving a car out of North Dakota and the last heard from him he was in Moorhead, believing himself safe there from extradition to North Dakota...[248]

Monday, August 25 through Friday, August 29, 1919: Blank Travels Back to Beach

He finally was discovered at Moorhead, Minn., where he...remained during the recent convention of the Townley newspaper men, who feted him and banqueted him and generally accorded him the honors due a hero.

Blank was seen in Jamestown on Monday night by a Beach citizen, whom he advised that he (Blank) was en route home to Beach with his family... Tuesday night Blank is alleged to have been seen at league hotel headquarters [in Bismarck]. Advice to this effect was wired Sheriff John Pierzina at Beach, and he forwarded instructions here to Sheriff Welch for the apprehension of Blank. Welch stated

---

[248] *The Bismarck Tribune*, Bismarck, North Dakota, August 19, 1919

today that he knew nothing of Blank's whereabouts, and the league hotel denied that he had registered there.[249]

Friday night Martin F. Blank…returned to [Beach] from Moorehead, Minn., where he had been for about ten days evading arrest on a charge of criminal libel, sworn out by State's Attorney R. F. Gallagher.[250]

Saturday, August 30, 1919: Blank Arrested

Early Saturday morning Blank was arrested and arraigned in justice court…and he was released on $2,500 bonds.[251]

As the month after Murrel's killing came to a close, four men had been charged with first degree murder. Three were out on bail pending trial. The Bowens' friend Martin Blank became a fugitive averting criminal libel charges, ultimately arrested. Their world continued to be turning upside down.

[249] *The Bismarck Tribune*, Bismarck, North Dakota, August 28, 1919
[250] *The Beach Advance*, Beach, North Dakota, September 5, 1919
[251] *The Beach Advance*, Beach, North Dakota, September 5, 1919

Fall 1919, Winter 1920

IN THE MONTHS AFTER MURREL'S DEATH, Maud was bereft. Widowed at 31, she was torn between anger and despair over losing her beloved husband; the need to give her six, soon to be seven, children consolation and encouragement to forge ahead; and, given their dire financial situation, immediate pressure to reestablish sources of income.

She navigated this while still being afraid for their lives. They were the only living witnesses to the shooting, save those accused. She was so fearful that she kept the doors of the farmhouse locked, entering and leaving through a window. She did not let the children out of the house at all. In her taped interview, Maud said that George Jeffrey told his sister (Offley's wife) that "the four" had intended to "get them all so no one would be left to tell the story."

Staying on the ranch seemed a perilous prospect. She and Murrel had another parcel of land roughly four miles northeast of Ollie, over the Montana border, including a house and outer buildings. With the help of family and friends, they left the Mallet Ranch. She would never live there again.

> *My husband was killed in 1919. We had seven children one of which was born after the death of my husband. In order to feed and clothe the children I had to go out and work in the fields and run the farm myself. The children had to go four miles to school.*

We moved over into Montana in 1920 where our neighbors were; the Martins, the Wangs, the Steens, the Starks, the Abrams, the Woodsends and the Hammonds.[252]

Maud was a survivor, and work was her salvation. She kept her deepest sorrows to herself and concentrated on running the new ranch. She tapped into her innate strength, enduring grief, loneliness, and the natural elements in order to stay on the property and raise her children. A story often told was that she "sided" her bedroom walls just a day before baby Paul was born on January 13, 1920, during the depths of winter. After the new baby arrived, she constructed a two-wheeled cart, pulled by a horse, in order to nurse him while she worked in the fields.

She fortunately had help from their loyal friend, Carl Thompson. Carl stayed on the Montana ranch as Maud's foreman for the next 21 years.

In addition to continuing to grow and harvest crops, she made extra money raising turkeys. Her turkey herd generally, and impressively, totaled 500 birds. When they were ready for market, she slaughtered and defeathered them, packaged them in barrels, and brought them to Beach to be shipped to Chicago. She sold them for 10 cents a pound. Another modest source of income was sewing backpacks for servicemen on behalf of the Red Cross.

The family saved money wherever they could. Maud redesigned and resewed the older children's clothing to

---

[252] *O'Fallon Flashbacks*, O'Fallon Historical Society, Baker, Montana, 1975

create outfits for the younger ones. Their family picture taken in the late 1920s depicts quite stylish ensembles despite the circumstances.

The Bowens' financial struggles would continue for years; although details are scant, per publication of North Dakota State Supreme Court decisions, Maud was forced to sue the Montana Life Insurance Company, appealing decisions multiple times through at least 1922.[253]

The Women's Auxiliary of the Nonpartisan League also took action to assist.

> *League members are raising funds for the relief of Mrs. M. K. Bowen, widow of the murdered rancher of Golden Valley, Bowen, because of his fight for the League, faced months of persecution and finally met a violent death. His cattle, valued at $30,000, were poisoned by his enemies and Mrs. Bowen was compelled to scrub floors for a living until her plight was brought to the attention of other Leaguers.[254]*

> *When M. K. Bowen, a League farmer of Golden Valley county, was murdered at the end of a series of persecutions which he had suffered because of his advocacy of the League, the Auxiliary clubs got behind a campaign to raise relief funds for his widow. To date more than $3,000 has been collected.[255]*

---

[253] *The Bismarck Tribune*, Bismarck, North Dakota, October 25, 1922
[254] *The Nonpartisan Leader*, Fargo, North Dakota, September 22, 1919
[255] *The Nonpartisan Leader*, Fargo, North Dakota, January 5, 1920

The desire to help extended across the state. Two of the communities mentioned in the following account, Donnybrook and Willow City, are over 200 miles and 300 miles, respectively, from Golden Valley County.

> *North Dakota women are outdoing the men in the present campaign to assist Mrs. M. K. Bowen and her little children...*
>
> *Donnybrook Club, No 18, Women's Auxiliary of the Nonpartisan League raised $142.18 [roughly $2,500 today] in collections at a picnic September 21. It was a drizzling chilly day, but the people turned out in large numbers to assist the widow and children of the murdered man.*
>
> *The members of the women's auxiliary of Willow City gave a picnic for the benefit of the widow and children on September 26.*
>
> *Mrs. Hans Quale of Sentinel Butte has submitted a plan for...auxiliary clubs to push a campaign to have all League men and women give $1 each and more if it can be spared. They are to send it to the League county paper, which is to appoint some person to receive these funds, keep an accounting of them and turn them over to the widow.*
>
> *The case of Mrs. M. K. Bowen needs immediate attention and should appeal to every member of the Nonpartisan League. It can be said with truth that M. K. Bowen was a martyr to the cause of the League. It was his uncompromising stand for the League on all occasions and*

his tireless fight against the gangsters that undoubtedly stirred up the hostilities that led to his death.

Mrs. Bowen is a strong supporter of the League and is a member of the Women's Auxiliary of Beach and Sentinel Butte. The loss of cattle, supposed to be from poisoning, preceding the death of her husband, left her practically destitute and deeply in debt. During the inquest the creditors seized practically everything of portable nature on the ranch. They were forced later to restore most of it, but this property is involved for the present and is no use to Mrs. Bowen.

The widow has six children, the oldest being only 11 years old. She will soon become the mother of another child. The property formerly owned by Mrs. Bowen is involved too much to yield anything to the needy family. Their support for some time must come from those who feel that they are worthy of aid from the organization and people for whom they have made almost inconceivable sacrifices.[256]

Maud said that the League raised $5,000 for them, the equivalent of nearly $90,000 today, and Governor Frazier delivered it to her personally.

A poignant article, written only eleven days after the Bowens' youngest son Paul was born, describes a visit paid to Maud by the NPL Auxiliary of Golden Valley County.

Try to picture this story.

---

[256] *The Bottineau Courant*, Bottineau, North Dakota, October 2, 1919

On our way over the hill from Beach everywhere seeing God's gentle kindness in covering every unsightly place with snow white purity. Passing the cemetery, glancing over at the recently made grave of M.K. Bowen, and on the way out to see the widowed mother and her newly born babe; thinking of that dear little fatherless babe, one wonders why the all gentle Father allows such cowardly things to happen in the beautiful world of his.

Reaching the end of our journey, we stop and wonder at the beauty of this spot. There nestling in the valley, the snow white hills way out beyond, here to see the old home of M.K. Bowen and his bride; hallowed with sweet memories and shrouded by one of the most terrible of tragedies. There it was that M.K. Bowen's brave young manhood was wiped out in a very few moments; all the story of his life was over; wiped out in the most cowardly way at the threshold of his own door.

Leaving this place of sweet memories and dark shadows, we find ourselves crossing over to the new home made by the fearless young mother. Before entering we listen to the sweet childish voices from within; being invited to enter we pass into a little home of immaculate cleanliness. The first to greet us is a handsome manly little chap with features we have seen before, the face so like that lying under a pall of snow. And here we see a picture most beautiful; one which should wipe away all sad thoughts; the brave young mother and her beautiful babe. We look in astonishment at the change; all the smoldering revengeful fire gone, nothing now but the mother love light in her eyes surrounded by a glorious wealth of red gold hair.

We see six pretty young faces, all glowing with pride in the sweet little babe; brave young faces they are, all ready to do and dare; fitting offspring of such a father and mother. It would indeed be strange to find them otherwise.

The same little chap who first greeted us, comes up smilingly once more and asks us why daddy does not come home to kiss that baby. Daddy loves babies. Again the look of tragedy in the mother's eyes, and we look with moist eyes at the sweet little face on its mother's breast, and we ask the Heavenly Father, if he could but turn back his universe and give us yesterday that we might see the brave young father in his great clean strength once more with his family.[257]

The 1920 Census, taken from January that year, just before Paul's birth, lists both Charles and Lois Epley and Carl Thompson as living with the family on the Montana land. The healing power of time, occupation, and the kindness of others helped Maud survive the unbearable. She was the epitome of the frailty and resilience of the human heart.

[257] *Golden Valley Progress,* Beach, North Dakota, January 23, 1920

Mary Bowen playing with baby Paul, Montana, 1920

Lois Bowen with brothers playing in background

Lois Bowen at the original Bowen homestead

Murrel K. "Kay" Bowen, Jr.

As Maud was reconstructing their lives in Montana, Pierzina and Gallagher were facing charges of negligence and incompetence in North Dakota. In the days following Murrel's death, supporters from across the state called for action.

> *While there has been nothing introduced to show that the state's attorney and attorney general were interested in stealing and destruction of cattle and killing of Bowen, many are not satisfied with the way the inquest is being conducted, and will appeal to the governor for removal of Sheriff Pierzina and Attorney Gallagher [illegible] full state protection sought for others whose lives have been threatened by murderers of Bowen. Impeachment proceedings against Langer are expected to develop.*[258]

> *No effort is being made by State's Attorney Gallagher to determine what connection if any the killing of Bowen has with the cattle poisoning that continued on his land for a year and a half.*[259]

> *A long list of charges have been drawn up by Nonpartisan league attorneys, based on findings reported by Seaman Smith...who was appointed by the governor as special investigator in the Bowen case.*

> *The charges against Gallagher include failure to protect the life of Bowen, though he is alleged to have known that Messrs. Taylor, Offley, Jeffrey and Stark...were armed*

---

[258] *Golden Valley Progress*, Beach, North Dakota, August 8, 1919
[259] *Golden Valley Progress*, Beach, North Dakota, August 8, 1919

when they applied to him for replevin papers for obtaining cattle held by Bowen, and owned by Offley.

The state's attorney is also accused of failing to assist in the prosecution of the four defendants.[260]

The cattle poisoning cases in Golden Valley county, leading to the murder of the victim, M. K. Bowen, a strong Leaguer, by men deputized by county authorities belonging to the gang, after he had vainly pleaded for protection of life and property, is another development that is convincing Leaguers that the organized farmers must go into local politics next election and thereafter, and that the state will not be safe for law, order and democracy until every nest of gangsters is routed from local power.[261]

Additional charges against Gallagher included failure to act after alleged irregularities in the sheriff's election the previous fall, through which Pierzina came to office, as well as failure to respond to the aggressions against the Rataezyks. Some of the charges against Pierzina were more salacious.

The charges against Sheriff Pierzina center around alleged failure to hold in jail the four men accused of killing Bowen, and of threats to kill Martin F. Blank, a Nonpartisan league publicity agent stationed there. Charges of drunkenness, of selling liquor, of employing

---

[260] *The Washburn Leader*, Washburn, North Dakota, September 12, 1919
[261] *The Bottineau Courant*, Bottineau, North Dakota, August 7, 1919

prisoners on his farm for his private benefit, also are made against the sheriff.[262]

...the charges [also] allege [a young woman] held illicit relations with the sheriff.[263]

During the hearing related to their removal from office, Maud, her brother Lee, and several friends and neighbors again found themselves testifying as to the events preceding and following Murrel's murder.

The hearing began Tuesday morning before Attorney T. J. Kruse of Mandan, named by Governor Frazier as referee, with a large crowd in attendance. The governor was presented by James Manahan of Minneapolis, and J. W. Lee of Rhame...John F. Sullivan of Mandan, T. F. Murtha, and W. F. Burnett of Dickinson, appeared for Gallagher and Pierzina.[264]

Both Sullivan and Murtha would go on to also serve as defense attorneys for the four men accused in Murrel's killing.

On Saturday, August 30th, Governor Frazier removed both Gallagher and Pierzina from their offices.

Saturday evening at six o'clock an order signed by Governor Frazier, suspending State's Attorney Gallagher and Sheriff John Pierzina from office was served on those

---

[262] *The Washburn Leader*, Washburn, North Dakota, September 12, 1919
[263] *The Washburn Leader*, Washburn, North Dakota, September 12, 1919
[264] *The Beach Advance*, Beach, North Dakota, September 19, 1919

gentlemen and they surrendered their offices to the county commissioners.[265]

R. F. Gallagher, states attorney of Golden Valley county, and John Pierzina, sheriff, were suspended from office...[charged] with delinquency in protecting M. K. Bowen, slain recently near Beach, from his alleged assassins. These men will be given an opportunity to defend themselves before Attorney T. J. Krause of Mandan September 16.[266]

The accused officials are confident they can refute all charges made in any fair court. In any event the matter will go the limit in the courts before it is ended, the accused officials say.

[The following Tuesday] The county commissioners... appointed C. L. Dawson, a young attorney lately returned from the war, as acting state's attorney, and E. E. Mikkelson, former chief deputy, as acting sheriff. The commissions are anti-Townley [i.e. anti-Nonpartisan League].[267]

As Governor Frazier's political opponents gained strength, this decision would unfortunately be short-lived. Late in January 1920, in the Morton County District Court, Judge Crawford ordered the reinstatement of both Pierzina and Gallagher. An attorney for Governor Frazier filed a motion with the Supreme Court for a change in venue, charging

---

[265] *The Beach Advance*, Beach, North Dakota, September 5, 1919
[266] *The Bowbells Tribune*, Bowbells, North Dakota, September 5, 1919
[267] *The Bismarck Tribune*, Bismarck, North Dakota, September 4, 1919

prejudice on the part of Judge Crawford, but the motion was denied.[268]

While no formal charges were brought against Attorney General Langer, similar feelings were cited against him:

> *Farmers are already writing in to Governor Lynn J. Frazier demanding a full investigation of the circumstances surrounding the slaying of M.K. Bowen...*
>
> *C. W. Reichert of Carrington says in his letter to the governor:*
>
> *"I just read in The Courier-News about the killing of M. K. Bowen at Beach. If this is true it seems as tho it is getting about time we were looking after Mr. Langer's office. I know you will attend to that end of the job, so far as the law will permit, and I would like to see him impeached from his office. If I can do anything for Mrs. Bowen and the children with my pocketbook or otherwise, let me know."[269]*
>
> *Evidence is accumulating to show that Attorney General Langer, acting apparently in harmony with the strongly hostile anti-farmer authorities of Golden Valley County, repeatedly refused to take adequate steps to investigate the death of hundreds of head of cattle, belonging to Mr. Bowen, and to apprehend the culprits, and that when under pressure a state detective was employed and*

---

[268] *The Bismarck Tribune*, Bismarck, North Dakota, January 21, 1920
[269] *Fargo Courier-News*, Fargo, North Dakota, August 4, 1919

evidence was discovered of cattle poisoning, Mr. Langer discharged the detective and failed to act.

The murdered man was a staunch member of the Nonpartisan League and incurred the deadly enmity of the county authorities by opposing them and circulating a petition against them charging them with having stolen an election for sheriff in 1918 and by asserting it was politics that prevented the running down of the cattle poisoners. The fact that Attorney General Langer is an inveterate foe of the Nonpartisan League is believed to account for the failure to investigate the cattle poisoning cases and give protection to Mr. Bowen – negligence, no doubt, responsible for his death.

Bowen wrote informing Langer of threats against Bowen's life. It seems that Langer would not take any course that might seem unfriendly to the anti-League politicians in Golden Valley county.[270]

For his part, that same January, Langer embarked on a speaking tour about the murder case.

Attorney General Langer today began a three days' speaking tour in Billings and Golden Valley counties, upon which he will be accompanied and introduced by C.L. Dawson, acting state's attorney of Golden Valley county and state president of the American Legion. Mr. Langer will speak in Beach, at Golva, where he will discuss the

---

[270] *The Producers News*, Plentywood, Montana, August 8, 1919

Bowen murder case; at Sentinel Butte, Belfield, and Medora.[271]

I am especially grateful for your kind invitation because it has given me the opportunity to present the facts in the Bowen cattle poisoning affair...It is to you people, neighbors of all that transpired, that I wish to present the facts now so grotesque and distorted by the reptilian press and its lying masters...[272]

As the months since Murrel's murder passed, resolution and harmony remained distant concepts.

[271] *The Bismarck Tribune*, Bismarck, North Dakota, January 15, 1920
[272] *Mandan Pioneer*, Mandan, North Dakota, January 23, 1920

~

The (Eventual) Trial

IN THE EARLY PART OF THE 20TH CENTURY, the legal process was no more expedient than it is today. The only trial that took place began nearly two years after Murrel's killing. Given the notoriety of the case, there was significant press coverage across the state throughout that time.

November 1919

Initially there was a push to hasten the start of the trial given Maud's impending due date.

> *A petition has been entered in the supreme court asking it to order a special term of the sixth district court to try the Bowen murder case. Lack of hotel accommodations is given as one of the reasons necessary for an immediate trial. Another is that Mrs. Bowen is soon to become a mother and may not be able to appear as a witness if the trial is postponed too long.*[273]

January 1920: Delay Due to Birth of Baby Paul

The expedited trial before Paul's birth on January 13th did not take place. The formal proceedings began during a special term of court on January 27th, presided over by Judge Crawford. Crawford was the same official Governor Frazier felt might be too prejudiced to rule in the reinstatement of Gallagher and Pierzina. Given her postpartum condition, Maud unfortunately could not attend.

---

[273] *Sioux County Pioneer*, Fort Yates, North Dakota, November 27, 1919

The formal criminal complaint, signed and filed by Gallagher, was read in open court. After the defendants entered a plea of not guilty, a new trial date was set for June 1st. A request to reduce Taylor's bond from $10,000 to $5,000 was also granted; he was the only defendant still in custody.[274]

> *The expected fireworks at this term of court have failed to materialize...The most notable case, that relating to the killing of M. K. Bowen, went over to June 1...owing to the fact that Mrs. Bowen, who recently became a mother, could not be present at this time...*[275]

June 1920: Delays Due to Absence of the Prosecution, Two Venue Changes

By June 1st, however, the previously named members of the prosecution team – Simpson, Nuchols, and Gallagher – were all indisposed and failed to appear. Presiding Judge Frank T. Lembke appointed an alternate prosecutor, H. A. Mackoff; Mackoff was a partner in Simpson's private practice in Dickinson.[276]

Both Maud and Mackoff submitted affidavits that day requesting that the trial be further postponed until Simpson could be present. Per Maud's statement:

> *...L. A. Simpson is the one who was out in Golden Valley and various other places to gather the evidence on behalf of*

---

[274] Minutes of Trial, January 27, 1920
[275] *The Beach Advance*, Beach, North Dakota, undated, approximately January 1920
[276] Judge Lembke Order, June 1, 1920

the State...and is the one who is best acquainted with all of the facts and hence best prepared to try the case...Simpson is now confined to his bed and will be unable to attend this trial at present, but that he will be able to attend the same in four or five days...Nuchols is now absent at Fargo where he is appearing before the U. S. Grand Jury in capacity of Assistant U. S. Attorney General and...it will be some time before he will be able to come to Beach.[277]

Mackoff concurred:

L. A. Simpson...has been sick and confined to his bed for a week ...and is under the care of a physician. [Mackoff articulated that he] does not know anything about the facts in the above case and has done nothing towards preparing said case for trial...Simpson has done all the work in...preparing ...for trial.[278]

By June 4th, Gallagher had returned to Beach. Despite Maud and Mackoff's requests to ensure Simpson was present, Gallagher, Mackoff, and Albert Sheets were confirmed for the prosecution team. Sheets was one of the officials that came to the Mallet Ranch in the Spring of 1919, whom Martin Blank referred to as the "...*youthful lawyer [who] pooh-poohed the idea of cattle poisoning.*"

In addition to ensuring a prepared prosecution team was in place, there was another pivotal issue to address. During the

---

[277] Maud Bowen Affidavit, June 1, 1920
[278] H. A. Mackoff Affidavit, June 1, 1920

ten months since the murder, *The Beach Advance* regularly published slanted accounts of the affair. As a result, Maud felt that a fair trial could not be held in Golden Valley County. She, S. A. Smith, Martin Blank, and E. O. Johnston all submitted affidavits to request a change of venue to a more neutral location.

> *...shortly after the killing...a great number of false rumors sprung up...and were widely circulated...that Bowen and his wife were the aggressors in the said shooting and that the defendants...were wholly innocent...and that tended to convey the impression that [Bowen] was a man of bad character and repute and of a quarrelsome nature and that he was a Socialist and a Radical...*

> *...the Beach Advance, a weekly newspaper published in the said City of Beach...contained what was alleged to be an accurate account of the details of the killing...secured by the representative of the said newspaper in interviews with the said defendants immediately after said shooting...*

> *...such articles...were repeated...in very bold type...nearly every week for several months thereafter, so that the story and the details of the said shooting became firmly fixed in the minds of the people of said county and tended to create a firm prejudice in the minds of said people...in favor of the said defendants and against [the Bowens].*[279]

---

[279] Maud Bowen, Martin Blank, S. A. Smith Affidavits, June 4, 1920; E. O. Johnston Affidavit, June 1, 1920

Proceedings to hear the request for change of venue took place on June 4th, with Judge Lembke presiding. Defense counsel Sullivan argued that there was no evidence that the rumors were not indeed fact, and that the trial should proceed immediately as planned in Golden Valley County. Sullivan was due to be *"...in the murder cases...and...riot cases of Sioux County...on the 15th [of the month],"* hence was keen to get started.[280]

Judge Lembke ultimately ruled *"...that the affidavits sufficiently set forth a cause for removal...[as] the people are prejudiced and the plaintiff cannot have a fair and impartial trial...".* He ordered the case be removed to Stark County and tried at the next term of court beginning mid-month.

> *District court took a sudden adjournment at noon today upon granting a change of venue in the Bowen case to Stark county, where it is expected it will be tried at the first term of court, probably about the middle of this month.*
>
> *The Bowen case was continued over until today because L. A. Simpson, special attorney general, was sick and could not be present when the case was called. This case is on for trial today, a large crowd being in attendance.*
>
> *...The libel case against Martin Blank also went over on motion of defense, on the ground that H. L. Halliday, defendant's attorney, was sick and could not try the case at this time.*[281]

---

[280] Transcript of proceedings for Change of Venue, June 4, 1920
[281] *The Beach Advance*, Beach, North Dakota, undated, approximately June 1920

The case did appear on the calendar for the next regular term in Stark County, beginning June 15th. However, in open court on June 24th, the defense filed an affidavit for another change of venue, citing prejudice against presiding Judge Lembke. That day Lembke signed the order to again change the venue, this time from Stark to Adams County.[282] The Adams County seat, Hettinger, is a considerable 125 miles from Beach.

Counsel for the defense filed an appeal to the Supreme Court of the State of North Dakota to send the case back to Golden Valley County[283], but that appeal was ultimately denied.[284]

January 1921: Delay Due to Defense Schedule Conflict

With its location settled, the trial was set to take place in Hettinger the following January. However, a new member of the defense team, one C. H. Starke, cited scheduling conflicts, resulting in yet another delay.

> *C. H. Starke, being sworn, says that he is one of the attorneys for the defendant... [and] that he is a member of the Legislature of this State; that the Legislature is in session...at Bismarck, N. D.; that [his] personal attendance upon the trial...is necessary...and prays that the trial of this cause be postponed until the next regular term of this court...*[285]

---

[282] Order for Change of Place of Trial, June 24, 1920
[283] Notice of Appeal, June 24, 1920
[284] Supreme Court Appeal Decision, November 9, 1920
[285] C. H. Starke Affidavit, January 5, 1921

Although Simpson initially moved for the trial to proceed, he ultimately conceded and agreed with presiding Judge Thomas Pugh that moving forward may have opened the possibility of any verdict being "reserved on a technicality." Judge Pugh thus ordered that the trial be postponed again, until the next regular term, "...*not less than sixty days after the adjournment of the present session of the Legislature.*"[286]

June 1921: At Last, the Trial

After two changes of venue and two additional delays, the trial was finally set to begin before Judge Harry L. Berry from the Sixth Judicial District. Given the considerable distance from Golden Valley County, the local Nonpartisan League Auxiliary rented a home for the Bowen family in Hettinger for the duration of the trial.

In parallel with Murrel's murder trial, Martin Blank continued to defend himself against libel charges, ultimately issuing a retraction in exchange for the charges being dropped.

> *The criminal libel charge against Martin F. Blank, former editor of the Golden Valley Progress, Nonpartisan paper, was dismissed in district court here upon the filing by Blank of a retraction of the charges he had made against R. F. Gallagher, state's attorney, at the time of the M. K. Bowen killing.*[287]

---

[286] C. H. Starke Affidavit, January 5, 1921

[287] *The Devils Lake World*, Devils Lake, North Dakota, June 22, 1921

Both the state and the defense submitted long lists of witnesses they planned to call; in press accounts it was said that *"About a hundred witnesses have been subpoenaed by the state and the defense."*[288] The defense even included Governor Frazier in its witness list.[289] [290] [291] The logistical complexity of scheduling so many appearances, especially as the trial location moved further and further away from Golden Valley County, was another factor in the delays.

Although finally with a confirmed location and date, the proceedings were not free of the dramatic events preceding them.

Monday, June 20 to Thursday, June 23, 1921: Jury Selection

The first item on the agenda was jury selection. That proved to be a daunting task, with numerous objections by both the state and the defense. Per Maud, Sullivan argued for jurors that favored the IVA; Simpson did the same for those that favored the Nonpartisan League. The original proposed panel was exhausted and twenty-four more were called.

> *With the original jury panel exhausted and 24 more men called, only nine jurors had been accepted up to noon [on Thursday, June 23]...it was expected the other three would be agreed upon early this afternoon and the trial be begun late today.*[292]

---

[288] *Adams County Record*, Hettinger, North Dakota, June 23, 1921
[289] Ennis Walter Taylor Affidavit, June 14, 1921
[290] Criminal Information, January 27, 1920
[291] Notice, September 16, 1920
[292] *The Fargo Forum*, Fargo, North Dakota, June 23, 1921

The jury secured to try the first man, Offley, after four days' examination …is composed of men about evenly divided in political faith, Leaguers and Independents, it is said.[293]

The jury was completed at 3 p. m…after counsel worked since Monday…[294]

The significant public interest, and resulting large crowds, exceeded the capacity of the courtroom; thus, arrangements were made for the trial to be held in the auditorium of the local high school.

The June term of the District Court opened here Tuesday afternoon, with the trial of E. W. Taylor, D. R. Offley, Ira J. Stark and George Jeffrey who are charged with the murder of M. K. Bowen… The case came here on a change of venue from Stark county. The attendance at the hearings the past three days has been very large because of the unusual interest aroused in the case arising from incidents happening shortly after the murder two years ago. The court room at the court house was found inadequate to take care of the crowd of interested legal luminaries, witnesses, prospective jurors and hundreds of spectators so the court adjourned and it was arranged to use the spacious auditorium at the school house as court room for the entire term of court.[295]

---

[293] *Grand Forks Herald,* Grand Forks, North Dakota, July 9, 1921
[294] *The Fargo Forum,* Fargo, North Dakota, June 24, 1921
[295] *Adams County Record,* Hettinger, North Dakota, June 23, 1921

"From the number of witnesses on hand for both the defense and state, it will take at least three weeks or more to try the case," said Attorney J. F. Sullivan of Mandan, for the defense.[296]

HETTINGER HIGH SCHOOL BUILDING.

Friday, June 24, 1921: Trial Opens, Prosecution Merry-Go-Round, Offley Confirmed as Defendant

There was also a dispute as to who was prosecuting the case, and who was to be tried.

At least four individuals were named to represent the state as part of the prosecution team: Simpson, Nuchols, one Mr. Oppegard, by then the state's attorney for Golden Valley County, and Peter Garberg, a senator from Adams County appointed by Judge Berry.

---

[296] *The Fargo Forum*, Fargo, North Dakota, June 23, 1921

*When the trial opened, Attorney L. A. Simpson objected to
the appearance of State's Attorney Oppegard in the
prosecution role because Oppegard was formerly employed
in the office of Keohane & Jones, attorneys of Beach, who
were retained by the defendants at the time of their arrest.*

*State's Attorney Oppegard answered the charge...stating
he was employed by Keohane & Jones, but insisted...he had
nothing to do with the case.*[297]

Judge Berry concurred and removed Oppegard from the
prosecution team. Interestingly, before his term as state's
attorney, Gallagher had also been in private practice with
Jones and Keohane. No one had objected to his participation
in the prosecution during the coroner's inquest, preliminary
hearing, or the ultimately postponed trials.

*This latest development in the murder trial...leaves
Golden Valley County without direct representation in the
prosecution of its own case. Judge Berry in disqualifying
Oppegard announced the appointment of Peter Garberg as
prosecuting attorney. Garberg is a Nonpartisan senator
from Adams County.*

*L. A. Simpson of Dickinson claims he has been authorized
by Attorney General William Lemke to conduct the
prosecution and Judge S. L. Nuchols, assistant United
States District attorney, has arrived from Fargo, with the
claim that he, too, has been employed by the attorney*

---

[297] *The Fargo Forum*, Fargo, North Dakota, June 24, 1921

general's office. Judge Nuchols was retained originally in the case by William Langer, former attorney general.

Attorneys J. F. Sullivan and T. F. Murtha are counsel for the defendants.[298]

The defense initially asked that Taylor be tried first.

Counsel for the defendants, asked that...E. W. Taylor...be tried first because he is not at liberty on bail...The prosecution, however, refused, and the case against Offley was called.[299]

Thursday, June 23 through Saturday, June 25: State Begins Their Case, C. A. McClure and George Tubbs Called

Once the prosecution merry-go-round was settled and the jury selected, the first witnesses were called. C. A. McClure, who was present when George Tubbs came to the Mallet Ranch to retrieve Offley's cattle, took the stand, followed by Tubbs.

Following a lengthy statement to the jury and the court, Attorney L. A. Simpson of Dickinson late yesterday afternoon called McClure as the first witness for the state. He was under cross-examination by the defense this morning.

McClure told of being at the Bowen farm when the hired man of D. R. Offley came over to get cattle held by Bowen. He was told to "tell Offley to come and get them himself."

---

[298] *The Fargo Forum*, Fargo, North Dakota, June 24, 1921
[299] *The Fargo Forum*, Fargo, North Dakota, June 24, 1921

McClure testified further that he went to the Bowen farm after the shooting July 31, 1919, and that he picked up five forty-five caliber shells and two thirty-two caliber shells, the forty-five shells fitted the gun of Taylor's, who was accused of the actual killing, but he could not connect up the 32 caliber shells in any way.

The defense will attempt to prove that Bowen was shot by Taylor in self-defense after he threatened with a gun four men who called at his farm with a replevin for the cattle held.[300]

Geo. Tubbs, a relative of the defendant Offley was the third witness called. He was in the employ of the defendant and testified that he had been sent over to the Bowen ranch to get the cattle that Bowen had penned up but was told by Bowen to tell Offley to come after the cattle himself. That he had remained at home after the departure of Offley for the Bowen place.[301]

Admissions by George Tubbs...that he was trying to testify according to a signed statement he had made to Seaman Smith, the special representative of Governor Lynn J. Frazier, and was trying to testify to "what they wanted" him to...put new twists into the case.

Tubbs, in his direct testimony Saturday, declared that Seaman Smith and others had told him, his employer (Offley), was a bad man and that he had met Seaman Smith

---

[300] *Grand Forks Herald*, Grand Forks, North Dakota, June 24, 1921
[301] *Adams County Record*, Hettinger, North Dakota, June 30, 1921

at the Carl Thompson place, Mrs. Bowen being there. He testified on direct examination by the state that he had seen the four men at the Offley place the afternoon of the shooting…that Ira J. Stark had a .45 caliber revolver and E. W. Taylor, D. R. Offley and G. R. Jeffrey had .32 caliber guns; that he had seen the men start for the Bowen farm with the "papers" to get the cattle.[302]

Monday, June 27, 1921: George Tubbs, Mary Bowen Testify for the State

After spending Sunday sequestered and guarded, the jury returned to hear testimony that Monday.

Members of the jury hearing the evidence are closely guarded day and night, and they spent Sunday in seclusion. No one is allowed to speak to any members of the jury at any time. Two bailiffs are constantly on duty.[303]

George Tubbs' cross examination began that morning.

On cross examination, Tubbs declared Stark was not present at all, and that he had only seen Offley and Jeffrey leave the place, and when they did it was for Beach to secure replevin papers for the cattle.

Tubbs then declared that Seaman Smith and "they" had sent for him, Tubbs, who went to South Dakota after the shooting; they had sent him a mileage book and an offer of $4 a day and expenses if he would return.

---

[302] *The Fargo Forum*, Fargo, North Dakota, June 27, 1921
[303] *The Fargo Forum*, Fargo, North Dakota, June 27, 1921

> *He then admitted that he was trying to testify according to the signed statement given Smith.*[304]

While eldest daughter Lois Bowen had been subpoenaed, there was likely a misunderstanding that she wasn't home the day Murrel was killed. Presumably as an alternate, Mary Bowen, just 10 years old, was called.

> *The small daughter of M. K. Bowen was today brought into the case as a witness for the first time. She was not questioned in the preliminary examinations, nor at the coroner's inquisition.*

> *Attorney L. A. Simpson…declared he had not known she would be a witness until a very few days ago.*[305]

> *Mary Bowen…told of her mother's actions following the shooting. Playing on the porch she heard the shots. Declared her mother shot at one of the men who came to see Bowen that day and she declared that a man named Taylor shot in the direction of her father from a hill sixty feet away. It was dusk she said when the shooting took place.*[306]

---

[304] *The Fargo Forum*, Fargo, North Dakota, June 27, 1921
[305] *The Fargo Forum*, Fargo, North Dakota, June 27, 1921
[306] *The Bismarck Tribune*, Bismarck, North Dakota, June 29, 1921

Tuesday, June 28, 1921: Mary Bowen, John "Hans" Boegli, and Daisy Wassman Testify for the State

Mary's testimony continued the following day, along with the account from the Bowens' ranch hand and neighbor, John "Hans" Boegli.

> The testimony of the young daughter of M.K. Bowen, Mary, and of the Bowen hired man, Hans Boegli, were features of today's session in the Bowen murder trial. The little girl testified that "she had never talked with mama or any one," nor told anyone anything about what she knew of the killing of her father until a couple of weeks ago.
>
> Boegli testified that he [heard] Bowen curse the four visitors [illegible] farm, that he heard two shots, [illegible] which there was a pause, followed by two more shots. He said he [illegible] the little girl cry "my papa is [illegible] and heard Mrs. Bowen shout "Hans, Hans, they've killed him." During this time, he testified, he was milking a cow on the farther end of the barn and did not stop milking. Boegli heard Mrs. Bowen calling to him, and finally she came to him and said: "Hans, they've killed him," This hired man witness averred positively that he replied. "I know it," and continued his milking.[307]
>
> [Boegli] said that he heard the words that preceded the shooting, but that he was milking at the time and kept on with the job during the entire affair. Mrs. Bowen called to

---

[307] *Grand Forks Herald*, Grand Forks, North Dakota, June 28, 1921

him that they had killed her husband but he said "I just kept on milking."[308]

The man further testified that the day of the shooting Martin Blank, league newspaper man, who recently retracted all his charges and statements against State's Attorney R. F. Gallagher, came to him and took Boegli and Mrs. Bowen to town where they talked over the whole matter with L. A. Simpson, Seaman Smith and Martin Blank.

The defense paid special attention to Boegli's description of the position in which Bowen lay.[309]

The state also called Daisy Wassman that day.

Mrs. Daisy Wassman, employed by Offley, testified that she had heard her employer make threats relative to Bowen stating that he would "get him."

Offley's attorneys are devoting all their time to building up the theory that Offley and the others shot at Bowen in self defense.[310]

---

[308] *The Bismarck Tribune*, Bismarck, North Dakota, June 29, 1921
[309] *Grand Forks Herald*, Grand Forks, North Dakota, June 28, 1921
[310] *The Bismarck Tribune*, Bismarck, North Dakota, June 29, 1921

Wednesday, June 29, 1921: Lee Plummer and Martin Blank Testify for the State

Lee Plummer, a brother of Mrs. Bowen, testified as to certain measurements he had taken. He told of the condition of the body following the shooting.

Martin Blank, former Beach editor, who became involved in criminal libel charges in connection with the case was on the stand Wednesday. He told of conversations he had had and measurements he had taken. Cross-examination of Blank was vigorous on the part of the defense.

[Blank] testified that he and Seaman Smith and Hank Bentley had gone to the farm. In fact Blank had been at the murder farm every day up to that time after the shooting and had searched on this particular day, Aug. 4, 1919, for shells. He recited in detail where the shells were found.[311]

On cross-examination Blank declared that only one place where shells were found had been marked. Nevertheless on Aug. 10, six days later, he had made the measurements as to the location of the shells which the state contends shows where various men stood when the shots were fired.

The large crowds which are gathering every day find little of an interesting nature. Up to date the trial has been devoid of any dramatic elements. It is expected within the next day or so that the state will put in evidence showing an alleged feud existing in the neighborhood and much of

---

[311] *The Bismarck Tribune*, Bismarck, North Dakota, June 30, 1921

the ground gone over in the investigation by the state may be retraveled in the prosecution.

The last three days have been given over almost entirely to testimony on details relative to the location of the body of the dead man, the points where empty shells of different caliber were found and other measurements made on the ranch.[312]

Thursday, June 30, 1921: The State Calls Sheriff John Pierzina and George Irving

As the trial neared July, summer temperatures soared to triple digits; trial spectators thinned out as a result. Next on the stand were Sheriff Pierzina and George Irvin, a former deputy sheriff and hotelier operating in Ollie.

With the thermometer in the court room over 100 degrees, spectators who have been thronging to hear the testimony in the trial of D. R. Offley… deserted and the jury sleepily listened to detailed evidence. The only point of consequence gained by either side was in the examination of former Sheriff John Pierzina of Golden Valley county. He identified various exhibits, told of arresting the defendants and on cross-examination told how E. W. Taylor, who is charged with the actual killing of M. K. Bowen, had called him over the phone, told him to come and get him if he wanted to arrest him and that he was ready to surrender himself.[313]

---

[312] *The Bismarck Tribune*, Bismarck, North Dakota, June 30, 1921
[313] *Grand Forks Herald*, Grand Forks, North Dakota, July 1, 1921

John Pierzina, former sheriff of Golden Valley county, who was removed from office by Governor Frazier and later reinstated, this afternoon was placed on the stand by the state.[314]

Pierzina...stated that Taylor had telephoned him that he had shot Bowen and he immediately went and placed Taylor under arrest. Following Taylor's arrest, Pierzina's deputies arrested three more defendants, all being held in jail 24 hours after Taylor's arrest.[315]

George Irving, a hotel man of Ollie, Montana, stated that both Taylor and Bowen had made threats to "get" the other.[316]

[Irving] told of alleged threats made by Taylor against Bowen in a conversation with Irving concerning money Bowen owed Taylor, that Taylor said he would kill him. On cross-examination, Irving said that the conversation was nothing but a joke and Taylor didn't mean anything.

[Irving] testified that Taylor had remarked to him that he, Taylor would "kill Bowen yet." When asked by defendant's counsel whether Bowen had ever made any threats regarding Taylor, the witness answered "yes." Attorney Simpson for the prosecution objected to the answer of the witness, but was overruled. The attorneys continued to wrangle about this when court adjourned.[317]

---

[314] *The Bismarck Tribune*, Bismarck, North Dakota, June 30, 1921

[315] *The Bismarck Tribune*, Bismarck, North Dakota, July 1, 1921

[316] *Adams County Record*, Hettinger, North Dakota, July 7, 1921

[317] *The Bismarck Tribune*, Bismarck, North Dakota, July 1, 1921

The other witnesses testifying, but whose statements brought out nothing new were Alvin Hoverson, Dan Cooper, Alvin Sanderson, Albert Sherva, Arnold Beach, Frank Sommers, Ed Honnold, B. L. Brigham, Mary E. Loebe, Dr. Sutter, Seaman Smith.[318]

Tuesday, July 5, and Wednesday, July 6, 1921: Maud Takes the Stand, Judge Berry Calls Two Surprise Witnesses

After a break for Independence Day, the trial resumed.

When court reconvened…following the holiday recess the state was granted permission by District Judge Berry to read into the record…testimony taken at the preliminary examination. The testimony of Dr. Stough, since deceased, was read, as was that of W. A. Cooper, another preliminary examination witness, who now is outside of the state.[319]

Dr. Stough's testimony was particularly important, as he was the physician who confirmed the wounds in Murrel's back, indicating a second shooter.

Maud also took the stand that day. Our search for publication of her testimony was largely unsuccessful; below is an account from July 6th, when she was "put through a severe, grilling cross-examination" by the defense.

Mrs. Bowen under cross examination…testified largely as at the preliminary examination to the effect that she had seen Taylor use a small handled .32 caliber revolver from

---

[318] *Adams County Record*, Hettinger, North Dakota, July 7, 1921
[319] *The Bismarck Tribune*, Bismarck, North Dakota, July 6, 1921

a distance of about two paces. She could not be shaken on this.[320]

Defense counsel...today began trying to pick to pieces the story told by the widow of the slain man. Attorney John F. Sullivan, of Mandan, and C.P. Murtha, of Dickinson, put Mrs. Bowen through a grilling cross-examination.

She was placed on the stand yesterday by the state and told the story of how Bowen was shot. According to the direct examination which followed the general line of questioning of the preliminary hearing she saw E.W. Taylor fire two shots at her husband as he was coming from the corner of the corral to the barn.

The only new bit of evidence introduced by the state was questions and answers given by Mrs. Bowen that she had personally secured a shot gun during the fracas and later placed it near her husband's body. Records of the preliminary examination showed that when county officials were called to the farm a shot gun was across Bowen's body in such a manner as to indicate he had held it in his hands when he was killed. It was about this that defense counsel gave Mrs. Bowen a severe cross-examination.[321]

This was a pivotal point in the case; in order to justify self-defense, Murrel would have had to be threatening the four men with a gun. Maud adamantly and consistently said that

[320] *The Bismarck Tribune*, Bismarck, North Dakota, July 7, 1921
[321] *The Bismarck Tribune*, Bismarck, North Dakota, July 6, 1921

Murrel was unarmed, and it was she who had the gun and placed it by Murrel's body.

Picture the scene on July 31, 1919, after Maud ran back to the house to phone for help, and until that help arrived. The four defendants were left unattended at the crime scene. They would have had ample opportunity to align on the events of the evening and possibly tamper with evidence, including changing the placement of the body or the gun Maud had used.

The same day Maud was cross-examined, Judge Berry made a surprise announcement related to the testimony of the physicians who examined Murrel's body.

One or a subset of three physicians, Drs. Maercklein, Stough, and Templeton, examined the body on three separate occasions. Dr. Maercklein was the first to do so, traveling to the Mallet Ranch with Sheriff Pierzina the night of the shooting.

The following day, he and Dr. Templeton together conducted another examination at the ranch and testified as part of the coroner's inquest. The day after that, as Maud inspected Murrel's clothing, she discovered two additional bullet holes in the back of his shirt that had not been seen during the coroner's inquest. She insisted another examination be done, which was completed by Drs. Maercklein and Stough in the Beach morgue. Per his testimony at the preliminary hearing, Dr. Stough confirmed that there were five wounds on Murrel's body, not three, and that the additional two were from .32 caliber bullets that entered Murrel's back.

Unfortunately, in September of 1920, nine months before the trial, Dr. Stough died of a sudden illness.

> *Dr. R. W. Stough of Beach, died yesterday at the Bismarck hospital following an illness of one week. Dr. Stough was one of the most prominent physicians in the state. He was graduated from the University of Illinois in 1905, at which time he went to Beach where he built up a very large practice.*
>
> *The death of Dr. Stough comes as a shock to his many friends. He motored with his family to the Yellowstone three weeks ago. While there he went in swimming and injured his nose while diving. The injury was not thought to be serious at the time and he drove home. Infection set in however, resulting in paralysis of the lower limbs and later of the whole nervous system.*[322]

Dr. Stough's death was another blow in a growing series of pivotal and unfortunate events. Judge Berry had initially allowed admittance of Dr. Stough's written testimony from the preliminary examination, but quickly reversed that decision. Without notice, he directly called Drs. Maercklein and Templeton to appear; although reportedly a surprise to both the state and the defense, this was an action the defense had previously requested.

---

[322] *The Bismarck Tribune*, Bismarck, North Dakota, September 13, 1920

Judge H. L. Berry, presiding in the trial of D. R. Offley for the murder of M. K. Bowen...sprung a surprise on both the state and the defense.

The defense counsel had been endeavoring to secure as witnesses two living doctors who had examined the body of Bowen...

The counsel for the defense objected to the introductions of testimony of Dr. Stough, since deceased, whose testimony given at the preliminary hearing was read into the records. Objection was based on the fact that they were unable to cross-examine him.[323]

The state held that this was expert testimony and did not need cross examination.[324]

Two other doctors were known to have examined the body. The state objected to the calling of these physicians. Judge Berry without announcing his action sent orders to the two physicians to report at Hettinger as witnesses and his announcement of their arrival was the first information either side of the case had of the subpoenas.[325]

Maud had testified *"... that she had seen Taylor use a small handled .32 caliber revolver from a distance of about two paces [about five feet]. She could not be shaken on this."*[326] However:

---

[323] *The Bismarck Tribune*, Bismarck, North Dakota, July 7, 1921
[324] *The Fargo Forum*, Fargo, North Dakota, July 7, 1921
[325] *The Bismarck Tribune*, Bismarck, North Dakota, July 7, 1921
[326] *The Bismarck Tribune*, Bismarck, North Dakota, July 7, 1921

The defense counsel J. F. Sullivan and T. F. Murtha seized upon this as a failure of the trial, for upon cross examination of Dr. Maercklein the physician asserted that he had examined the body at the farm following the murder when he had been in the company with the coroner and also at the undertaker's. He declared that it was impossible shots could have been fired from such close range, both because of the nature of the wound and the absence of the powder marks.[327]

Upon further questioning Dr. Maercklein said five bullets had penetrated Bowen's body, that three of the bullets were of .45 calibre and that a fourth had lodged in the brain was of the same calibre and that the fifth, not found undoubtedly was of the same calibre.[328]

…Under cross examination [Dr. Templeton] declared that the bullet wound in Bowen's left arm near the elbow was in about the position…as if he were holding a gun in his hand preparatory to shooting and that examination of his body showed one bullet wound in the chest to have been caused by the bullet which passed through his arm. Three bullets had entered the body from the left side in the same angle and had lodged in the right side of the body, the physician said. The bullets and wounds were from a .45 caliber gun he said, again disputing the testimony of Mrs. Bowen that Bowen was shot with a .32 caliber "white

[327] *The Fargo Forum,* Fargo, North Dakota, July 7, 1921
[328] *The Bismarck Tribune,* Bismarck, North Dakota, July 7, 1921

handled" gun. His testimony corroborated that of Dr. Maercklein.[329]

Drs. Maercklein and Templeton's testimonies were particularly damaging. They disputed the presence of two different caliber bullets, diminishing the possibility of a second shooter, and validated the idea that Murrel had been holding a gun, giving credence to the self-defense argument.

> *The main claim of the defense will be based on the statement of Dr. Maercklein...that Bowen had raised his right arm to level his gun thus exposing his side. The defense admits and claims that Taylor shot Bowen with a .45 caliber revolver but that he shot him only after Bowen had gone to the barn and obtained a gun.*[330]

Friday, July 8, 1921: The State Rests, the Defense Opens Their Case, Ennis Taylor on the Stand

Just over two weeks after the start of the trial, the state rested, and the defense began presentation of their case. During defense attorney Sullivan's opening statement, he announced that in a break from common practice, all four defendants would take the stand.

> *"We have nothing to conceal and nothing but the whole story to tell, and to tell it to the jury," said Attorney J. F. Sullivan...*

---

[329] *The Beach Advance*, Beach, North Dakota, July 15, 1921
[330] *The Bismarck Tribune*, Bismarck, North Dakota, July 7, 1921

"That is why a few precedents in legal practice will be broken. We will place each and everyone of the persons accused of murder on the witness stand," the attorney added.

"Witnesses to prove the reputation of the deceased as a fighting man, witnesses to prove Bowen had made threats against Offley and others, giving cause to Offley for taking two special constables and friends with him when he went to Bowen's ranch to get his cattle, which he said Bowen had taken up; witnesses to testify of threats made by Bowen against Offley of which Offley never heard, will follow Stark on the stand after which Jeffrey will be examined and finally Offley placed on the stand on his own defense," said Attorney Sullivan. "While Offley is the only defendant in the present trial, all four are charged with the murder and all four will take the stand."[331]

Ennis Taylor was the first of the accused to testify.

"I shot, don't know how many times, but until he dropped," said E. W. Taylor...when he was called Friday morning as the first witness for the defense in the case of state against Offley.

The story of Taylor is the story...about which the whole defense is based. Upon examination today he declared that Bowen locked up Offley's cattle, that Offley had sent legal means to secure their return and that Taylor and Stark

---

[331] *The Bismarck Tribune*, Bismarck, North Dakota, July 9, 1921

were sworn in as constables. With [George Jeffrey], a fourth man, they went to the Bowen farm.

Taylor served the papers and Bowen started to swear at Taylor and the other men. Offley went to the upper corral to inspect his cattle and Bowen went to the gate to release them after the replevin papers had been served.

"When did you feed and water them last?" asked Offley, according to the witness Taylor.

"Today, yesterday and the day before," said Bowen.

"Well, Bowen, they don't look it," said Offley.

Bowen then said: "I have taken all the blank blank blank from you I am going to take!" he said.

Bowen started for the barn.

Taylor shouted "stop."

Bowen threw Taylor aside and ran to where he kept his gun – a sawed off shotgun.

"Don't touch that gun," ordered Taylor.

Bowen reached for the gun, swearing meanwhile. Took the gun from its place, raised it towards his shoulder and started to turn.

"I shot him and kept shooting at him until he dropped. If I had not he would have killed me, Offley and all of us," said the witness.[332]

Saturday, July 9, 1921: Defense Calls Ira Stark, Jury Allowed to Go Home

The blazing hot day began with completion of the state's cross examination of Taylor.

Late yesterday afternoon [Taylor] was cross-examined by L. A. Simpson... He repeated his story and held up this morning under a severe grilling.[333]

Shortly before noon, Stark took the stand.

Ira J. Stark...under direct examination...corroborated the story told by E. W. Taylor. He was unshaken under grilling questions fired by attorneys for the state.

Stark declared that he was sitting on his horse listening to the talk of Bowen with Offley and Taylor; that Bowen began cursing the four men who came to replevin the cattle belonging to Offley which Bowen had penned up, and that Bowen ran for the barn. He did not see Bowen when Taylor shot first, but did see Bowen fall. The witness swore that Bowen was holding a "two handed gun" when he dropped.[334]

[332] *The Beach Advance*, Beach, North Dakota, July 15, 1921
[333] *The Bismarck Tribune*, Bismarck, North Dakota, July 9, 1921
[334] *The Ward County Independent*, Minot, North Dakota, July 14, 1921

...Stark corroborated the testimony previously given by [Taylor] that Bowen had cursed the four men who called to replevin cattle and had run to the barn to get his gun, that he heard Taylor shoot and saw Bowen when he dropped. He declared that Bowen was holding a gun.[335]

"I heard two shots coming from the direction of the house," Stark said. Then he testified that he saw Mrs. Bowen running from the house, carrying a rifle and endeavoring to get a shot at one or another of the four men.[336]

According to news accounts, temperatures reached an incredible 126 degrees, leading to an early adjournment that afternoon. After being sequestered thus far, the jury was allowed to return home until Monday morning "on their honor." This was another surprising twist, three-quarters of the way through the trial.

The courtroom Saturday was like an oven, the thermometer registering 104 in the courtroom while a thermometer placed outside the building in the sun, ran up to 126 degrees and was then taken in to prevent its bursting.[337]

The court adjourned at 4 o'clock Saturday afternoon...[338]

Members of the jury who have been under close guard since the trial opened three weeks ago, were placed on their

[335] *The Bismarck Tribune,* Bismarck, North Dakota, July 11, 1921
[336] *The Ward County Independent,* Minot, North Dakota, July 14, 1921
[337] *The Ward County Independent,* Minot, North Dakota, July 14, 1921
[338] *The Bismarck Tribune,* Bismarck, North Dakota, July 11, 1921

honor Saturday and allowed to return home over Sunday.[339]

It was believed by Maud and friends of the Bowens that at least one juror was coerced or possibly bribed during that recess.

Monday, July 11, 1921: Stark Cross-Examined by the State

The judge allowed the jury to go home over Sunday and cross-examination of Stark was taken up this morning. [He] repeated the story told Saturday.[340]

Following cross-examination of Stark, character witnesses will be placed on the stand, and it is expected that...Jeffrey, a third accused man, and D. R. Offley, now on trial for Bowen's murder, will be placed on the stand shortly.[341]

Tuesday, July 12, 1921: Character Attacks, George Jeffrey Testifies

One of the defense's tactics was to paint Murrel as an aggressive, argumentative hothead, ready for a fight at every turn. A far cry from the devoted husband and father who danced with his daughters and made sandwiches for the children at the end of a long day.

---

[339] *The Ward County Independent*, Minot, North Dakota, July 14, 1921
[340] *The Bismarck Tribune*, Bismarck, North Dakota, July 11, 1921
[341] *The Ward County Independent*, Minot, North Dakota, July 14, 1921

Defense counsel...today announced their intention of placing witness after witness on the stand to testify to the character of Bowen.

"We will continue putting witnesses on the stand to prove the reputation and character of Bowen as a bad man, until the court stops us," said Attorney J. R. Sullivan, of the defense today. "We are prepared to summon every resident of Bull Run township, Golden Valley county."

Already about a dozen character witnesses are in Hettinger prepared, it is said, to testify that the murdered man was...of a quarrelsome nature and a "bad man."

The defense today will make use of Sheriff Pierzina, originally called as a state witness, and planned, also, on placing Hans Boegli, hired man of the Bowens, on the stand for the defense.

Judge H. L. Berry, presiding, made no comment relative to the expressed intention of the defense to summon an army of character witnesses.[342]

After that level-setting by Sullivan, the character witnesses were called.

Charles G. Huffman, farmer, living near the Bowen place, was the first of the long list of character witnesses called by the defense. Bowen, he said, was "a dangerous man. He had a reputation of always carrying a gun." This was the opinion of everyone who knew Bowen, the witness

---

[342] *The Fargo Forum*, Fargo, North Dakota, July 12, 1921

asserted. [343]*...and said that twenty persons had told him [so].*

Under cross examination, L. A. Simpson...demanded of the witness that he name the men who had talked with him concerning Bowen and had said he was a dangerous man. Huffman did. The names were immediately listed by ...the defense as additional character witnesses whom they will call. [344]

Next, Sam Fisher testified; Fisher had put up bail funds for both Jeffrey and Stark.

Sam Fisher, another farmer neighbor of Bowen's, took the stand shortly before noon, testifying to a threat made by Bowen, also as to his general reputation... [345]*...as a "Quarrelsome bad man." On cross examination, Atty. L. A. Simpson...asked, "Are you a Nonpartisan or an independent?"*

Atty. J. R. Sullivan...objected, and his objections were sustained. Four more character witnesses were questioned on the reputation of Bowen. All told of the general belief that he "was a dangerous man." Under cross examination the witnesses made the case stronger by developing the fact that many people had trouble with the deceased. Then Simpson launched into questions objected as political. Most of the objections were sustained.

---

[343] *The Fargo Forum*, Fargo, North Dakota, July 12, 1921
[344] *The Bismarck Tribune*, Bismarck, North Dakota, July 12, 1921
[345] *The Fargo Forum*, Fargo, North Dakota, July 12, 1921

Attorney Sullivan then in open court told Simpson: "Go ahead and put in your political stuff, we'll quit objecting, and when we get through we will prove that politics had nothing to do with the killing."[346]

Two more neighbors, Loren Bearfield and Frank Haigh, testified similarly. Bearfield had also posted bail for Stark.

...L. A. Bearfield and Frank Haigh, all of whom were residents of that neighborhood at that time were so-called character witnesses who stated that they had heard Bowen make threats and that he had the general reputation of being a bullying bad man and that the deceased habitually carried a gun.

John H. Haigh, banker at Carlyle, Montana, George Christianson, former clerk of court of Golden Valley, were next called by the defense...[347]

George Christianson had posted bail for Offley.

...followed by W. E. Blue, Guy Lovell and Edw. Eagan.[348]

Guy Lovell, Beach, was placed on the stand by the defense. He declared "Bowen had trouble with about everybody in the community," and "he was always bragging about what he was going to do to somebody."

Blue said that two or three weeks before the shooting...Bowen...told him he would "get Offley by the

---

[346] *The Fargo Forum*, Fargo, North Dakota, July 13, 1921
[347] *Adams County Record*, Hettinger, North Dakota, July 14, 1921
[348] *Adams County Record*, Hettinger, North Dakota, July 14, 1921

law within two weeks and if he couldn't get him by law he would get him with a gun."

The court stopped the defense after the ninth character witness, declaring enough evidence has been introduced for the purpose of the record.

Judge Berry also issued an order limiting the threats made by Bowen to those communicated [directly] to Offley and the other defendants.[349]

Several Golden Valley County officials were also called on behalf of the defense, primarily to call into question whether Boegli had been coerced in providing his previous statements.

[Heath], clerk of court of Golden Valley county and Judge Stoddard, justice at the inquest were also called.[350]

[Heath] of Beach testified that after the preliminary hearing, Hans Boegli, hired man at the Bowen farm, came to him on business relative to proving up his homestead. According to Heath, Boegli told him, "I had to lie like hell" at the preliminary examination, "but I've gotten away from them now and can tell a different story." Boegli has been almost constantly with Mrs. Bowen and Seaman Smith… On cross examination Heath added more facts to his story.

---

[349] *The Fargo Forum*, Fargo, North Dakota, July 13, 1921
[350] *Adams County Record*, Hettinger, North Dakota, July 14, 1921

Boegli's veracity further was questioned in examination of Led Stockwell...who was at the Bowen home at the night of the tragedy.. [351] Stockwell, at present sheriff of Golden Valley county, but at that time deputy sheriff, testified as to particulars and talks he had with Mrs. Bowen and John Boegli the day he stopped at the Bowen ranch on his way to arrest Offley, Stark, and Jeffrey.

John Boegli...was recalled and when questioned regarding the remarks he had made to Stockwell denied he had talked to him at all on that occasion.

M. Sherman, another witness called by the defense stated that the testimony of John Boegli when on the witness stand here a week or so ago did not correspond at all with what Boegli had told him shortly after the shooting.[352]

[Sherman] testified to hearing Mrs. Bowen and Hans Boegli in the Rice drug store at Beach, talking over the line of testimony Boegli...was to give, Boegli seeming to be unwilling to testify to what Mrs. Bowen wanted him to relating to the gun found on Bowen's body.[353]

The defendants then again took the stand, beginning with Jeffrey.

Jeffrey...occupied the stand all day Tuesday... Counsel for the defense took about an hour and a half with the witness and the balance of the day Jeffrey was under cross-

[351] *The Fargo Forum*, Fargo, North Dakota, July 13, 1921
[352] *Adams County Record*, Hettinger, North Dakota, July 14, 1921
[353] *The Beach Advance*, Beach, North Dakota, July 15, 1921

examination... Offley had asked him to ride over with him to the Bowen farm and help drive back the cattle after the constables had served the papers and secured them for him, he said.

He repeated some of the curses which Bowen had delivered prior to his dash to the barn for his gun which was followed by the shooting. Bowen raised his gun to shoot, the witness said, and Taylor shot first.[354]

Wednesday, July 13 and Thursday, July 14: Offley Takes the Stand

The heat has at times been almost unbearable but the shower yesterday afternoon had a cooling and refreshing effect that was greatly appreciated by the sweltering people in the court room.[355]

As promised by defense attorney Sullivan, Offley was next to take the stand.

D. R. Offley was placed on the stand Wednesday in his own defense. Practically the whole day was given over to the examination of the witness by the defense attorneys, the whole story of incidents prior to and at the time of the shooting being developed to the minutest detail.

---

[354] *The Beach Advance*, Beach, North Dakota, July 15, 1921
[355] *Adams County Record*, Hettinger, North Dakota, July 14, 1921

"I bought a revolver," he said, "because I had heard of threats Bowen had made and I wished to protect myself against Bowen."[356]

The witness declared he believed he had reason to fear personal violence and told of seeking legal means of recovering from Bowen the cattle which Bowen had penned up.[357]

He admitted this fear and named friends and neighbors who had advised him of threats made by Bowen. He bought a revolver and told about it on the theory that if Bowen knew he had a gun, Bowen would not assault him, he insisted on cross examination.

Questioned as to why four armed men were necessary to get his cattle on the trip in which Bowen was killed, Offley declared that he believed there was safety in numbers and it would minimize the hazard. "I had no hatred for Bowen, just fear of what he might do," the witness declared.

Offley was put through about six hours of grilling by the prosecuting attorneys.[358]

Friday, July 15 and Saturday, July 16, 1921: Final Witnesses Called, Including Defense's "Star"

On the final days of the trial, the defense took every opportunity to call into question any potential evidence

---

[356] *The Beach Advance*, Beach, North Dakota, July 15, 1921
[357] *Grand Forks Herald*, Grand Forks, North Dakota, July 14, 1921
[358] *The Beach Advance*, Beach, North Dakota, July 22, 1921

negating their position, beginning with recalling Maud to the stand.

> *Mrs. Bowen called in rebuttal denied the statement made by John Haigh that she had told of a conversation with her husband wherein Bowen remarked to her that he would shoot the fellows that came to get the cattle, after which she had said "Murrel what good would it do you to shoot them." On cross examination by Mr. Sullivan, however, she admitted that this conversation had in fact occurred.[359]*

> *Defense counsel objected to the repetition of testimony.[360]*

Two of the defense's final witnesses included Gale Clark and James Davis.

> *A statement was made by Gale Clark, former Golden Valley farmer now residing in Minnesota, that he had called at Bowen's place the day before Offley did, and secured nine head of his cattle which Bowen had penned. Clark paid Bowen $5 per head for alleged damages and Bowen said he would get his money's worth out of the 45 head belonging to Offley. He said he saw a thirty-thirty rifle and a revolver in the house.*

> *James Davis, hardware dealer at Carlisle, Montana, told of Bowen buying ammunition and declaring he would "get Offley and those fellows by law or else with a gun."[361]*

---

[359] *Adams County Record*, Hettinger, North Dakota, July 21, 1921
[360] *Grand Forks Herald*, Grand Forks, North Dakota, July 16, 1921
[361] *Grand Forks Herald*, Grand Forks, North Dakota, July 16, 1921

The defense seemed to save whom they viewed as their strongest witness for the end of the trial – the sheriff of Wibaux County, Montana, Arthur Barclay.

> That Bowen two days before he was killed had declared he would kill the man that came after Offley's cattle, was the startling piece of last minute testimony put in by the defense in the trial of D. R. Offley for Bowen's murder. The defense immediately afterward rested its case late yesterday afternoon.
>
> Sheriff Barclay of Wibaux county, Montana, was placed on the stand by the defense. He declared that he had seen M. K. Bowen in Carlisle two days before the shooting. Bowen was talking to a group of men which the sheriff joined. He told about taking up cattle which had strayed into his pastures.
>
> "I heard him say he had taken up a bunch of cattle and heard Bowen say 'I am going to shoot the fellow who comes after them,'" the sheriff said.
>
> Under cross-examination, attorneys for the state attempted to shake the sheriff's testimony, but he declared that he did not know any of the four defendants, the only man connected with the shooting whom he knew personally being the man who was killed.

"I remembered the statement of Bowen because the killing occurred two days after and it was impressed on my mind," he said.[362]

[Barclay] testified that Bowen during the day prior to his death, had been in Ollie, Mont., and in conversation with him had declared he had to hurry home because Offley was coming after his cattle and that "they may walk or ride to my place but they'll carry them home."[363]

As a direct result of the testimony given by Sheriff Barclay, Judge H. L. Berry, presiding, reversed his ruling that only threats alleged to have been made by Bowen, and which had been communicated to Offley be allowed in the evidence. The judge ordered returned to the record all testimony of non-communicated threats which he previously had ordered out.

"This testimony is competent evidence to show whether Bowen or Offley was the aggressor. The jury will take full cognizance of this testimony," said Judge Berry.[364]

In another unfortunate turn, Judge Berry reversed his previous ruling that only threats made directly by Murrel to Offley (as opposed to those allegedly made when Offley was not present) would be admitted, allowing the floodgate of "character witness" testimony to be considered by the jury.

---

[362] *Grand Forks Herald*, Grand Forks, North Dakota, July 16, 1921
[363] *Grand Forks Herald*, Grand Forks, North Dakota, May 19, 1926
[364] *Grand Forks Herald*, Grand Forks, North Dakota, July 16, 1921

Monday, July 18, 1921: Defense Closing Arguments

Following ten days of testimony, the defense rested.

> *After a few minor witnesses recalled...the state made a short argument. [Attorneys] J. F. Sullivan...and...T. F. Murtha...addressed the jury for a total of four hours, resting the case for the defense at 5 o'clock Monday.*

> *They outlined incidents leading up to the shooting; recalled to the jury the dozen or more threats made by Bowen against Offley; reiterated the claim made by E. W. Taylor and admitted and insisted he did the actual shooting and in self-defense; called special attention to the testimony of the Montana sheriff who heard Bowen say he would kill the man who came after the cattle, and paid scant or no reference to alleged political charges originally brought into the case by the Nonpartisan league leaders. The defense counsel called special attention of the jury to the fact that testimony showed conclusively that Offley personally had nothing to do with the shooting, in fact didn't do it at all, and that absolutely no evidence had been introduced to show any previously arranged plot for violence against Bowen.*[365]

Tuesday, July 19, 1921: State's Closing Arguments, Jury Instructions and Deliberations, Another Change of Venue

Closing arguments were concluded the morning of July 19. That afternoon, jury deliberations began.

---

[365] *Grand Forks Herald*, Grand Forks, North Dakota, July 19, 1921

The state this morning in rebuttal argument made no well defined argument to connect Offley with the killing of Bowen, the state rather seeming to rely on the jury finding that any one of the other three men accused of the murder...killed Bowen, expecting evidently that the jury would find Offley an accessory or abettor of the slaying.

Judge H. L. Berry at 1 o'clock this afternoon began his charge to the jury and it was expected the jury would be given the case at 2:40. An early decision is looked for.[366]

While the jury deliberated, the attorneys and Judge Berry discussed arrangements for the next trial to be held, the State vs. Ennis Walter Taylor. In what appears to be a surprise to Simpson, defense attorney Sullivan announced that the venue would change yet again, from Adams to Burleigh County.

Mr. Sullivan: It is stipulated between the State of North Dakota and the defendants...that the venue ...be changed from the County of Adams...to the county of Burleigh...for trial before the Hon. W. L. Nussle...

Mr. Simpson: ...it cannot be tried now in Adams county, nor within the next thirty or forty days of this time?

The Court: ...we cannot try it within that time in this county.[367]

---

[366] *Grand Forks Herald*, Grand Forks, North Dakota, July 19, 1921
[367] Clerk Minutes of Trial, July 19, 1921

The exchange confirming the third change of venue took place in 15 minutes, and Judge Berry signed the order.

Wednesday, July 20, 1921: The Verdict

After roughly twelve hours of deliberation, the jury returned a verdict of not guilty.

> *A verdict of not guilty was returned at 2 a. m. today, by the jury which tried D. R. Offley for the alleged murder of M. K. Bowen.*

> *Indications this morning were that the murder charges against Ira J. Stark and G. R. Jeffrey would be dropped as there is far less evidence to connect either with the shooting, or alleged connivance at murder, than there was in the case against Offley.*[368]

After the verdict, defense attorney Sullivan made several points to the press to minimize the influence politics had in the case.

> *"The verdict of not guilty is absolute proof of the fact that the Fargo Courier-News, The Nonpartisan Leader and the subsidiary league newspapers collected money for Mrs. Bowen upon absolutely false pretenses," said Attorney J. F. Sullivan…*

> *Mr. Sullivan referred to the fact that following the shooting and political capitalizing of the death of the league member, the league newspapers took up a collection for the*

---

[368] *The Fargo Forum*, Fargo, North Dakota, July 20, 1921

poor widow of the league member who was killed by the I. V. A.s.

"I think it rather significant, too," said Sullivan, "that the political value of charges gone with elimination of Langer, Pierzina and Gallagher from office, that the Fargo Courier-News made no effort to cover the trial and throughout the five weeks of the trial ignored the case, or gave it scant attention in news stories clipped from other papers."[369]

After being retained shortly after the preliminary examination hearing in 1919, Sullivan was a consistent and highly effective architect of the defense's position. While Simpson's strong reputation led Maud to select him as the lead prosecutor for the state, his illness and legal troubles of his own may have been insurmountable distractions.

Accounts of the trial in press outlets were often slanted, but one of the strongest examples was from *The Fargo Forum.* Their coverage of the verdict ("Jury in Session Eight Hours; Widow Berates Men on Street," July 20, 1921) included several statements that one man from Adams County felt necessary to correct. O. C. Bergland, who attended the trial, wrote a letter to the editor of the *Fargo Courier-News* with his own account.

...most of the I.V.A. papers throughout the state have by this time made their comments on this trial and the

---

[369] *The Fargo Forum*, Fargo, North Dakota, July 20, 1921

outcomes of it and these comments contain about as much truth as is ordinarily found in the 'kept press.'[370]

The Fargo Forum[371]	O. C. Bergland Account[372]
Offley was discharged from custody by Judge Berry, who complimented the jurymen on being attentive in giving all testimony consideration. "You were judges of the facts in the case and your decision is necessarily right," he said.	*This statement by the Forum is a pure fabrication, a lie. The judge made no such remark.*
The assembly hall in the high school building of this little city was jammed with people waiting to hear the verdict. There was little doubt as to the outcome, and with the announcement of the foreman, a ripple of applause started which was stopped by court officers.	*This is another lie. In addition to the regular court officials there were six I.V.A. present and no more.*

[370] *Fargo Courier-News*, Fargo, North Dakota, July 26, 1921
[371] *The Fargo Forum*, Fargo, North Dakota, July 20, 1921
[372] *Fargo Courier-News*, Fargo, North Dakota, July 26, 1921

The Fargo Forum[371]	O. C. Bergland Account[372]
The jury which freed Offley this morning included seven men who have been affiliated with the Nonpartisan League.	*Another lie, the jurors, who had affiliated with the League, were promptly challenged and the defense…employed an I.V.A. attorney for that express purpose.*
At no time during the eight hours' deliberation of the jury was there question as to the results. Time was required, juryman said, to consider all charges of the judge.	*On the first ballot the jury stood six to six. A member of the jury whose wife was exceeding interested in this trial from the beginning dropped the remark that 'We had a hard time to bring ___ over to our side.' This man being without a doubt an honest and upright man who was willing to do what was right, but unable to read a sentence of the judge's charge and who was in plain English bulldozed by the others.*

The *Fargo Forum*[371]	O. C. Bergland Account[372]
This morning [Mrs. Bowen] met seven of the jurymen. She became furious at seeing them and walking rapidly to them on the street, she unbraided them unmercifully for their verdict of not guilty. "You're a bunch of crooks," she shouted. "You were fixed by big business. The whole trial was a frame up." Mrs. Bowen was led away by friends.	*A short time thereafter the prince of the I.V.A.s here was seen on the principle street of Hettinger surrounded by the prisoners not yet tried and the gentleman who was just acquitted extending his congratulations and expressions of sympathy, Mrs. Bowen was at the same time walking past them crying like a child and wondering whether it was safe for her to return with her seven small, fatherless children to her former home where her husband had been shot.*

Bergland made several other points.

> *Our district court adjourned after spending 25 days grinding out the facts in the Bowen murder case, or rather the case of the state of North Dakota against Taylor, Stark, Jeffrey, and Offley. These gentlemen demanded separate trials and only the case of Offley was tried here. Some of our prominent I.V.A. entertained the prisoners royally*

while they were here and took the greatest interest in the trial and jury from the start. In fact the prisoners expressed their sincere regrets to have to part with such good-hearted Christian friends that they had made during the trial. We suggest that it would be proper for some of these friends to send a delegation to Bismarck next month in order that they may contribute their 'bit' to the cause of the other three defendants when on trial there.

Think of four strong, husky men armed with automatic guns and rifles going like a squad of soldiers to the quiet home of M. K. Bowen; surrounding him in his own barn yard with nothing in his hands with which to protect himself, nothing about his body, except a shirt, a pair of o'alls and a pair of shoes; shooting him down like a dog; claiming to the court, and to the world, that they were afraid of Bowen; pleading self defense; and that a jury of 12 supposedly sane, intelligent men believed the story and acquitted (him) them. What a travesty on justice, what a stain on the fair name of Adams County, which has always in the past had a reputation for meting out at least partial justice to the persons guilty of crime.[373]

The day that Maud and the Bowens' friends and family had been waiting for only brought more agony and hopelessness. Delbert Offley was now free. Ennis Walter Taylor was to be tried the following December in Bismarck, nearly 200 miles from Golden Valley County. The possibility of seeing justice for Murrel's murder was rapidly fading.

---

[373] *Fargo Courier-News*, Fargo, North Dakota, July 26, 1921

STATE OF NORTH DAKOTA,   IN DISTRICT COURT,
COUNTY OF ADAMS   SIXTH JUDICIAL DISTRICT.

STATE OF NORTH DAKOTA,
                  Plaintiff,

            vs.   V E R D I C T.

ELLIS WALTER TAYLOR,
DELBERT H. OFFLEY,
IRA J. STARY, and
GEORGE JEFFREY,
                  Defendants.

            We, the jury, duly impanelled and
sworn to try the above entitled action, find the
defendant, Delbert H. Offley, not guilty.

            Dated this 20 day of July, 1921.

                              B J Price
                                        Foreman.

CLERK OF
Clerk of District Court,
Adams County, N. D.
Filed at Hettinger, N. D, this
20th day of July 1921
at 2 o'clock
                  L M Howell
                        Clerk.

Verdict of Not Guilty, July 20, 1921

246

Orphaned, then Dismissed

TAYLOR'S TRIAL DID NOT TAKE PLACE that December. It had been stipulated that the case be tried by Judge Nuessle, but he was not presiding during that term. Reaching an alternative agreement was hindered as Simpson was no longer connected to the case.

> *[The trial] growing out of the Bowen murder in Golden Valley county, which was agreed upon for trial [in Burleigh County] before Judge Nuessle, probably will not be held this term because Judge Nuessle is not presiding. Leslie Simpson...said that his connection with the case had ceased, as he had been under the authority of former Attorney General Lemke...*[374]

A year later, in December 1922, there was again a dispute over the jurisdiction.

> *[Taylor, Stark, and Jeffrey] probably will not be tried in the Burleigh county district court for murder. The case, a part of the "Bowen murder case" which originated in Golden Valley county, was stipulated to be tried before Judge Nuessle here by L. A. Simpson, special prosecutor, and J. F. Sullivan, attorney for the defendants. According to attorneys the district court of this county has no jurisdiction in the matter.*[375]

When they appeared on the docket another year later, in December 1923, the remaining three cases were described as

---

[374] *The Bismarck Tribune,* Bismarck, North Dakota, December 6, 1921
[375] *The Bismarck Tribune,* Bismarck, North Dakota, December 19, 1922

"orphaned." Simpson had retired from prosecuting the case. Nuchols also stated he was "out of the case." The current Attorney General, George Shafer, stated that "his administration had not been concerned with the case."

> *The first criminal case listed on the calendar, that of the state against [Taylor, Stark, and Jeffrey], for the murder of M. K. Bowen…will not be tried, William Langer, partner of S. L. Nuchols, listed as attorney for the state said. L. A. Simpson of Dickinson, who prosecuted Bert Offley on the same charge, was in the city today and said he had retired from the case…*

> *District court, which opened here yesterday, has three "orphan" murder cases on the criminal calendar [that of Taylor, Stark, and Jeffrey]. Subsequently the cases were transferred to Burleigh county and Judge Nuessle, then district judge, declined to assume jurisdiction. However, the papers remained here and the cases went on the court calendar. An effort was made to have the cases transferred back to Adams county, and the court also declined jurisdiction, because they had been transferred to Burleigh county, according to Attorney-General George Shafer.*

> *Shafer…said that his administration had not been concerned with the case, but because the state's attorney of Golden Valley county is disqualified, some action probably will be taken.*[376]

---

[376] *The Bismarck Tribune*, Bismarck, North Dakota, December 4, 1923

In 1926, the cases were again scheduled to be tried in Burleigh County; again, the trials did not take place. Given the prolonged process, Taylor's bondsman requested his money back, thus Taylor was again incarcerated. Sullivan continued to push for a dismissal.

> *"When we find a court willing to assume jurisdiction, we will move for dismissal of charges against Walter Taylor on the grounds of lack of prosecution on the part of the state," said Attorney J. F. Sullivan...in comment on the famous "Bowen murder case"...which bobbed up again Monday like a wrath of the past after five years of inaction. Meanwhile Walter Taylor, surrendered by his bondsmen is in the Morton county jail.*

> *"Taylor has served more than two and a half years in jail; he has not been the master of his own fortunes for nearly seven years, and the court's instructions during the Offley trial was such as to practically acquit Taylor. For five years the case has been dropped and we will present this lack of prosecution on the part of the state in a plea for dismissal," said Attorney Sullivan today.*

> *State's Attorney Halliday of Beach declares prosecution has lagged while the courts threshed out the matter of jurisdiction and insists that the second defendant, Taylor...shall be tried.*

> *And Taylor, resignedly occupying a cell in the Morton county jail adds: "I hope so."[377]*

After years of jurisdiction challenges, postponements, and disengagement by the original prosecutors, on January 14, 1927, all charges against the three remaining defendants, including Taylor, the confessed killer, were formally dismissed. Adding to the long series of unfortunate events, the court reporter from Offley's trial in Hettinger unexpectedly died before creating a transcript. The majority of the state's witnesses had moved out of the area. Frazier had been removed from office. Simpson had abandoned the case. No one with the authority to do so was willing to push for the trials to be held.

Request for dismissal came from the newly elected state's attorney for Golden Valley County, J. A. Miller.

> *The so called "Bowen Murder Case," which has caused much comment in North Dakota during the past seven years, has been dismissed.*
>
> *Judge J. A. Coffey, in Burleigh County District Court, today ordered the case against E. W. Taylor, Ira J. Stark, and George Jeffrey charged with first degree murder in connection with the death...of Murrel K. Bowen...dismissed after J. A. Miller, State's Attorney of Golden Valley County, had presented a motion requesting*

---

[377] *Grand Forks Herald*, Grand Forks, North Dakota, May 19, 1926

such action. The motion was approved by Attorney General George Shafer.

State's Attorney Miller stated in his motion that the question of the innocence or guilt of the other three was indirectly submitted to the jury at that time in as much as the jury was instructed if it believed any of the defendants went to the Bowen place with the intention of killing Bowen or committing any unlawful act, it should find the defendant guilty.

Taylor, the motion sets forth, has already been incarcerated in jail for almost three years. He was arrested on July 31, 1919 and held in jail until after the completion of the Offley trial in 1921. He was then out on bail until February, 1926, when his bondsmen surrendered him to the sheriff because of the delay in the proceedings.

The other defendants have been at liberty on bail since the time of their arrest.

With changes of venue and other complications, a curious case of lost jurisdiction arose, several district judges refusing to assume jurisdiction.

The three cases finally were transferred to Burleigh county.

Many of the witnesses in the case have since moved away, according to Miller, who stated that 18 of the 28 important state witnesses are now residing outside of North Dakota, which would make it difficult to prosecute the case at this *time. In addition, the court reporter who took the testimony in the Offley case died before making a transcript of his notes. The first trial cost the county over $25,000, Miller said, and further prosecution of the defendants would be a "disastrous additional financial punishment" in view of the present financial condition of the county's taxpayers. Several hundred taxpayers have signed a petition asking dismissal of the case, he told the court.*[378]

The long, arduous legal process ended with no convictions for any wrongdoing against the Bowens, seven and a half years after Murrel's death.

By this time, three of the four defendants had left Golden Valley County. Only George Jeffrey appears to have stayed in the area; by the 1940s he was working for Frank Haigh.[379]

As of 1925, Delbert Offley had moved his family to Fort Yates, North Dakota, where he again ran a mercantile. They eventually relocated to Oregon, settling in Springfield, operating a grocery and liquor store.[380] He died in 1964 at the age of 81.[381]

Like Offley, Ira Stark initially moved to Fort Yates, eventually settling in South Dakota, where he died of pulmonary tuberculosis at the age of 38. His funeral was

[378] *The Fargo Forum*, Fargo, North Dakota, January 15, 1927
[379] WWI and WWII Draft Registration Cards, National Archives
[380] *The Oregonian*, Portland, Oregon, July 24, 1941
[381] US Social Security Records

held in the United Brethren Church at Ollie, and he was buried there in the family plot.[382]

Relatives of Stark have told Murrel's descendants they have the gun he carried the day of the shooting. Interestingly, his niece became a friend of Ada Bowen Rustad's eldest daughters. The niece said she admired Ada for "never holding against her that her uncle had killed [Ada's] father."

By 1930 Ennis Taylor was living in Meagher County, Montana, north of Bozeman, with his wife, brother, and sister-in-law. There he had again found employment as a ranch worker. He died in 1962 at the age of 81.[383] [384]

[382] *The Fallon County Times*, Baker, Montana, October 18, 1934
[383] United States Federal Census, 1930
[384] *The Billings Gazette*, Billings, Montana, February 10, 1962

Looking Back, Looking Forward

THE TRAGEDY OF MURREL'S DEATH, with no legal accountability for it, is the product of a long series of "what ifs."

Would his death have been prevented if he hadn't taken the county sheriff and state's attorney to task over the years? If he hadn't been so successful, becoming the largest landowner in the township? If he hadn't joined the Nonpartisan League, or been such a visible supporter? If he hadn't come across those men on horseback late one night, possibly in the midst of cattle rustling? If the cause of his cattle being poisoned and stolen had been resolved? If investigator Frank Evans' formal reports of the cattle poisoning aligned with what he'd told Maud? If the Bowens had successfully relocated to Canada, or elsewhere? If Murrel hadn't penned up Offley's cattle that one time, rather than driving them back as he'd always done? If Carl Thompson had been at the Mallet Ranch on the day Murrel was killed?

Would someone have been convicted of his murder if the accused had been immediately incarcerated separately as Judge Stoddard had ordered? If the state had provided a consistent prosecution team? If such a high-powered defense attorney had not been involved? If Dr. Stough hadn't died before he could testify at the trial to establish a second shooter? If his preliminary hearing testimony had been admitted into evidence? If Judge Berry hadn't called Drs. Maercklein and Templeton to testify? If the jury hadn't been allowed to return home, having otherwise been sequestered? If jurisdiction yoyo-ing hadn't held up the final three trials, including that of a confessed shooter?

Any one of these or a dozen other variables could have created a different outcome. Ultimately, Murrel's life may be best summarized in two of poet Virgil's lines about divine intervention... "fortune favors the bold"... yet... "fate will find a way."

The Bowen family's story was one of extremes, from influence, prosperity, and contentment to heartbreak, poverty, and a fight for survival. Thanks to sheer will and the help of loyal and loving friends and family, Maud was able to rebuild their lives.

By the time the final three cases were dismissed in 1927, Maud was fully settled on the Montana land, continuing to raise the youngest children there. Eldest daughter Lois was married with a young family of her own. Mary would be married within a few months. Eldest son Bud had gone to live with Murrel's parents in Iowa. Ada had gone to live with the Epleys for a time.

While Maud never lived on the Mallet Ranch again, eldest daughter Lois moved there with her husband Arnold. They lived and raised their five sons on the property for 14 years, and in 1933, the family would suffer another unimaginable loss there.

> While living at the Mallet ranch, [Lois' son] Bobby lost his life in Teddy Lake and almost cost Lois hers.

Per Lois:

> *"When I was a kid, we used to run all over in the lake and catch frogs. There was no danger of deep water because the deepest part was only up to your chest. In the spring of 1933, we'd had lots of rain and the water had washed down a side of a bank where they had developed a spring year ago and it made a big whirlpool. My brother, Bud, and Arnold had been watering a horse a few days before and they noticed the horse kind of half disappeared. They laughed and thought how funny it was, never thinking that the water was washing out a hole. Bobby walked out in the water and fell into the whirlpool. The oldest boy (Dwight) was home with me. Maybe I could have put a rope around him, for he could swim a little and maybe he could have rescued Bobby. Instead I sent him out to the field after his dad. Bobby had been in the water for awhile and Arnold was a mile away in the field. I went in after Bobby and I thought, 'Gee, I can just walk in there after him.' I fell in over my head and that really surprised me. It was terrible! I couldn't swim. It (floor of lake) was slippery and sort of like a funnel. I guess I just wasn't supposed to die then. I just splashed until I finally felt a little slippery wall and finally made it to shallow water. I always thought it was a miracle I ever made it out."*[385]

When Murrel and Maud's youngest son Paul was married in 1940, Maud sold the Montana property to him and returned

---

[385] *The Fallon County Times*, Baker, Montana, May 19, 1994

to her childhood home of Harlan, Iowa, where she lived for the next 23 years.

Tragedy had also continued to strike Murrel's family there. His sister Hazel's fiancé, Phil West, contracted typhoid fever during a trip to Canada and he died shortly before they were to be married. That loss, in addition to her brother's death, led to a nervous breakdown from which Hazel did not recover. She was admitted to the mental hospital in Clarinda, spending several decades there before transferring to a home for the elderly at Logan. She died there on March 14, 1976, at the age of 88.[386]

In 1966, at age 78, Maud again moved west, to Baker, Montana. Baker is 22 miles southwest of Ollie, not far from where she and Murrel had lived, and close to where her daughters Lois and Ada had settled with their families. She spent the rest of her days there, living on her own in a small white shotgun-style house on the east side of town.

> *I now live in Baker, Montana where I have many friends and where I can be near to some of my children.*
>
> *The names of our seven children follow; Mrs. Arnold Beach (Lois), Mrs. Don Scott (Evelyn), Mrs. George Waterland (Mary), B. B. Bowen (Bud), M.K. Bowen, Mrs. Gordon Rustad (Ada) and Paul Bowen. I have 33 grandchildren, 72 great grandchildren and 3 great, great grandchildren.*[387]

---

[386] Written accounts by eldest daughter Lois Bowen Beach
[387] *O'Fallon Flashbacks*, O'Fallon Historical Society, Baker, Montana, 1975

These numbers were from 1975; she and Murrel would have many more great-grandchildren, great-great-grandchildren and beyond.

The living room of Maud's home in Baker was the center of all activity. She loved spending time with family and friends, and frequently entertained. She preferred tea to coffee and always had tea, crumpets, and conversation ready for visitors. She continued to quilt and crochet and would often offer guests an afghan or quilt to take home. She loved playing music; while she couldn't bring her piano from Iowa, she bought a small keyboard. She still had the precious Victrola phonograph and often listened to music on it.

Her extreme dislike of dishwashing never changed; she had a habit of storing dirty dishes in the pantry or even a closet. When visitors asked if they could help, she would readily reveal the piles of dishes. Although never purchasing an automatic dishwasher, she liked to keep up with the times; given her similar dislike of peeling potatoes, she delighted in discovering the instant variety.

Her later years were no less active than her youth. Despite her children's protests, she continued to drive her own car into her late eighties, even making solo trips back to Iowa at the spry age of 88. She also continued to be active as a member of the Baker Community Church and Baker Senior Citizens Center.

In the twilight of her life, she finally reminisced about her life with Murrel, making this book possible; her love for him continued long after his mortal life ended. She passed away on October 16, 1979, at the impressive age of 91. She would once again take her place at his side, buried next to him in the Beach Cemetery.

The Bowen family circa late 1920s
Back: Kay, Evelyn, Bud, Paul
Front: Ada, Maud, Mary, Lois

Maud Bowen at the Montana ranch; close friend Carl Thompson, who helped her run it for 21 years

Maud, the farmer/rancher

March 10,1933   MRS. MAUD BOWEN, Box33, Ollie, Fallon
Brand for cattle on right ribs
Brand for horses on left thigh
Vent for both below origins A-640

Maud's brand – M Lazy H

Bud Bowen in Harlan, Iowa with grandparents B. B. and Mary Bowen and aunt Hazen Bowen

Murrel's sister, Hazel
Bowen, and her
fiancé, Phil West

Phil died of typhoid
fever shortly before
their wedding

Fill West Harlon Fa

Arnold and Lois Bowen Beach

Mary Bowen Waterland with husband George and daughter Dorothy

Evelyn Bowen Scott

Bryce Buel "Bud" Bowen

Murrel K. "Kay" Bowen, Jr.

Ada Bowen Rustad

Kay and Ada both played basketball for Ollie High School

Youngest son Paul Bowen

Paul and his wife, Gladys Shepherd Bowen

Paul on the Montana Ranch

Lois Bowen Beach's son, Bobby, who drowned
in Teddy's Lake on the Mallet Ranch in 1933

Maud's 88th birthday celebration in 1976

M. K. and Maud Bowen gravesite, Beach Cemetery, Beach, North Dakota
[...with Maud's misspelled headstone!]

～

Additional Context

THESE FINAL CHAPTERS PROVIDE FURTHER DETAILS about local and state officials, other key parties, and even institutions such as the press that influenced the arc and outcome of this story.

Key Influencers

TRAVELING THROUGH THE AREA TODAY, a beautifully rugged and pastoral vision of rural America, it seems incredulous that murders were fairly common there at the beginning of the 20th century. The unusual attention that Murrel's killing garnered stemmed from his relationships with those in the highest offices in the state and the dramatic events leading up to it.

He had a strong relationship with the governor. He sought help directly from the attorney general for the cattle poisoning. On a local level, he frequently tangled with the county sheriff and state's attorney, which may have been the biggest factor leading to his death. The following provides additional information about these individuals, each having some influence on events preceding and succeeding Murrel's death.

North Dakota Governor Lynn Frazier

Lynn Joseph Frazier was elected the 12th governor of North Dakota in 1916 on the NPL ticket, and re-elected in both 1918 and 1920. His road to the highest office in the state was an atypical one, however.

> *Prior to his career in state and national politics, Frazier was a farmer and school teacher [from*

Lynn Frazier

Hoople, North Dakota]. He completed his bachelor's degree at the University of North Dakota, graduating with honors in 1902.[388]

Frazier had never intended to take over the family farm, but the early deaths of his father and brother forced his hand. He had planned to be a doctor.[389]

As a young farmer, Frazier became involved in local politics, serving on the township board and school board. When the Nonpartisan movement began in 1915, Frazier became an active participant.[390]

A more jaunty account of his rise to governor:

After graduating from the University of North Dakota, he came back home and married, took up farming on the old home place, and addressed the astonished cows and chickens in fancy Greek and Latin cuss-words. The Nonpartisan League went up to Hoople one day, yanked Mr. Frazier off his plow and made him governor, since which time he has become the most cussed and discussed executive in the United States. He is a Republican, a Scotchman, and a Methodist with five children.[391]

The NPL wanted to run a "real farmer," and Frazier was exactly that. He had no political experience and ran as an outsider.

---

[388] State Historical Society of North Dakota
[389] The Bank of North Dakota Story
[390] State Historical Society of North Dakota
[391] *The Bismarck Tribune*, Bismarck, North Dakota, June 14, 1918

...he was regarded by the League's leadership, particularly William L. Lemke, as the ideal candidate for Governor. He was an uncomplicated man who spoke humbly and in short utterances. Bald, stout and plainly dressed, there was nothing flashy or even "professional" about him.[392]

Almost unknown was this reserved, scholarly, university graduate living upon a farm about nine miles from any given point, a sturdy, level-headed person whose previous ambition had been to be a good citizen and cultivate the soil with scientific skill. The executive committee heard of him in the midst of a consideration of twenty other candidates, and was so much impressed with the accounts that it sent hot-foot after this wonder. It found him a perfect Cincinnatus, although unconscious of the fact. Clad in overalls, he was steering a load of fence-posts over the bleak prairie, and wound his reins around the handle of the brake when he stopped to greet the messenger summoning him instantly to Fargo on grave business. His knees knocked together when he finally grasped the fact that some persons wanted him to be governor; he had never made a public speech in his life.[393]

He neither smoked nor drank. He had no ambition to seek office. The office sought the man. He was so grateful for his education at University of North Dakota that he named his twin daughters Unie and Versie. He used no off-color language. When the call came to him that he had been nominated for the governorship, he apologized that he

---

[392] The Bank of North Dakota Story
[393] *The Story of the Nonpartisan League*, Charles Edward Russell, May 1920

could not come immediately because he was wearing his overalls.[394]

Frazier believed in the power of government to protect the "common man" – farmers and laborers.

> *The NPL successfully sponsored a number of radical changes in legislation during Frazier's administration. Some of these changes included the establishment of state-owned industries: the Bank of North Dakota and the State Mill and Elevator. An Industrial Commission, consisting of the governor, attorney general, and commissioner of agriculture and labor, was established to oversee the operations of the state-owned industries. The state hail insurance system was overhauled, and a graduated income tax and an inheritance tax were introduced. One constitutional amendment established a procedure for the recall of public officials.*[395]

By 1920, however, the popularity of the Nonpartisan League had taken a steep decline. Frazier was challenged for the governorship by Attorney General Langer and reelected by a narrow margin. He and the NPL were branded Socialists by the IVA opposition, and he was recalled during the middle of his third term.

> *Unfortunately for Frazier and the Nonpartisan League, the bottom dropped out of the North Dakota economy at the end of the 1910's. Fueled by the general deflation in*

---

[394] The Bank of North Dakota Story
[395] State Historical Society of North Dakota

commodity prices that occurred in the aftermath of World War I, agricultural income declined significantly in the state, and the process was further aggravated by the onset of the drought that would plague the states of the Great Plains for more than a decade.

By 1921, the situation seemed dire. A shortfall in tax revenue forced the Frazier Administration to borrow money to cover the cost of government, but the state's private banks refused to assist the state government in the refinancing of the debt.

Furthermore, the Nonpartisan League's relative lack of political experience made its efforts to deal with the economic crisis seem clumsy and inept, and many of the state's newspapers turned against Frazier and the party. When it became apparent that the state-owned Bank of North Dakota was bordering on insolvency, Frazier's opponents began to campaign for his removal.[396]

The investigation was led by a familiar face, John Sullivan.

The recall event was led by the North Dakota Independent Voters Association... In a campaign that blamed Frazier for the state's economic woes and which highlighted his anti-war stance during World War I, Frazier was voted out of office [by a margin of 4,000 votes] and replaced by Republican and Independent Voters Association member Ragnvold A. Nestos.[397]

---

[396] Marquette University Law School
[397] Marquette University Law School

> *Ironically, [the procedure for the recall of public officials he signed] was immediately put to use in the recall of Governor Frazier and the rest of the Industrial Commission.*[398]

Frazier was the only state governor to be recalled from office in the 20th century. It would be 80 years, until 2003, that another governor would be recalled – California's Gray Davis.[399]

After his recall, Frazier returned to his farm in Hoople. His stay there was short-lived, however, as the NPL endorsed him for the U. S. Senate in March 1922. He won a seat the following fall and continued to work for progressive legislation benefiting farmers.

In 1940 he was defeated in his re-bid for Senate by his old rival, William Langer.

> *Frazier somewhat unexpectedly lost his Senate seat in 1940, when he was defeated in the Republican primary by his sometimes rival William Langer... Langer's decision to challenge Frazier appears to have been more personal than political, as the two men largely saw eye-to-eye on most issues.*[400]

He again returned to his farm in Hoople, and died there on January 11, 1947.

---

[398] State Historical Society of North Dakota
[399] Marquette University Law School
[400] Marquette University Law School

North Dakota Attorney General William Langer

William ("Wild Bill") Langer was one of the most colorful, controversial, and important politicians in the history of North Dakota.[401]...he was described as "tempestuous," "swashbuckling," and "thoroughly unpredictable in his actions and attitudes."[402]

William Langer

Langer was born on a farm near Casselton [North Dakota] in 1886. Young Langer demonstrated his intelligence and forceful personality while still a student. He graduated as valedictorian of his high school class (Casselton 1904) and graduated from UND in 1906. He passed the bar exam, but was too young to practice law. He then entered Columbia University in New York City and graduated at the top of his class.

He turned down job offers in New York to return to North Dakota... He began his law practice at Mandan and was elected state's attorney of Morton County. He vigorously prosecuted offenders of the prohibition laws [and] was backed by the Nonpartisan League in his successful bid for attorney general and governor.[403]

Langer quickly earned his "Wild Bill" moniker. After being elected state's attorney of Morton County in 1914, *"he swore*

---

[401] State Historical Society of North Dakota
[402] United States Senate
[403] State Historical Society of North Dakota

out 167 warrants against prohibition-era liquor dealers and vice operators during his first day on the job."[404]

His high-profile raids were common across the state, as reported in colorful press accounts.

> *...there certainly is a ghost of a spoiled party stalking back and forth on the road between the 2 cemeteries near Beach where a sensational little one-act tragedy in dry life was staged recently... [after] seizure and dragging to its doom some $1,430 worth of whiskey, some bonded, some bulk, but all guaranteed to have a kick. It was in jugs, in gallon tins, in quart, pint, catsup and medicine bottles, enough to float a ship...*

> *The spoiling of the party was accomplished by members of Attorney General Langer's "Flying Squadron," and as a result four men await trial for attempting to instill a distilled pep in a coca-cola world.*

> *In order to make the Golden Valley country trip complete, six men at Golva, one in Beach and one at Sentinel Butte were arrested for selling cigarettes, operating punch boards or slot machines.*[405]

> *"Bill" Langer's "Flying squadron" is headed this way. Just when it will arrive no one can tell, not even "Bill" himself and he wouldn't tell if he could. The squadron*

[404] *The Fargo Forum*, Fargo, North Dakota, November 1, 1988
[405] *The Weekly Times-Record*, Valley City, North Dakota, October 16, 1919

visited Devils Lake and fined several fellows charged with selling cigarettes.[406]

In 1920, Langer made a bid for governor against incumbent Frazier, backed by the "Anti-Townley" faction; he had broken with the NPL shortly after Murrel's death.

> *He [made] a series of stinging attacks against NPL officials and what [he] saw as attempts to abuse the League's newly won power. NPL founder A. C. Townley branded Langer a traitor, while Langer countered that Townley was "greedy for power, hungry for money," and had lied to farmers.*[407]

> *The Burleigh County Anti-Townley club was formed here yesterday at a convention of anti-Townleyites from all over the county...the convention...endorsed Attorney General William Langer for governor...[and] pledged anew the faith to destroy Townleyism's grip on Burleigh county and strenuously and devotedly work to defeat the league candidates in the November general election.*[408]

Frazier defeated Langer in that race, but Langer later mended fences with the Nonpartisan League and won the governorship on that ticket in 1932, serving two terms.

> *...following the onset of the Great Depression in 1929, the Nonpartisan League regained political control in North Dakota under the leadership of former apostate William*

---

[406] *The Ward County Independent*, Minot, North Dakota, September 4, 1919
[407] *The Fargo Forum*, Fargo, North Dakota, November 1, 1988
[408] *The Bismarck Tribune*, Bismarck, North Dakota, April 7, 1920

Langer, who had rejoined the Nonpartisan League in the late 1920's. The Nonpartisan League programs of the early 1930's, which included mortgage relief measures and a ban on corporate farming, were highly reminiscent of the programs of a decade earlier.[409]

...Langer set about reforming his image and revising the League. In speaking engagements and a prolific letter-writing campaign, he distanced himself from the IVA and argued that he had attacked the League's personalities but remained true to its principles.[410]

In 1936, he won reelection to his second gubernatorial term. During his final tenure, funding was secured for improving old age pensions and child welfare.[411]

He continued to follow in his political rival's footsteps, defeating Frazier to take over his U.S. Senate seat in 1940, *"...an office he held from 1941 until his passing in 1959."*[412]

Murrel sought assistance from Langer to determine the cause and perpetrators behind his cattle being poisoned; despite numerous investigations, no one was charged with the crime.

---

[409] Marquette University Law School
[410] *The Fargo Forum,* Fargo, North Dakota, November 1, 1988
[411] State Historical Society of North Dakota
[412] State Historical Society of North Dakota

Golden Valley State's Attorney Richard Francis Gallagher

[R. F. Gallagher was born in] 1880, in Oak Grove, Minn. [He] obtained his B. A. and law degree from the University of Minnesota in 1905 and 1906. He practiced law at Staples, Minn., before moving to Beach, N. D., in 1910.

R. F. Gallagher

While at Beach he was active in Democratic politics and operated a weekly newspaper for a few years, besides practicing law. He served as Golden Valley states attorney and city attorney and was a candidate for state attorney general in about 1920.[413]

When he was recalled from office in September 1919, John Sullivan represented him in his successful bid to have the decision reversed. Shortly after being reinstated to office, Gallagher left Beach and moved to Mandan, where he joined Sullivan's law firm.[414] Gallagher and Sullivan were also neighbors in Mandan; the Gallaghers lived just a block away from Sullivan's mansion on Fourth Avenue Northwest.

At the same "Anti-Townley Club" convention in April 1920 where Langer was endorsed for governor, Gallagher was endorsed for attorney general.

...Took similar action in regard to the candidacy of R. F. Gallagher, state's attorney of Golden Valley county, who

---

[413] *The Bismarck Tribune*, Bismarck, North Dakota, February 12, 1952
[414] *The Bismarck Tribune*, Bismarck, North Dakota, February 12, 1952

is running for the office of attorney general on the anti-league ticket.

Enthusiastically applauded a speech by Mr. Gallagher flaying the socialistic doctrines and practices of the Nonpartisan league leaders and administration.[415]

He was not successful in that election, but continued private practice as part of Sullivan's firm until setting up his own practice in 1932. He was eventually appointed to a Morton County judgeship in March 1951, and died the following year at the age of 71.[416]

Golden Valley County Sheriff John Ignatius Pierzina

[John I. Pierzina] was born [in Arcadia, Wisconsin] Nov. 20, 1875...and married Hattie Giemza in 1898...The couple moved to Beach in 1907 where they farmed a number of years. After his retirement from the farm, Mr. Pierzina was an implement dealer at Beach and later purchased a service station and a bus depot. In late years he had owned and operated the Big Chief Cabin Camp at Beach.[417]

Frazier removed Pierzina from office stemming from his actions related to Murrel's murder and a number of other charges.

[415] *The Bismarck Tribune*, Bismarck, North Dakota, April 7, 1920
[416] *The Bismarck Tribune*, Bismarck, North Dakota, February 12, 1952
[417] *The Winona Daily News*, Winona, Minnesota, January 19, 1957

The charges against Sheriff Pierzina range from crime in office to immorality and habitual drunkenness. The principal charge is that he refused to incarcerate the four alleged murderers of Mr. Bowen when they were placed in his charge and that he permitted them to lounge around the jail unguarded. He is also charged with attempting to conceal evidence against the slayers and with threatening to shoot Martin Blank. He is held to be an accessory to the fact in the murder of Rancher Bowen.[418]

Charges of drunkenness, of selling liquor, of employing prisoners on his farm for his private benefit, also are made against the sheriff.[419]

The charges also included "illicit relations" with a young woman, Mary Alice Halstead; they would marry a short time later.[420]

Mary Halstead, a young woman who was attacked in the charges against Pierzina, has retained an attorney to prosecute a damage suit...[421]*...in the sum of $25,000 each against the six men who signed the charges against Sheriff Pierzina and State's Attorney Gallagher...the charges allege [she] held illicit relations with the sheriff.*[422]

Pierzina died in Beach in 1957, at the age of 81.[423]

[418] *The Bowbells Tribune,* Bowbells, North Dakota, September 5, 1919
[419] *The Washburn Leader,* Washburn, North Dakota, September 12, 1919
[420] *The Bismarck Tribune,* Bismarck, North Dakota, September 25, 1920
[421] *The Bismarck Tribune,* Bismarck, North Dakota, September 4, 1919
[422] *The Washburn Leader,* Washburn, North Dakota, September 12, 1919
[423] *The Winona Daily News,* Winona, Minnesota, January 19, 1957

Coroner Harry Lewis Rice

H. L. Rice

Rice was a pharmacist who ran the Rice Drug Store in Beach, also elected coroner of Golden Valley County.

This popular drug firm [Lee & Rice] was formed in April [1913], when H. L. Rice became a partner in the business formerly conducted by his present associate, P. H. Lee. Mr. Rice came to Beach in 1910 from Ellsworth, Wis., where had had been engaged in the practice of dentistry, being a graduate of the Detroit Dental College. His first business venture here was in the real estate business and farming and he still handles some land and conducts a section farm with marked success. In April he joined Mr. Lee in the present enterprise and the combination is making a success which speaks much for the combination.[424]

He eventually owned and ran the business outright.

Rice was summoned to the Mallet Ranch on the evening of Murrel's killing and oversaw the coroner's inquest the following day. In September 1919 Coroner Rice testified in the office removal cases of Pierzina and Gallagher, stating Pierzina *"...had done his full duty on that occasion and at the inquest the following day, that all the men connected with the killing had been arrested and brought to town that night..."*[425]

---

[424] *Golden Valley Chronicle*, Beach, North Dakota, December 12, 1913
[425] *The Bismarck Tribune*, Bismarck, North Dakota, September 19, 1919

Coroner Rice was also summoned to be a witness at Offley's trial in Hettinger but not put on the stand.

North Dakota Sixth District Judge Harry L. Berry

Judge Berry was born in Martin County, Minnesota, on November 25, 1871. After graduating from Mapleton High School, he entered the University of Minnesota studying law, received his law degree from the University in 1903.

H. L. Berry

He then moved to North Dakota where he practiced law at Anamoose, Harvey, Stanton, and Killdeer, North Dakota. He served two terms as State's Attorney of Mercer County. He was elected Judge of the Sixth Judicial District of North Dakota in 1920, served in that capacity until his death on July 16, 1944.[426]

Several of Judge Berry's decisions during the trial may have been pivotal: not allowing the written testimony of Dr. Stough which established the likelihood of a second shooter, calling Drs. Maercklein and Templeton who negated a second shooter possibility and supported that Murrel had raised a gun, allowing the jury to be unattended toward the end of the trial, and admitting all character witness testimony.

---

[426] State of North Dakota Courts

Defense Attorney John F. Sullivan

John Sullivan

Another Iowan, Sullivan was born in Estherville in 1884, graduating with honors from the University of Minnesota School of Law, then coming to Mandan, North Dakota, in 1907. He was "called to Mandan to install a card system he developed for the recording of abstracts which is widely used today." After originally joining the firm as a stenographer, he eventually took over the law practice of J. M. Hanley, forming Sullivan, Kelich, and Sullivan.[427]

> *He always worried about all his cases: the ones he worried about the most he always won. He suffered from the occupational hazard of ulcers...*[428]

He was one of the principals in the 1921 investigation of the Bank of North Dakota that led to the recall of Governor Frazier.[429]

Outside of his law practice, he operated the historic Parkin ranch on the Cannonball River south of Mandan.

> *The ranch, located approximately 30 miles south of Mandan, was large enough to support upwards of seven hundred head of cattle. John's outdoor recreation was the weekends he spent at the ranch.*

---

[427] *The Bismarck Tribune*, Bismarck, North Dakota, June 8, 1950
[428] Mandan Historical Society
[429] *The Bismarck Tribune*, Bismarck, North Dakota, June 8, 1950

When the Oahe Dam was built, many acres of the Cannonball Ranch were lost. John offered the government the opportunity to lease the land for $1.00 and that he retain ownership of it. The government insisted on buying the land and offered John a specific sum. John felt it was not enough, so they went to court and the final settlement received more than twice what they offered.[430]

He was also a director in several prominent businesses, including the Montana-Dakota Utilities Company.[431] He and his wife bought a large home on Fourth Avenue Northwest in Mandan that was likely considered a mansion in its time; it now operates as the Weigel Funeral Home.

Sullivans entertained a great deal in their home. Domestic help was easy to get before World War II, so the dinners that were serviced were always six or seven course meals. Mrs. Sullivan stated, "We entertained like mad except during the wars. Everything was very formal. The men always wore evening clothes."

One dinner party…was after the dedication of the new Bridge across the Missouri River…A roast duck dinner with all the trimmings was served to twenty guests.[432]

He also had a cottage on Lake Melissa, near Detroit Lakes, Minnesota, where he died in 1950.[433]

---

[430] Mandan Historical Society
[431] *The Bismarck Tribune*, Bismarck, North Dakota, June 8, 1950
[432] Mandan Historical Society
[433] *The Bismarck Tribune*, Bismarck, North Dakota, June 8, 1950

He initially became involved by representing Pierzina and Gallagher in their bids to be reinstated after being removed from office by Governor Frazier in the fall of 1919; shortly thereafter Sullivan became lead defense attorney for the four men accused of killing Murrel.

It is curious why a wealthy, successful, well-known attorney from Mandan would defend three small ranchers and one itinerant farm worker from the rural part of the state, hours from Mandan. The case dragged on for seven years; he presumably took the case pro bono, or his fees were paid by interested parties with means. He may have been personally interested to move against Frazier and the other officials backing Bowen, or enlisted to do so by others wishing the same.

Prosecution Attorney Leslie A. Simpson

L. A. Simpson

Leslie Simpson was a well-known and respected State Senator and attorney living in Dickinson, North Dakota.

Mid-October 1889: Two weeks before North Dakota statehood, Leslie Simpson stepped off a train from Minneapolis and decided that he liked what he saw. He rented an office above the First National Bank building on Dickinson's Main Street and threw himself into the formation of the new state as well as his law practice.

These were turbulent times in North Dakota, but Simpson never shied away from controversy or a fight. While conducting a rough and tumble frontier law practice, he jumped into the middle of equally tough political battles. Four years after his arrival, he was elected to the North Dakota House of Representatives. He served 4 years in the House. The citizens of Stark County next elected Simpson to the North Dakota Senate. He continued to serve as a State Senator until 1912. He was elected president pro-tem of the Senate in 1909. Simpson was considered a strong friend and fierce opponent in those steamy political times.

[He] made national newspaper headlines, as the lawyer for "Dakota Dan," a rancher from Dickinson who claimed to be Daniel Blake Russell, the long-lost youngest son of deceased Massachusetts State Senator, Daniel Russell…Whoever could prove to be Daniel Blake Russell would be heir (along with an older brother, William) to Senator Russell's large fortune…equal to $9 million to $13 million today.

The trial began in Boston, Massachusetts on September 20, 1909. Simpson was described at various times by the Boston Globe and the Boston Post as having "a sweet, musical voice, a very pleasant and agreeable smile and a most winning and agreeable personality." During the trial, opposing counsel, Robert W. Nason, admitted that Simpson was "as keen a lawyer as I have ever met…." The newspaper accounts of the trial also referred to the small, bronze button that Leslie Simpson always wore. President Roosevelt had given it to Simpson to commemorate

Simpson's service as a Roughrider during the Spanish American War.[434]

Although Simpson, and Dakota Dan, were unsuccessful in this claim, he maintained a strong reputation across the state. The firm he founded in 1889 still operates in Dickinson as the Mackoff Kellogg Law Firm.[435]

Per Maud, she chose him to represent the state in the cases against the four accused men because of this well-known reputation. Unfortunately, he did not live up to her expectations. He did not raise the cattle poisoning, the invasion of Offley's cattle onto the Bowens' land, Murrel's trip to Canada to find a new home, his putting the Mallet Ranch up for sale, or the lack of attention paid by authorities to Murrel's complaints. The defense put many witnesses on the stand to assail Murrel's character, but Simpson did not counter with testimony from the Bowens' many friends.

Simpson's closing was cited as a "short argument," that the state "made no well defined argument," while defense attorney Sullivan gave a four-hour closing statement. There may have been extenuating circumstances affecting Simpson's focus on the Bowen case. He had been in poor health to the extent of not appearing on the trial date in June 1920; it was eventually postponed for another year. Concurrently with the 1921 murder trial in Hettinger, he was also fighting obstruction of justice charges.

---

[434] Mackoff Kellogg Law Firm History
[435] Mackoff Kellogg Law Firm History

A.R. Boxrud, former Northern Pacific railroad conductor at Dickinson, N. D., and who has been a fugitive from justice for the last three years, was arrested by federal detectives in Chicago at 6:30 p.m. yesterday...

Boxrud faces two indictments, one in which he is charged jointly with Leslie Simpson, Dickinson attorney, and T. N. Hartung, former Stark county sheriff, with "conspiring to obstruct justice," and the other with the theft of goods valued at approximately $5,000 from Northern Pacific boxcars at Dickinson.[436]

Dr. Raymond Ward Stough

Dr. Stough was one of the most prominent physicians in the state. He graduated from the University of Illinois in 1905, at which time he went to Beach where he built up a very large practice.[437]

It is estimated that not more than one physician in 2,000 has an experience of this character in the course of a life practice.[438]

Dr. Stough had served several terms as coroner for Golden Valley County. He was one of the three physicians that examined Murrel's body in the 48 hours after his death and testified during the preliminary hearing in Beach.

---

[436] *Jamestown Weekly Alert*, Jamestown, North Dakota, May 26, 1921
[437] *The Bismarck Tribune*, Bismarck, North Dakota, September 13, 1920
[438] *Jamestown Weekly Alert*, Jamestown, North Dakota, July 6, 1905

The body had first been examined at the coroner's inquest by Drs. Maercklein and Templeton. They found only three bullets had entered the body on Murrel's left side. The following morning, Maud found additional bullet holes in the back of Murrel's shirt and requested another examination. Dr. Stough joined Dr. Maercklein in examining the body in the morgue in Beach. During this examination, the doctors concluded that five bullets had entered Murrel's body; Dr. Stough testified as such during the preliminary hearing that August.

Unfortunately, Dr. Stough died unexpectedly in September of 1920. At the trial in Hettinger, Judge Berry first allowed admittance of Dr. Stough's written testimony but later reversed that ruling given defense attorney Sullivan's objections that Dr. Stough could not be cross-examined.

Dr. Charles John Maercklein

Maercklein was born in Wisconsin in 1876, about 43 at time of Murrel's murder. He graduated from the Wisconsin College of Physicians and Surgeons in 1902.[439] By 1910 he was living in North Dakota, first Lidgerwood, followed by Gackle, then Bowman, where he and his wife Martha were still living as recently as September 1918.[440] [441] [442]

---

[439] Application for License before the Wisconsin Board Medical Examiners 1902
[440] WWI and WWII Draft Registration Cards, National Archives
[441] *The Sheboygan Press*, Sheboygan, Wisconsin, October 14, 1961
[442] United States Federal Census, 1910

There, he ran into trouble; per an article from the *Bowman County Pioneer*:

> *Dr. C. J. Maercklein, who came here from Gackle, N. D. last…is out on a $2,000 bond for his appearance at the next district court for trial on the charge of adultery, preferred by a businessman of Bowman.*
>
> *That Maercklein is around now is probably due to the fact that the man who swore out the complaint was not armed with a revolver when his wife told him that crime had been committed when Maercklein had been called to treat her in his capacity as a physician. Maercklein admitted the accusation at the time in the presence of others, and according to the husband, asked him if there was not some way in which the matter could be settled. To this the half crazed husband replied that not money would settle it, and that only the blood of the physician could settle it.*
>
> *Maercklein then got away and[443]…went to the jail for protection, and locked himself in during the absence of the sheriff.[444]*
>
> *…he called up an attorney, and he with the justice of peace visited the jail about 11 o'clock Saturday night. He then swore out a warrant for the husband charging blackmail and a threat to his life, but this warrant was not served.*
>
> *A warrant charging Maercklein with the offence above stated, was served however, and Sunday afternoon*

---

[443] *The Bowman County Pioneer*, Bowman, North Dakota, May 2, 1918
[444] *The Fargo Forum*, Fargo, North Dakota, May 8, 1918

> *Maercklein was released on $1,000 bail until Monday*
> *when he put up a bond of $2,000 for his appearance in*
> *district court in June.*[445]

Per Ada Bowen Rustad's handwritten note, Maercklein came to Beach from Rhame, North Dakota, in February 1919, five months prior to Murrel's murder. In just nine years he had relocated to five different towns across the state.

He first examined the body the night of the shooting, and he and Dr. Templeton were also called to the Mallet Ranch for the coroner's inquest the following day. The two concluded that only three 45 caliber bullets had entered the left side of the body.

After Maud noticed two additional holes in the back of Murrel's shirt, she insisted the body be examined again. Coroner Rice agreed and called on Drs. Maercklein and Stough to re-examine the body. This time the two doctors concluded Murrel had been shot five times, not three. Dr. Stough testified as such in the preliminary hearing in August 1919; it may have been a factor in the resulting first-degree murder charges.

Dr. Maercklein's testimony at the trial in Hettinger had the opposite effect. His account suggested that Taylor must have been at a distance, that only one caliber bullet was used, and that it appeared Murrel was raising his arm, as if to be aiming a gun. His testimony validated the key tenet of self-

---

[445] *The Bowman County Pioneer*, Bowman, North Dakota, May 2, 1918

defense, although Maud vehemently testified that Murrel did not have a gun.

Maercklein moved back to Wisconsin in 1925, where he continued to practice medicine in Sheboygan and Red Granite. He died there in 1961 at the age of 85.[446]

[446] *The Sheboygan Press*, Sheboygan, Wisconsin, October 14, 1961

Role of the Press

THE EARLY 1900s WAS A BOON for the newspaper industry – this was the era of William Randolph Hearst and Joseph Pulitzer competing in "yellow journalism" to see who could sell more papers by maximizing drama and sensationalism. Theodore Roosevelt also coined the term "muckrakers" in response; while it was meant as a pejorative term by Roosevelt, it eventually took on favorable connotations of social concern and courageous investigation. Charles Edward Russell, a leading reform writer of the era, penned possibly the first book about the rise of the Nonpartisan League in 1920.

North Dakota had its own competitive news industry. By 1910, more than 344 newspapers were published in the state, compared to fewer than 100 today.[447] Each in its own way tended toward sensationalism to sell papers and gain political support.

As the Nonpartisan League gained more attention, becoming more of a threat to business as usual, newspapers became a tool to attempt to suppress its growth.

> *Newspapers in the state that were owned, controlled, financed, or influenced on the side of the coterie known as the Old Gang, vehemently warned the farmers against what they termed "a band of swindlers now traversing our state and defrauding our farmers through subscriptions to a mythical new political league," and the name of the "Six-*

---

[447] State Historical Society of North Dakota

dollar Suckers" was invented for those that had already yielded to the siren song of the adventurers.[448]

In the fall of 1915, the NPL launched its own paper, *The Nonpartisan Leader*, and farmers also began to financially support community-owned papers.

> *The movement in North Dakota...did not start from a desire to reform the press. It was a defensive measure. North Dakota farmers on organizing into the Nonpartisan league found the local press, which they had been supporting, was almost solidly against them. It not only refused to tolerate their new point of view but the editors did not seem to try to comprehend it. They started to defeat it by scoffing and from that went to misrepresentation and abuse.*

> *The reason for this was that in former years the farmer had not taken an interest in politics. He had accepted it as he found it, taking for public sentiment the policies that were really of interest to the small clique of politicians and money lenders who had been using the political organizations to further their own ends.*

> *The blind fury of the editors against the Nonpartisan league can only be explained by assuming that the editors and the small group in touch with them felt that their special privileges were being threatened.*[449]

---

[448] *The Story of the Nonpartisan League*, Charles Edward Russell, May 1920
[449] *The Nonpartisan Leader*, Fargo, North Dakota, June 24, 1918

The Nonpartisan Leader, June 17, 1918

The Nonpartisan Leader was not the only paper that brandished a strong point of view. The state's newspapers soon appeared divided into those that favored the NPL and those that favored the opposition IVA party.

Smaller, scrappier papers, including the *Golden Valley Chronicle, Golden Valley Progress, The Bottineau Courant, The Bowbells Tribune,* the *Fargo Courier-News,* the *Jamestown Weekly Alert,* the *Producers News,* and the *Ward County Independent,* tended to favor the NPL.

Larger statewide newspapers tended to favor the IVA, including *The Bismarck Tribune*, published from the state capital, and the *Fargo Forum*, published from the state's largest city. Some smaller publications, however, also appeared to be IVA sympathizers, including *The Beach Advance* and the *Adams County Record*.

Given the political undertones and involvement of officials at the state level, news outlets from across the state had a field day with the Bowen case, often using highly charged language and rhetoric.

NPL-slanted papers generally reported the more human side of the story, such as the Bowens' cattle being poisoned, Offley's cattle repeatedly grazing on the Bowens' winter pasture, and the Bowens' fearing so much for their safety that they put their ranch up for sale and contemplated a move to Canada. During the trial their papers gave more credence to Maud's testimony.

IVA-favorable outlets were more apt to brand NPL members as "radicals," and during the murder trial gave more weight to the credibility of the defense, amplifying Murrel's reputation as a volatile and caustic character, and emphatically stating that politics did not enter the equation. They also tended to depict Maud as an unstable, hysterical woman.

While researching this book, a curious challenge arose.

In July of 2022, we visited the Golden Valley County Museum, which keeps an archive of newspapers from the area, including the *Golden Valley Progress*. Oddly, there was a gap in the available papers, beginning with the first publication after the murder, and including the subsequent several years. Hence, none of the more detailed coverage of Murrel's death and subsequent trial is part of the record. The first issue missing was the invaluable August 8, 1919 publication, including Martin Blank's firsthand account of the coroner's inquest and Paul Greer's trip to the Mallet Ranch within a week of the murder. Fortunately, Maud saved the August 8th edition, and daughter Ada had copies made which many members of the family still have.

The *Golden Valley Progress* presumably continued to publish detailed accounts of the next several years' events, including the trial. Those accounts would have been in the missing issues.

One final example of the collision of the press, politics, and "silk stockings vs. overalls" is as follows. The tale brings together several names already seen in this story, but we begin with a new one, J. Wells Brinton, editor of the *Golden Valley Chronicle* – *"A Farmers' Paper Published for and by the Farmers," "A Newspaper that Causes Comment in a*

J. Wells Brinton

Town that is Talked About." The *Chronicle* was owned by a group of shareholders, the majority being farmers of the county, including Murrel, as well as Offley, Charles Woodsend, and Frank and John Haigh.[450]

Its rival paper, *The Beach Advance*, was "owned and controlled" largely by current and former county officials and attorneys, including Gallagher, Mark Jones, John Keohane, and John Madison.[451]

Brinton's experience is a marquee example of how dangerous being a newspaper editor in the early 1900s could be, even in a small town.

It appears Brinton may have come to Golden Valley County shortly before the Bowens; he married in Beach in September 1909 after being *"...prominent the past two years in the rapid development of the Golden Valley district."*[452] Not long after, the fray began. By 1910 he was facing both libel and assault charges.

> *There are two criminal cases against J. W. Brinton, editor of the Beach Chronicle; one charging criminal libel, and one for assault. These are cases growing out of the old political feud at Beach... James Haigh [was] charged with assault with a deadly weapon, upon the person of Leonard Stockwell, is now on trial. This is one of the feud cases from Beach, growing out of the Brinton quarrel.*[453]

450 *Golden Valley Chronicle*, Beach, North Dakota, November 20, 1914
451 *Golden Valley Chronicle*, Beach, North Dakota, May 16, 1913
452 *The Dickinson Press*, Dickinson, North Dakota, September 18, 1909
453 *The Bismarck Tribune*, Bismarck, North Dakota, March 13, 1910

Brinton was eventually cleared of all charges, defended by Leslie Simpson,[454] but deadlier trouble was around the corner. In the fall of 1912, late one night, an arsonist attempted to destroy the building where Brinton produced the *Chronicle* and lived with his wife, who was expecting their first child, in an apartment on the second story.

> *The Beach Chronicle is in ashes and the site of what was its beautiful home is marked by smoking ruins. It was a total loss. The loss on the building and contents will reach $35,000 and was partially insured.*
>
> *The flames were seen about 11 p.m., and almost immediately there was a terrific explosion that rocked the building. Editor Brinton and his wife were sleeping upstairs and the plastering fell upon them and china fell to the floor from the mantel and the plate racks. The entire building seemed to be in flames all at once. It was impossible to save a thing.*
>
> *There had been much bitterness in Beach and Editor Brinton has been a zealous factor in the fight.[455]*

Two months later, Brinton had the paper up and running again and published his own account of the incident.

> *As will be remembered…the Chronicle suffered a severe damage on the night of September 4 – from a fire originating from an unknown cause in the basement of the Chronicle building. The damage amounted to about*

---

[454] *The Devils Lake World*, Devil's Lake, North Dakota, June 2, 1911
[455] *The Fargo Forum*, Fargo, North Dakota, October 8, 1912

$500.00 and was fully paid by the insurance companies. The windows in the back part of the basement were burned out from this fire and had not been replaced on October 5, a month later, when the second fire and explosion destroyed the entire building and its contents.

Neither fire could be accounted for, and both originated in the same part of the building at the same hour and on wet stormy nights. No gasoline was kept in the building to cause fire or explosion and no fire was in the furnace on the nights mentioned.

The writer and wife lived in rooms in the rear of the second floor, which contained all our household goods and personal effects. On the night of October 5 we returned from the moving picture show at about nine o'clock and retired for the night. About two hours later Mrs. Brinton was awakened by smoke coming in through the open window of the bedroom, and, thinking at first it was smoke from a train, did not become alarmed for several minutes, but finally aroused the writer, who, realizing it was coming from the lower part of the building, ran to the back door and was about to open it when the explosion occurred, shaking the building and cracking the plastering overhead. Realizing that the fire was in the building, I drew on a pair of trousers and an overcoat and went down the front way to the ground to find the entire basement and first floor a mass of flames and smoke, which forbade entrance. The fire alarm had not yet sounded and only two parties, aside from myself, were on the ground. Few if any saw the fire before the explosion took place.

Finding that nothing could be saved from the lower part of the building and knowing that the building was doomed, I turned my attention to my wife, who, like myself, hurried from the building scantily clothed, and escorted her to the home of her sister, Mrs. Lloyd, in the southeastern part of town. So violent had been the explosion that when I returned to the building it was on fire to the roof and nothing could then be saved from the second story. H. W. Peek, my father-in-law, who was visiting with us and sleeping in our apartments, lost all his clothing and personal effects also, escaping with scant clothing. He recovered the only articles saved from the building, two fur coats and a suit of clothes that hung in a hall closet near the outside door. Aside from this the writer and his wife lost everything in the way of household effects, even our watches which lay on the dresser in the bedroom; piano, furniture, books, clothing, pictures, etc., amounting to nearly $2,500.00…The entire loss of building and contents was about $35,000.00, over $25,000.00 of which was sustained by the writer…

Mrs. Brinton also lost about $75.00 worth of baby clothes, bed, etc., which had just been gathered together to care for J. W. Brinton, Jr., who put in an appearance just seven days after the fire, and who would have had but the clothes that God gave him had it not been for the generous shower of baby paraphernalia which the good women of Beach gave *his mother, and it is with thoughts of appreciation that we mention it here.*[456]

This brazen, unpunished attempt on the Brintons' lives would still be fresh in the minds of some seven years hence, when Murrel was killed.

When J. W. Brinton was editor of a local paper seven years ago, he made the same fight that is being made for law and order by Martin F. Blank of the Golden Valley Progress. Mr. Brinton also was postmaster, and lived in rooms above the office.

One night a charge of dynamite was placed under his building and the place was wrecked. Mrs. Brinton was about to become a mother. No one was ever punished for the dynamiting.

Experiences of this sort, and they are numerous, where crimes have been perpetrated without punishment led many people here to fear that the slaying of the rancher would go by default in the same way.[457]

In June 1913, the next major chapter of Brinton's story took place when he published a fiery headline: *"Murdered! Chief of Police Shot and Killed Fred Blumsun."* Blumsun ran a pool hall in town and had previously told Brinton that he expected some kind of trouble from the Chief of Police, J. W. Gowers. Gowers admitted the shooting, but claimed self-

[456] *Golden Valley Chronicle*, Beach, North Dakota, December 13, 1912
[457] *Golden Valley Progress*, Beach, North Dakota, August 8, 1919

defense, saying Blumsun had thrown a rock at him. Brinton wrote:

> *Gowers has been a very unpopular policeman. He is a heavy user of liquor and has been in several questionable mixups when it was said he was under the influence of liquor. His acts, however, have always been upheld by the city officials and he will be defended in the present case by City Attorney Gallagher.*

> *This morning when the shooting became generally known, great excitement prevailed and remarks of lynching were heard. Protests were heard on every hand because Gowers was not confined in jail.*[458]

Sounds familiar. At the conclusion of the preliminary hearing that followed, no charges against Gowers were brought. By July 4 he was a free man and reinstated as Chief of Police. Brinton went on to publish the verbatim testimony from the hearing in its entirety, taking up many pages of the *Chronicle* for weeks, finally concluding at the end of August.

As this weekly reminder of the affair continued to appear in the paper, Brinton was attacked in downtown Beach. Per an eyewitness account:

> *On Saturday afternoon last, about 4 o'clock, I was on the front street between the Golden Valley Bank and Hoverson's Hardware Store, that I saw the fight between J. W. Brinton and Robert Wand; when I first saw them*

---

[458] *Golden Valley Chronicle*, Beach, North Dakota, June 20, 1913

they were clinched, I saw Policeman Gowers standing near them and saw him release Brinton's hold on Wand's hand and then saw Wand strike Brinton about the head and face and get him down in the gutter where he choked Brinton. I heard Brinton say to Gowers while Wand was striking him, "You are a fine policeman, why don't you stop this," or words to that effect, and Gowers replied, "if you say you got enough I will put him off." Gowers at no time attempted to part the men and when they parted Gowers stood smiling at Brinton.

Just before the assault was committed Gowers and Wand were seen talking together and many believe the acts of the two men were prearranged; that Gowers was on hand to assist...

Wand had no grievance against Brinton, except that he was a warm personal friend of Gowers and did not approve of the position taken by the Chronicle against Gowers for killing Blumsun...

Wand is a heavy booze fighter, but whether he was under the influence of liquor at the time is not known...Wand has considerable of a reputation as a rounder and bar room fighter, in fact, one of his friends recently made the remark that he would bet $100 that Wand could "beat up" any man in Beach. It was therefore natural that he should be selected to pull-off the "ruff stuff."

Mr. Brinton, who appears as though he had had an encounter with a wild cat, says he hopes the next man called upon to assault him will have his finger nails trimmed.[459]

In protest for Gowers standing by during the assault, Brinton solicited the mayor of Beach to remove Gowers from his position as chief of police. However, then City Attorney Richard Gallagher intervened, stating the mayor had no such authority. Brinton led an effort to discredit Gallagher's claim, and the mayor ultimately removed Gowers. Brinton published a few choice comments about Gallagher, aka "Fighting Dick."

> *A bunch of citizens soon showed the city attorney a point of law and his friend, the gunman, was discharged. Gallagher should take a correspondence course in North Dakota law – and follow it up with a night school term in oratorical etiquette so that he would be able to get up and address a gathering without insulting everyone present...Let "Fighting Dick" dream of his lost battles, as long as we beat him to a frazzle in the real fight – and proved to the people of this section that he is a revengeful, spiteful, quarrelsome, villainous, cowardly fighter – and a poor loser. Dream on Fighting Dick about your lost battles of yesterday...*[460]

> *Attorney Gallagher, Jefferson and Jones of the Advance Publishing Company, charged that Brinton of the Chronicle was promoting factionalism in Beach. Now Let's See. Gallagher fought county division when the town was*

---

[459] *Golden Valley Chronicle*, Beach, North Dakota, August 8, 1913
[460] *Golden Valley Chronicle*, Beach, North Dakota, August 8, 1913

united for division; when Beach citizens contributed over $5,000 to that cause. Gallagher used county funds by his approval of expenditures as state's attorney, to fight the creation of Golden Valley county. Gallagher, because the voters of Billings county defeated him for office, created factionalism in Beach by attempting to organize a boycott against a Beach institution [that institution was the Chronicle]. Gallagher created factionalism in Beach by carrying on a personal prosecution at the taxpayers expense just to satisfy his personal hatred for a Beach citizen. Gallagher, as city attorney, promotes factionalism by insulting and abusing Beach citizens who appear before the board of aldermen to transact business. Gallagher, as a defeated politician, promotes factionalism by asking the citizens of Beach to get revenge for him on his political opponents.

We could go on, but what's the use. We will simply ask: WHAT HAS GALLAGHER EVER DONE FOR HARMONY IN BEACH? And M. H. Jefferson. What has he ever done for harmony in the city of Beach? And Mark Franklin Jones. What has he ever done for harmony in Beach. Has he not orated and engendered factionalism ever since he landed in the city? This trio of trouble makers are fine examples of harmony are they not? Bless you, dear reader, they make their bread and butter by factionalism, strife, and political, legal, and personal warfare. They are lawyers, or supposed to be. They are engaged in the newspaper business. WHY? Why are lawyers engaged in newspaper publishing? IS IT FOR HARMONY'S

SAKE? THINK YOU. They are in the newspaper business to rule or ruin. They are attempting to control and run the affairs of Beach and the Golden Valley – politically – and to slander, condemn, punish and abuse anyone and everyone who dare oppose them. Jefferson made his brags that he dictated the majority of the appointments of Golden Valley county – and he and his gang propose to continue to control affairs. But it remains to be seen whether they will in the future. Gallagher – Jefferson – Jones comes about as near spelling harmony as war spells peace.[461]

Notice was taken by other news outlets across the state.

The chief of police at Beach has been discharged by the mayor of the town, the trouble arising out of an assault committed upon the editor of The Chronicle. – Fargo Forum.

As the Slope County News says: "It looks like it has developed into a cutting, slashing, murdering of the Chronicle editor." That paper further says, in commenting on the newspaper situation at Beach: "Were there some public principle in question the fight might be justified, but the blood thirsty fighting, just to see the crimson decoration on a brother, looks like poor journalism."[462]

The press and politics would formally collide, and trouble would again crescendo, the following March, when Brinton announced his candidacy for mayor of Beach.

---

[461] *Golden Valley Chronicle*, Beach, North Dakota, September 12, 1913
[462] *Golden Valley Chronicle*, Beach, North Dakota, August 15, 1913

The Chronicle man was informed this morning that his name had been selected, at a caucus of his friends last night, as a candidate for mayor, and that petitions are now being circulated to place his name on the ballot. Being that it is the wish of our friends, and not our enemies, we have consented to enter the fight, for a fight it will be, with the friends of honest government, and a desire to represent the people of Beach rather than to dictate to them, on one side and the friends of Gangism, Gowerism, and Graft on the other. We will have no apologies to make to anyone. – J. W. Brinton[463]

In a hotly contested race, including claims of voter harassment, Brinton won the election by just two votes.

In one of the most exciting and bitter city elections ever held in the city of Beach, J. W. Brinton…was elected mayor over J. P. Smith, president and manager of the Golden Valley Telephone company, by a vote of 151 to 149.[464]

Brinton gave a rousing speech at the Beach Opera House the evening before the election. The next morning, rival paper *The Beach Advance* published a special edition, describing an assassination attempt on its editor, R. O. Zollinger, during the night. Murrel was noted as one of the first people on the scene after hearing the shots. Given the heightened feelings about the race, he had likely come to Beach to hear the

---

[463] *Golden Valley Chronicle*, Beach, North Dakota, March 13, 1914
[464] *Golden Valley Chronicle*, Beach, North Dakota, April 10, 1914

speeches and take part in the general discourse leading up to the election.

> *While seated at the desk in the Progress office, R. O. Zollinger, who edited the write-up of the Advance election special, was shot at the hour of about 12:30 this morning.*

> *That he escaped instant death by the merest margin is a miracle. The weapon used was an automatic pistol of 30 or 32 calibre...The bullet...cut a neat hole in the glass and penetrated nearly through the back of the heavy office chair in which Zollinger was sitting, the inside of the chair being greatly splintered and the veneer loosened by the force of the bullet, which stopped just as it was about to penetrate through. The shot...was plainly heard in nearly all parts of the city, and a number of persons, among whom were Wm. O'Connor, a farmer residing near Carlyle, M. K. Bowen, also of Carlyle, J. Kidder of Trotters, Bob Fuller, Jesse Page, E. D. Logan, Harry Waters, Horace Ball, A. R. Hoffman and a number of others.*

> *It is rumored throughout the city and commonly believed that the dastardly attempt was the revengeful act of some disgruntled individual or individuals who had taken offense at the election edition of the Beach Advance which appeared Saturday night, and was commonly known to have been edited by Zollinger... His fearless pen has brought upon him the insane wrath of those whom he has*

attacked in past and present political crises, but he still
lives to continue his activities in the newspaper field.[465]

The splintered chair Zollinger occupied is still on display at the Golden Valley County Museum. Brinton dismissed the assassination attempt as a fabrication to discredit him and sway the election.

> *An extra was printed following the affair and used as campaign thunder on the streets on election day. It was insinuated that Brinton, or his friends, attempted to take Zollinger's life on account of the bitter attack made on Brinton in the Beach Advance...Little credit has been given the story and there seems to be no effort on the part of the peace officers to investigate the matter.*[466]

One of Brinton's first actions as mayor was to remove the city auditor, the chief of police...and City Attorney Gallagher.

> *Atty. Gallagher, following the day of his discharge, filed with the mayor his resignation, while the old auditor and chief...refused to recognize the mayor's removal, and in the meantime Beach has two auditors and two chiefs of police. Just what will be the next move has not been given out by either side, but the situation is attracting a great deal of attention around town.*[467]

[465] *The Beach Advance*, Beach, North Dakota, April 6, 1914
[466] *Golden Valley Chronicle*, Beach, North Dakota, April 10, 1914
[467] *Golden Valley Chronicle*, Beach, North Dakota, April 24, 1914

The defeated candidate in the mayoral race, J. P. Smith, also filed a notice to contest the results; he was represented by attorneys Gallagher, Keohane, and Jones.

Along with naming a new city attorney and city auditor, Brinton appointed a familiar face, S. A. Smith, as the chief of police. Brinton's appointees were under constant challenge, and much city council business seems to be taken up by motions to nullify the appointments, only for them to be re-confirmed by Brinton. Given the seesawing, Smith was not receiving pay for his services as chief of police. This dragged on for months.

> [Seaman's] appointment as chief of police was again rejected by the anti-Brinton aldermen last Monday night. Mr. Smith has served as chief of police for over five months without pay under the Mayor's appointment. Unable to freeze him out, the enemies of the Mayor have commenced a campaign of slander against him.[468]

> The Beach Advance refers to Mr. Smith in its last issue as a "fat loafer, a bum, a criminal, a big dog, a tramp and a law breaker with the brains of a box car."[469]

> The fight against him has been made vicious because of his candidacy for sheriff against John Madison whom the aldermen, R. F. Gallagher, Mark Jones, and the Beach Advance hope to elect. Mr. Madison, it will be remembered, arrested a Brinton voter on election day and

---

[468] *Golden Valley Chronicle*, Beach, North Dakota, October 9, 1914
[469] *Golden Valley Chronicle*, Beach, North Dakota, October 2, 1914

threw him in jail without a warrant and prevented him from voting at the instigation of Mark Jones.[470]

Mark Jones admitted that he interfered with voters and used profane language in the polling places – and prevented one man from voting at all...[471]

By such tactics the Gallagher-Jones paper expects to elect John Madison for sheriff.[472]

To the gang's chagrin, Smith was elected Golden Valley County sheriff that November by a margin of over 100 votes.

I will do my best to show my appreciation of the honor and confidence they have placed in me. I will work in harmony with anyone Mayor Brinton appoints as chief of police, to clear the city of Beach of all blind piggers, boot leggers and disreputable characters, and I sincerely hope and trust that those whom so bitterly opposed and condemned me before this election will call me a friend at the end of my term. Very sincerely yours, S. A. Smith.[473]

That month, the farmer-shareholders of the *Chronicle*, including Murrel, attempted to turn the tide of the "War in Beach" through a published statement which was run for several weeks.

We, the undersigned, stockholders in the Golden Valley Chronicle wish to place before the citizens of Golden Valley

---

[470] *Golden Valley Chronicle*, Beach, North Dakota, October 9, 1914
[471] *Golden Valley Chronicle*, Beach, North Dakota, April 24, 1914
[472] *Golden Valley Chronicle*, Beach, North Dakota, October 2, 1914
[473] *Golden Valley Chronicle*, Beach, North Dakota, November 6, 1914

our attitude on various conditions that exist at present in Beach and Golden Valley County, so that both the citizens and editor of the Chronicle may know our sentiments and trust that they will be respected by the editor and appreciated by the patrons of our paper.

The Golden Valley Chronicle is owned in a large degree by farmers in Golden Valley County, and we are interested in making it a credit to both farmers and business men in our county, believing that a square deal to both, and a mutual understanding of each others welfare, will bring the business interests and the farmer interests closer together, and eventually each will realize that the future development of either depends largely upon its close relationship to the other.

...[we] urge that all attempts to continue a disgraceful and immoral combat through the local newspapers be ignored by the Golden Valley Chronicle, and allow the volumes of filth and malice to return unchallenged to the source from which it came, and thereby permit to the upholders of further continuance of strife that has existed in the past, to bathe in their own slime.

We as farmers believe the time has come, if not long past, when the citizens of our county should register their disapproval of further continuance of a condition that will in time involve the entire county, and further disgrace its inhabitants, and possibly cause the destruction of human lives.

Further let us cease to discuss who is responsible for the "War in Beach," rather let us consider who will endeavor to stop it...by signing their names to this communication, [the farmer stockholders] go on record as opposed to the continuance of the "War in Beach." Also opposed to the purpose of some to carry that war out among the farmers, and create a warring spirit between the farmers whose only purpose can be to stir up strife among our citizens, thereby causing litigation among the farmers in proportion as exists in Beach; create business for the lawyers, and fees, at the farmers expense. The farmers are too busy trying to exist to add to their further troubles.

Let us eliminate the "War in Beach." Will you enlist? Then cut it out![474]

This statement is eerily foreboding; there would be a warring spirit between the farmers, there would be destruction of human lives.

[474] *Golden Valley Chronicle*, Beach, North Dakota, November 20, 1914

∽

Acknowledgements

THE INITIAL INSPIRATION FOR THIS BOOK was the memories of Maud Plummer Bowen, both happy and heartbreaking. The second source was the growing desire of Murrel's descendants to know more about him, including his grandchildren, great-grandchildren, great-great-grandchildren and now great-great-great-grandchildren, one of whom even carries the first name "Bowen." During their lifetimes, much of this information has not been readily available.

Special acknowledgement must also be paid to two of Murrel and Maud's daughters – the eldest and the youngest. Among their children, Lois Bowen Beach maintained the clearest memories of her father, and diligently documented and preserved personal accounts as well as many of the photographs and records included and referenced in this book. Ada Bowen Rustad also documented key details and made numerous copies of the invaluable August 8, 1919, edition of the *Golden Valley Progress*, which many of the Bowens' descendants still have. We hope they would be proud.

Many thanks to Martha Rustad Townsend, the Bowens' granddaughter and a career librarian, who discovered several of sources used – including from the Library of Congress, of course!

Additional sources, with thanks to their helpful and enthusiastic staff, included:

Adams County Courthouse, Hettinger, North Dakota

Golden Valley County Courthouse, Beach, North Dakota

State Historical Society of North Dakota, Bismarck, North Dakota

Mandan Historical Society, Mandan, North Dakota

Golden Valley County Museum, Beach, North Dakota

Jasper County Genealogical Society, Newton, Iowa

Thanks to the original newspaper copies preserved by Lois and Ada, and an invaluable subscription to Newspapers.com, information was sourced from many press outlets across North Dakota and beyond.

Finally, no one is more responsible for this story being published than Murrel's granddaughter, Janice Rustad Lininger, daughter of Ada Bowen Rustad. It could not have been done without her tireless in-depth research, passion for understanding the details, and commitment to honoring her grandparents. Congratulations, Mom.

～

About the Authors

Janice Rustad Lininger is a lifelong educator – and student. She is the daughter of Murrel's youngest daughter Ada, the 17-month-old toddler he was feeding as the four men came onto the Mallet Ranch. After attending the same country school as her mother, aunts, and uncles in Ollie, Montana, she graduated from Baker High School. Using a loan from the Bowens' dear friend Carl Thompson and working her way through, she earned a Bachelor's degree in Elementary Education from Montana State University Billings (then Eastern Montana College). She began her teaching career in Opheim, followed by Lewistown, before moving back to Baker. Her indirect research for this book started during many afternoons stopping for tea at her grandmother's house on the east side of town, when Maud would reminisce about good times and bad.

She married third generation North Dakotan Nate Lininger and moved 46 miles east to Bowman, North Dakota, where they raised their two children and she continued her career, working with students with special needs. After 55 years in Bowman, she relocated to Arizona to live closer to her son, Michael. She is thrilled to see the publication of this testament to her grandparents.

Kari Lininger-Downs is a proud native North Dakotan and career management consultant. She has always enjoyed writing and loved working on this book with her mom, developing tremendous awe and admiration for her great-grandparents and their children. She is a graduate of the University of Minnesota's Carlson School of Management and holds an MBA from the University of Michigan. She lives in Boston's South End with her husband, Matthew.

～

Reference Maps

North Central United States, South Central Canada

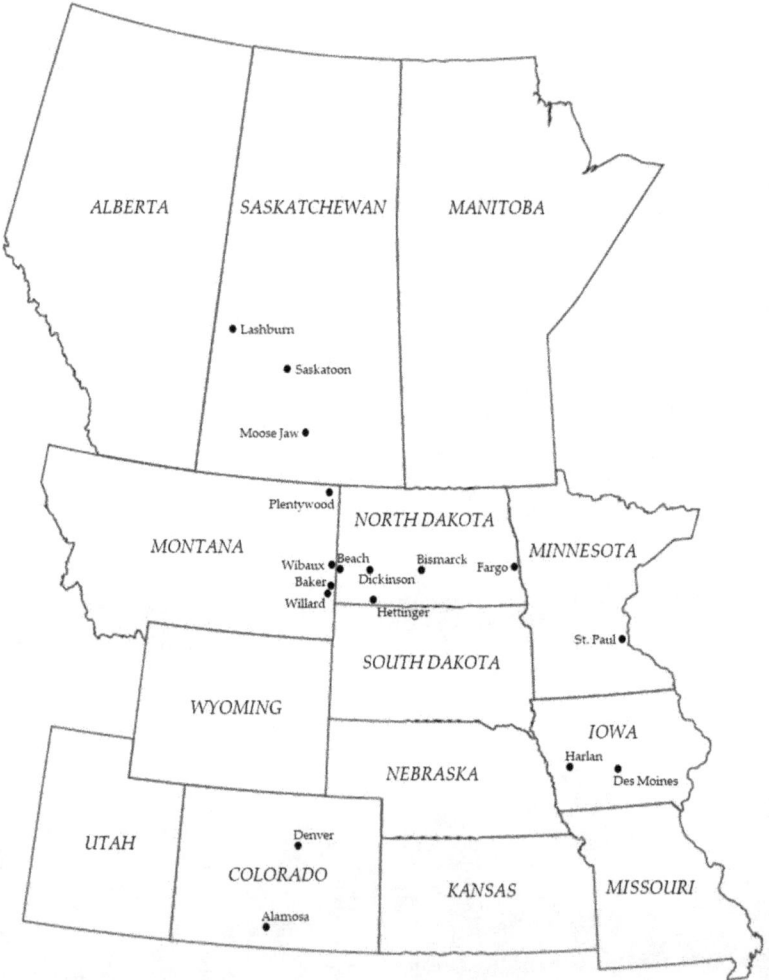

ALBERTA

SASKATCHEWAN

MANITOBA

● Lashburn

● Saskatoon

Moose Jaw ●

Plentywood ●

NORTH DAKOTA

MONTANA

Wibaux ● Beach ●   Bismarck ●   Fargo ●
Baker ●   Dickinson ●
Willard ●   Hettinger ●

MINNESOTA

St. Paul ●

SOUTH DAKOTA

WYOMING

IOWA

Harlan ●

NEBRASKA

Des Moines ●

UTAH

Denver ●

COLORADO

KANSAS

MISSOURI

Alamosa ●

500 MILES

State of North Dakota

Bull Run Township, Golden Valley County, North Dakota

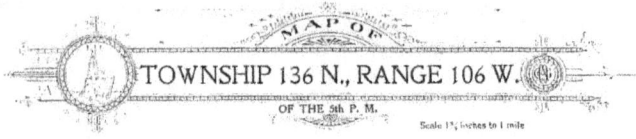

Plat Map of Bull Run Township, marking the property of M. K. Bowen and the neighbors involved in his murder

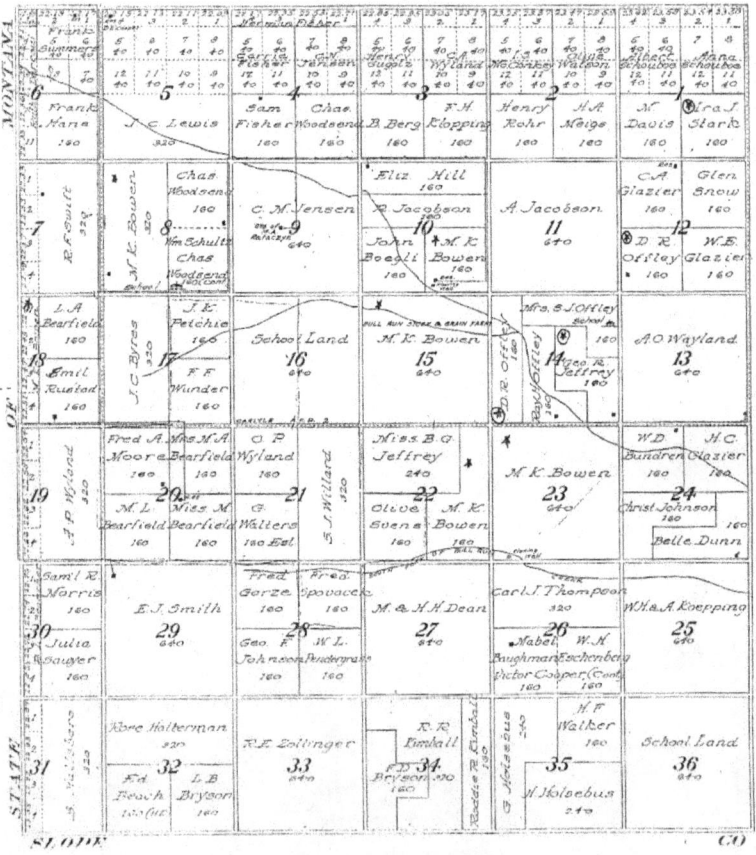

Individual Index

Given the large number of people mentioned in this story, a brief description of their relationship to the Bowens is below.

Barclay, Arthur: Sheriff of Wibaux County, Montana, located across the state line, abutting Golden Valley County; Barclay was one of the last witnesses called by the defense at the trial in Hettinger. He was reportedly the defense's strongest witness, likely due to his position in law enforcement. He claimed to have heard Murrel making threats pertaining to Offley.

Beach, Arnold: Husband of the Bowens' eldest daughter, Lois Bowen Beach, also called to testify for the state at the trial in Hettinger. He and Lois moved onto the Mallet Ranch after they were married.

Bearfield, Loren: Neighbor of the Bowens in Bull Run Township; he owned a quarter of land in Section 18. Several of his family members also owned land in the township. He put up a portion of Ira Stark's bond funds and testified in Hettinger as one of the character witnesses for the defense, saying he heard Murrel make threats against Offley and was a "bullying bad man."

Berry, Harry L.: North Dakota Sixth District Judge who presided over the trial in Hettinger; see "Key Influencers" chapter.

Blancher, Philipp: A neighbor and friend of the Bowens that served as one of the jurors at the coroner's inquest the day after the murder.

Blank, Martin: Editor of the *Golden Valley Progress*, a Beach newspaper owned by J. W. Brinton. Blank wrote several impassioned accounts and opinion pieces following Murrel's murder; it appears he felt the loss and injustice against the Bowens deeply. These accounts resulted in libel charges against him, which were dropped when he agreed to write a retraction. Months before Murrel's murder Blank made a trip to Bismarck to petition Attorney General Langer to continue investigations into the cattle poisoning. Murrel wrote to Blank from his trip to Canada, which Blank published in the paper. The night of the murder Blank came to the Mallet Ranch and demanded the suspects be taken into custody, tussling with Sheriff Pierzina in the process. He continued to advocate for Maud and for justice, reporting when the defendants were walking freely, supporting the trial being moved from Golden Valley County due to bias, and testifying at the preliminary hearing and the trial in Hettinger.

Blue, Walter E. "Doc": Farmer in Golden Valley County. Blue was a character witness for the defense during the trial in Hettinger. He stated Murrel told him he would "get Offley by the law within two weeks and if he couldn't get him by law he would get him with a gun."

Boegli, John "Hans": The Bowens' ranch hand when they lived on the Mallet Ranch, who also owned a quarter of land in Section 10, bordering the Bowens on the east and south. He testified that he helped chase Offley's cattle off the Bowens' property and was milking a cow in the barn on the day of the murder. He seemed to want to avoid making any definitive statements against Offley.

Bowen Rustad, Ada: Murrel and Maud's sixth child and youngest daughter, born on the Mallet Ranch. She was the 17-month-old toddler he was feeding when the four men came to the ranch on July 31, 1919. Ada documented several key details reflected in this book and had copies made of the invaluable August 8, 1919 issue of the *Golden Valley Progress* newspaper that many family members still have. She is also the mother and grandmother of the authors of this book.

Bowen, Brice Buel "B. B.": Murrel's father, a Civil War veteran and farmer/rancher in Shelby County, Iowa. Murrel's parents raised the Bowens' eldest son (and B. B.'s namesake), Bud, in Iowa after Murrel's death; see "We Begin at the Beginning" chapter.

Bowen, Bryce Buel "Bud": Murrel and Maud's fourth child and eldest son, born on their original homestead land in Section 8. He was six years old when his father was killed and went to live with his grandparents in Iowa shortly thereafter.

Bowen, Elizabeth "Betty" Spicer: Murrel's great-grandmother, who was captured by a Native American tribe in 1773 and released 18 months later; see "We Begin at the Beginning" chapter.

Bowen Scott, Evelyn "Happy": Murrel and Maud's third child and third daughter, born on their original homestead land in Section 8. She was seven years old when her father was killed. Along with her older sister Mary and younger brothers Bud and Kay, she was playing outside in the yard when the four men came to the Mallet Ranch. When the shooting started, she gathered Bud and Kay and ran to her father in the barn while Maud and Mary went into the house to find a gun. Per Maud, the shock of the day created a white streak in her hair that she wore the rest of her life.

Bowen, Freelove Rose: William Bowen's first wife. William and his second wife Nancy were Murrel's paternal grandparents.

Bowen, Hazel: Murrel's younger sister; Hazel was artistic and musical, educated at the art institute in Chicago. After the deaths of her fiancé and brother she suffered a mental breakdown and was hospitalized for much of her life.

Bowen Beach, Lois: Murrel and Maud's eldest child and first daughter. She was ten years old when her father was killed. She had been staying with Maud's niece and her husband, the Epleys, about 50 miles away in Willard, Montana when the murder happened. Lois and her husband Arnold moved to the Mallet Ranch after they married; their son Bobby tragically drowned in "Teddy's Lake." Lois preserved many of the personal accounts, records, and photographs included in this book.

Bowen, Mary Prudence Sewell: Murrel's mother; she and his father raised the Bowens' eldest son, Bud, in Iowa after Murrel's death; see "We Begin at the Beginning" chapter.

Bowen Waterland, Mary: Murrel and Maud's second child and second daughter, likely named for his mother, born on their original homestead land in Section 8. She was eight years old when her father was killed, turning nine weeks later. She was playing in the yard with three of her siblings when the four men came to the Mallet Ranch. When the shooting started, she went with Maud into the house to find a gun. She was put on the stand during the trial in Hettinger.

Bowen, Murrel K., Jr. "Kay": Murrel and Maud's fifth child and second eldest son, born on their original homestead land in Section 8. He was three years old when his father was killed.

Bowen, Nancy Agness: Thomas Bowen's first wife, who died in 1791. Thomas and his second wife Betty were Murrel's paternal great-grandparents.

Bowen, Nancy Enochs: William Bowen's second wife; mother of Brice Buel "B. B." Bowen and Murrel's paternal grandmother.

Bowen, Paul: Murrel and Maud's seventh child and youngest son, born on their Montana land six and half months after Murrel's death.

Bowen, Thomas: Murrel's great-grandfather, who immigrated to the United States from Wales in the 1760s.

Bowen, William: Murrel's paternal grandfather, son of Thomas and Betty Spicer Bowen; father of Brice Buel "B. B." Bowen.

Brinton, J. Wells: Founder and editor of the *Golden Valley Chronicle* newspaper. He was elected Mayor of Beach in 1914 and attended the first

NPL convention in Fargo with Murrel in 1916; he was part of the main stage program and later became A. C. Townley's secretary. His father and brother were also newspapermen, a dangerous profession in the early 1900s. The building he built in Beach to house the newspaper's printing press, a post office, and an apartment he lived in with his wife was destroyed by arson in 1912. See "Role of the Press" chapter.

Bundren, William D.: Friend and neighbor of the Bowens who owned a quarter of land in Section 24 of Bull Run Township. He testified during the coroner's inquest and the preliminary hearing in Beach; his son George was listed as a potential witness for the state during the trial at Hettinger.

Christensen, George: Former clerk of court for Golden Valley County, who ran on the IVA ticket. He put up a sizeable $7,000 for Offley's bail money (over $130,000 today), and testified for the defense as a character witness, citing Murrel as a "bullying bad man."

Clark, Gale: Clark testified for the defense at the trial in Hettinger, saying that he came to the Mallet Ranch the day before the murder and purchased nine of Offley's cattle for $5 a head. He stated that Murrel told him he'd "get his money's worth out of the 45 head belonging to Offley," and that he saw guns in the Bowen home.

Cooper, W. A.: Neighbor from Golden Valley County who testified at the preliminary hearing in Beach. He had moved out of state by the time of the trial in Hettinger, thus the transcript of his testimony from the preliminary hearing was used.

Crawford, William C.: The Sixth District judge who allowed and set bail for the four defendants in August 1919. He also ruled to reinstate Gallagher and Pierzina, although Governor Frazier raised that he was too prejudiced to rule in that decision. He also presided over the original court session in January 1920, when the trial was postponed given Maud had recently given birth.

Davis, James: Hardware store owner from Carlisle, Montana, who testified for the defense at the trial in Hettinger. He said that Murrel bought ammunition from him and declared he would "get Offley and those fellows by law or else with a gun."

De Morès, the Marquis: Fellow Frenchman and friend of Pierre Wibaux. He was an entrepreneur who established a meat packing plant in the current town of Medora, North Dakota, which is named for his wife. See "Call of the West" chapter.

Epley, Charles: Husband of Maud's niece, Lois; the Epleys were close to the Bowens and called "Uncle and Auntie Ep" by the Bowen children. Joining Murrel, Charles was among the party that explored Canada as a potential relocation option in July of 1919.

Epley, Lois: Maud's niece, daughter of Maud's older sister Jennie. The Epleys lived roughly 50 miles from the Bowens in Willard, Montana and were called "Uncle and Auntie Ep" by the Bowen children. The Bowens' eldest daughter Lois was staying with the Epleys in Willard when Murrel was killed.

Evans, Frank: Investigator from the Montana Stock Growers' Association called in by the North Dakota attorney general's office to determine the cause of the Bowens' cattle being poisoned. Per Maud, he corroborated Murrel's theory that poison had been added to Lewis Lye, used as a livestock supplement, or the powder used to keep flies off the cattle. She said Evans also found the shoeless hoof print that was likely from Stark's horse. She held him in high esteem and requested he return to Beach after Murrel was murdered. However, newspaper accounts of his formal affidavit tell a different story; he may have felt pressure to not implicate local authorities.

Fisher, Carrie: Neighbor of the Bowens in Bull Run Township; she owned a quarter of land in Section 4. She was the daughter of Samuel Fisher; they were both on the list of witnesses for the defense but it is unclear if she was called to the stand. Her sister Ettie put up a portion of the bail money for Stark.

Fisher, Samuel: Neighbor of the Bowens in Bull Run Township; he owned a quarter of land in Section 4. He was a witness called to Gallagher's office over the Rataezyk "hog affair." He put up a total of $8,500 in bond money for Jeffrey and Stark (over $150,000 today). He testified at the trial in Hettinger that Murrel had made threats against Offley and was a "quarrelsome bad man." His daughter Carrie was also on the list of witnesses; his daughter Ettie put up a portion of the bond for Stark.

Fleet, Martin: Friend of the Bowens from Ollie who came to the ranch the night of Murrel's murder. He testified at the coroner's inquest and preliminary hearing and was on the list of witnesses for the state at the trial in Hettinger, but it is unclear if he was called to the stand. He stated that George Jeffrey "had it in for Bowen" and heard Jeffrey say that he would "get" Murrel, and if he didn't, Taylor would; that he was "sure going to finish [Murrel]."

Frazier, Lynn: Governor of North Dakota; see "Key Influencers" chapter.

Gallagher, Richard F.: Golden Valley County state's attorney; see "Key Influencers" chapter.

Garber, Hugh Goode "H. G.": Attorney and special agent of the United States Department of Justice originally from Indiana but stationed in North Dakota, sent by the attorney general's office to investigate the cattle poisoning. He and Murrel apparently became close; they were business partners in growing flax on some of the idle parcels in the area, and Murrel sold a stake in the Mallet Ranch to Garber, likely stemming from financial strain of the cattle poisoning and theft.

Haigh, Frank: Vice president of the First National Bank in Carlisle and one of the "real substantial farmers of the county."[475] He testified as a character witness for the defense at the trial in Hettinger, saying Murrel was a "bullying bad man." George Jeffrey later worked for Haigh sometime after the case against him was dismissed.

Haigh, James: Brother of Frank Haigh and son of John Haigh. He was listed as a witness for both the state and the defense during the trial in Hettinger. He was allied with Brinton and the "overalls" side of the "war in Beach," charged with assault with a deadly weapon against Leonard "Led" Stockwell in 1910, but later acquitted. When Brinton was elected mayor of Beach, he appointed Haigh as city auditor.[476]

Haigh, John H.: Father of Frank and James Haigh, and director of the First National Bank in Carlisle. He testified for the defense in the trial at Hettinger, saying Maud relayed to him a conversation she had with Murrel, when Murrel said, "he would shoot the fellows that came to get the cattle," after which she replied, "Murrel what good would it do you to shoot them."

Honnold, Ed: Friend of the Bowens who came to the Mallet Ranch on the night of Murrel's murder. Ed testified at both the coroner's inquest and preliminary hearing that Taylor had told him in a Carlyle pool hall that he had some trouble with Bowen and that "[Taylor] was going to get the s—of a b—… if he had to get him with a rifle in the Badlands." He was listed as a witness for the state at the trial in Hettinger, but it is unclear if he testified.

Hoverson, Henry Alvin: Friend of the Bowens who testified at both the coroner's inquest and preliminary hearing, as well as for the state at the trial in Hettinger.

---

[475] *Golden Valley Chronicle,* Beach, North Dakota, December 1, 1916
[476] *Golden Valley Chronicle,* Beach, North Dakota, July 31, 1914

Huffman, Charles: Farmer from southern Golden Valley County. Called as character witness for the defense during the trial in Hettinger, who said that Murrel was a "dangerous man," and everyone who knew Murrel felt the same.

Irving, George: At various times a hotel owner and deputy sheriff; he was at odds with Brinton during the "war in Beach." Irving was called as a witness for both the state and the defense at the trial in Hettinger. He stated that Taylor told him he would "kill Bowen yet," but also said he heard Murrel make threats against Taylor.

Jeffrey, George: One of the four men accused in Murrel's murder; he was the brother-in-law of Delbert Offley; who was married to Jeffrey's sister Emma. He also owned a quarter of land in Section 14 of Bull Run Township; he shared Section 14 with Offley and Offley's brother and mother.

Jones, Mark: Lawyer in Beach, at various times in private practice with M. H. Jefferson, John Keohane, and Gallagher. Along with Keohane, Jones represented the four defendants during the preliminary hearing in August 1919. Cited by Brinton as being one of the leaders of the "gang" in the "war in Beach."

Keohane, John: Former state's attorney for Golden Valley County and a lawyer in Beach, at various times in private practice with Gallagher and Mark Jones. Keohane and Jones were the initial attorneys for the defendants during the preliminary hearing in Beach before Sullivan took over the defense.

Langer, William "Wild Bill": North Dakota attorney general; see "Key Influencers" chapter.

Lemke, William: At various times, he served as vice president of the Nonpartisan League, an attorney working with then Governor Frazier, and North Dakota attorney general following Langer. As attorney general he confirmed Simpson as lead prosecutor for the trial in Hettinger.

Loebe, Mary: Court reporter for Golden Valley County that documented the testimony at the preliminary examination hearing in Beach and testified for the state during the trial in Hettinger. Her transcription of the preliminary hearing is unfortunately not part of the court records at the Golden Valley Courthouse.

Lovell, Guy: Hardware store owner and brother of M. H. Lovell, a former alderman in Beach; they were both at odds with Brinton during the "war in Beach." He testified as a character witness for the defense at the trial in

Hettinger, saying Murrel "had trouble with about everybody in the community," and "…was always bragging about what he was going to do to somebody."

Mackoff, Herbert A.: Partner in Simpson's private practice in Dickinson, brought in as a member of the prosecution team when Simpson, Nuchols, and Gallagher did not appear at the trial set for June 1920. Along with Maud, submitted an affidavit requesting to postpone the trial until Simpson could be present.

Maercklein, Charles: Physician who examined Murrel's body, and testified during the coroner's inquest, preliminary hearing, and trial at Hettinger; see also "Key Influencers" chapter.

McCarthy, M. C.: Golden Valley County auditor whom Murrel accused of election fraud during the contest where Pierzina was elected sheriff over Warren Woodward, the NPL candidate. Murrel petitioned to Gallagher to remove McCarthy from office, one of the high-profile challenges Murrel made to Gallagher's diligence in performing his duties as state's attorney.

McClure, Charles A.: Friend of the Bowens who came to the Mallet Ranch on the night of Murrel's murder, and testified at the coroner's inquest, preliminary hearing, and the trial in Hettinger. He stated that he picked up five .45 caliber shells and two thirty-two caliber shells at the scene.

Milne, Grace: Friend of the Bowens who had relocated to Lashburn, Saskatchewan, Canada; the Milnes hosted the party that went to Canada to explore potential relocation options in July 1919.

Niece, Orville A.: Dentist from Beach who sold the Mallet Ranch to the Bowens. Dr. Niece came with Sheriff Pierzina and Coroner Rice to the ranch on the night Murrel was killed and was present at the coroner's inquest the following day.

Nuchols, S. L.: Judge from Mandan who was appointed by Attorney General Langer to help prosecute the case, beginning with the preliminary hearing in Beach, along with Simpson and Gallagher. Nuchols was part of the prosecution merry-go-round at the beginning of the trial in Hettinger. By 1923 he was in private practice with Langer and stated he was "out of the case."

Offley, Delbert: One of the four men accused in Murrel's murder, who owned a quarter of land in both Sections 12 and 14 in Bull Run Township. His cattle were repeated found on the Bowens' winter pastures; he spearheaded the effort to secure replevin papers and deputize Taylor and

Stark in order to retrieve his cattle after Murrel decided to hold them rather than driving them back to Offley's land. He was seen by the Bowens' ranch hand, Hans Boegli, inside the barn when Murrel was shot, and Maud states that it was Offley that fired the fatal shots in Murrel's back.

Offley, Emma Jeffrey: Wife of Delbert Offley and sister of George Jeffrey, two of the four defendants in Murrel's murder. Maud stated that Jeffrey told Mrs. Offley that they had planned to kill the entire family so no one would be alive to tell the story.

Oppegard, G. J.: By the time of the trial in Hettinger, he was then state's attorney for Golden Valley County. He had previously been in private practice with Keohane and Jones, who served as defense counsel during the preliminary hearing in Beach, thus Simpson objected to his participation. Judge Berry concurred, but oddly no one applied the same argument in allowing Gallagher to be a part of the prosecution team during the preliminary hearing and several of the eventually postponed trials.

Palmer, Peter: A neighbor and friend of the Bowens that served as one of the jurors at the coroner's inquest the day after the murder.

Pierzina, John: Golden Valley County sheriff; see "Key Influencers" chapter.

Plummer, David Levi "Lee": Maud's brother, who also relocated with his wife Myrtle from Iowa to Southeastern Montana around the same time as the Bowens came to North Dakota. Maud and Lee were very close; he was an invaluable source of support for her after Murrel's murder.

Plummer, Harriet "Hattie" Beems: Maud's mother; see "An Iowa Bride" chapter.

Plummer, William Taylor: Maud's father; see "An Iowa Bride" chapter.

Rataezyk, Mike: Friend of the Bowens who worked on a neighboring farm in Section 9 of Bull Run Township. Mike enlisted Murrel's help when he accused Charles Woodsend and Stark of stealing his pig and when he alleged Stark and Taylor tried to shoot Mike and his wife Mary. Through these incidents, Murrel again challenged Gallagher's diligence in performing his duties as state's attorney. The last picture taken of Murrel was on Easter Sunday 1919, when he, Maud, and the children went with the Rataezyks to church services. Mike was also present at the coroner's inquest.

Rice, Harry: Golden Valley County coroner; see "Key Influencers" chapter.

Roosevelt, Theodore: Twenty-sixth president of the United States. He was a cattle rancher in North Dakota in the 1880s and became a friend of Pierre Wibaux; he shot a buffalo on the land that became the Mallet Ranch, and the Mallets named the spring-fed lake on the property "Teddy's Lake" in his honor. The Bowens' grandson tragically drowned in that lake in 1933. See "Call of the West" chapter.

Rustad, Emil: Neighbor of the Bowens in Bull Run Township, who owned a quarter of land in Section 18. Emil was named as a witness for both the state and defense at the trial in Hettinger and testified at the preliminary hearing in Beach. He was also enlisted by Mike Rataezyk to provide a statement to Gallagher during the "hog incident." Emil's son Gordon would later marry the Bowens' youngest daughter, Ada, and is the grandfather and great-grandfather of the authors of this book.

Sewell, Samuel: Murrel's maternal grandfather, father of Murrel's mother Mary; the Sewells and their son Albert relocated from Iowa to Colorado in 1888.

Sewell, Sarah Jane: Murrel's maternal grandmother, mother of Murrel's mother Mary; the Sewells and their son Albert relocated from Iowa to Colorado in 1888.

Sheets, Albert: Assistant attorney general whom Langer sent to investigate the cattle poisoning in the Spring of 1919. He was described in the press as the "...youthful lawyer [who] pooh-poohed the idea of cattle poisoning, and gave his opinion that the cattle had died from eating fermented grain." Sheets was also briefly named to the prosecution team when the trial was set to begin in June of 1920.

Simpson, Leslie: Prosecution attorney selected by Maud. He also served under Theodore Roosevelt as a member of his "Rough Riders" during the Spanish American War; see "Key Influencers" chapter.

Smith, Seaman: Appointed Beach chief of police by Brinton and elected to two terms as sheriff of Golden Valley County. Smith later worked for the state under Governor Frazier. After the murder Smith was sent to Beach by Frazier as a "special investigator" to both restore order, given the defendants were often seen walking free on the streets, and to help with the investigation of the murder. His work became fodder for Frazier's decision to remove both Gallagher and Pierzina from office. He testified at the preliminary hearing in Beach, supported the request to move the trial from Golden Valley County given bias, and testified for the state at the trial in Hettinger.

Spicer, Lydia: Mother of Elizabeth "Betty" and William Spicer, Jr.; Lydia was Murrel's great-great-grandmother, killed during a retaliatory Native American raid on the Spicers' farm in Southwestern Pennsylvania.

Spicer, William: Father of Elizabeth "Betty" and William Spicer, Jr.; William was Murrel's great-great-grandfather, killed during a retaliatory Native American raid on the Spicers' farm in Southwestern Pennsylvania.

Spicer, William, Jr.: Brother of Betty Spicer Bowen and Murrel's great-great-granduncle, who, along with Betty, was captured by a Native American tribe in 1773, fully integrating and spending the rest of his life with them.

Stark, Ira J. "Jay": One of the four men accused in Murrel's murder, who owned a quarter of land in Section 1 in Bull Run Township. He was just 23 years old at the time of Murrel's murder. He was involved in both alleged aggressions against the Rataezyks.

Stockwell, Leonard "Led": Stockwell came to the Mallet Ranch on the night of Murrel's murder when he was deputy sheriff. He was later elected Golden Valley County sheriff. He was part of the "war in Beach" and had an altercation with James Haigh; Haigh was charged over the incident but later acquitted. Stockwell testified at the trial in Hettinger for the deo[--[fense.

Stoddard, A. M.: Justice of the peace in Golden Valley County, who authorized Offley's replevin papers, deputized Taylor and Stark, and presided over the preliminary hearing. He ruled during the hearing that Taylor be charged with murder in the first degree, and Offley, Jeffrey, and Stark as accessories to the crime.

Stough, Raymond: Former Golden Valley County coroner and physician who discovered the additional wounds in Murrel's back; testified during the preliminary hearing but unfortunately died nine months prior to the trial in Hettinger; see also "Key Influencers" chapter.

Sullivan, John: Represented Gallagher and Pierzina in their bid to be reinstated to office after Governor Frazier removed them. Sullivan became lead defense attorney for the four defendants after the preliminary hearing. He also led the investigation resulting in Governor Frazier's removal from office; see also "Key Influencers" chapter.

Taylor, Ennis Walter: One of the four men accused in Murrel's murder. He came to the area as part of a cattle drive from Texas. He found work on threshing crews and as a ranch hand and worked for the Bowens in both capacities. He and his wife Mary lived in a small apartment on the Mallet Ranch when he worked for the Bowens. He and Offley were most often cited as making threats against Murrel.

Templeton, Thomas: One of three physicians that examined Murrel's body. Templeton conducted an examination during the coroner's inquest, when the body was still in the barn, by accounts covered with dirt and manure and in low light conditions. He testified at the trial in Hettinger, corroborating Maercklein's assertion that only .45 caliber bullets were used, and that the position of the wounds indicated Murrel was holding a firearm.

Thompson, Carl: Loyal friend, neighbor, and ranch hand of the Bowens, owning 320 acres in Section 26 of Bull Run Township. He fought in WWI and returned from the war just a day before Murrel was murdered. The day of, he had been away from the Mallet Ranch retrieving his horse, which he had boarded with a neighbor during the war; he avowed that if he had been present, it would not have happened. He served as a juror at the coroner's inquest but oddly was not listed as a witness at either the preliminary hearing in Beach or the trial in Hettinger. Carl supported Maud and the family for the following 21 years, serving as her foreman on the Montana property. He generously loaned Janice Rustad Lininger $500 for her college education (almost $6,000 today).

Townley, Arthur C.: Bankrupt flax farmer from Golden Valley County that founded the Nonpartisan League; see "Rise of the Nonpartisan League" chapter.

Tubbs, George: Nephew and ranch hand of Delbert Offley; Tubbs was the first to try to retrieve Offley's cattle after Murrel penned them in the Bowens' corral. He testified for both the state and the defense at the trial in Hettinger, stating that he had been coerced by S. A. Smith to make certain statements during Smith's early investigation.

Twichell, Treadwell: North Dakota state legislator who allegedly said "the farmers should go home and slop the hogs and leave governing of the state to the politicians," which became a rallying cry in the formation of the Nonpartisan League.

Wand, Robert: Accused by J. W. Brinton of physically attacking Brinton on the streets of Beach in front of Chief of Police Gowers, leading to Gower's removal from office. Per Brinton, Wand was retaliating for statements made by Brinton in the *Golden Valley Chronicle*.

Watson, William: Neighbor of the Bowens in Bull Run Township who allowed them to live in a sod house on his property when they came to North Dakota in 1908.

West, Phil: Fiancé of Murrel's sister Hazel who died of typhoid fever shortly before they were to be married.

Westrope, William Taylor: Maud's nephew, son of Maud's elder sister Mary, and namesake of Maud's father W. T. Plummer. William came to the Mallet Ranch the night of Murrel's murder and testified at both the preliminary hearing and the trial in Hettinger.

Wibaux, Pierre: French cattle baron who established the W-Bar Ranch on the North Dakota-Montana border, at one time one of the largest cattle owners in the United States; Murrel worked on the W-Bar for a summer in the early 1900s. See "Call of the West" chapter.

Wood, Frank: Farmer from Deering, North Dakota; co-author and first enlistee in the Nonpartisan League. See "Rise of the Nonpartisan League" chapter.

Woodsend, Charles: Neighbor of the Bowens whose land in Section 8 bordered the Bowens' homestead property. Per Maud, they had been friendly with the Woodsends, often playing cards and socializing. Things may have soured when Murrel supported the Rataezyks in their accusations against Woodsend for stealing their pig. Woodsend put up a sizeable $5,000 for Stark's bail, over $90,000 today. He was listed as a witness for the defense during the trial at Hettinger.

Zollinger, Ross O.: Editor of *The Beach Advance*, "rival" paper to the *Golden Valley Chronicle. The Advance* was thought to support the "silk stocking" side of the "war in Beach." Zollinger wrote that there was an attempt made on his life the night before Brinton was elected mayor, and Murrel was one of the first on the scene. Zollinger also owned the entire 640 acres of Section 33 in Bull Run Township.

Bibliography

We Begin at the Beginning

[1] *Spicer Massacre, June 4, 1773*, Wright, Dr. Clarence C., based on an account given by Thomas and Betty Bowen's daughter Nancy at a family reunion in 1889; Wright is Nancy's great-grandson and Betty's great-great-grandson

[2] Written accounts by the Bowens' eldest daughter, Lois Bowen Beach; property of Bowen-Beach-Rustad-Lininger Family

Photos and images property of the Bowen-Beach-Rustad-Lininger Family

Call of the West

[3 8 9 10 12 13 19 21] "The Romantic Story of the W-Bar Ranch," September 1906, published in the *Montana Homeseeker*, Helena, Montana

[4 11] "Wibaux," Healy, Donna, May 19, 2002, *The Billings Gazette*, Billings, Montana

[5 7] "Pierre Wibaux, cattle king," Welsh, Donald Hugh, 1950, *Graduate Student Theses, Dissertations, & Professional Papers. 3221*

[6] North Dakota Cowboy Hall of Fame website, https://northdakotacowboy.org/

[14 15 17 18 20] *Theodore Roosevelt and the Dakota Badlands*, Brooks, Chester L. and Mattison, Ray H., 1958, National Park Service, reprinted in 1962 and 1983 by the Theodore Roosevelt Nature and History Association, Medora, North Dakota

[16] "Gateway to Montana," Inbody, Kristen, July 7, 2013, *Great Falls Tribune*, Great Falls, Montana

[22] State Historical Society of North Dakota website, https://www.history.nd.gov/

[23] *The Story of the Nonpartisan League*, Russell, Charles Edward, May 1920, Harper & Brothers Publishers

Images of Pierre Wibaux and cattle branding on the W-Bar Ranch, "The Romantic Story of the W-Bar Ranch," September 1906, published in the *Montana Homeseeker*, Helena, Montana

Image of the Marquis de Morès, National Park Service website, https://www.nps.gov/thro/

Image of Theodore Roosevelt, Dickinson State University collection via National Park Service website, https://home.nps.gov/thro/

Image of the Chateau de Morès, North Dakota GenWeb website, https://www.usgwarchives.net/nd/goldenvalley/postcards/

An Iowa Bride

[24] Personal account by Maud Plummer Bowen, *O'Fallon Flashbacks*, 1975, O'Fallon Historical Society, Baker, Montana

Photos and images property of the Bowen-Beach-Rustad-Lininger Family

Their Adventure Begins

[25] Personal account by Maud Plummer Bowen, *O'Fallon Flashbacks*, 1975, O'Fallon Historical Society, Baker, Montana

[26] "Inside Facts Antedating Bowen Killing Show Futility of Boss' Campaign to Discredit Langer," August 6, 1919, *The Bismarck Tribune*, Bismarck, North Dakota

[27] State Historical Society of North Dakota website, https://www.history.nd.gov/

Photos and images property of the Bowen-Beach-Rustad-Lininger Family

Life on the Prairie

[28 33] Personal account by Maud Plummer Bowen, *O'Fallon Flashbacks*, 1975, O'Fallon Historical Society, Baker, Montana

[29 33 34 35 37] Written accounts by the Bowens' eldest daughter, Lois Bowen Beach; property of Bowen-Beach-Rustad-Lininger Family

[30] "Tales of the Town," October 22, 1915, *Golden Valley Chronicle*, Beach, North Dakota

[31] "Seniors Into View," Dyke, Carol, May 19, 1994, *Fallon County Times*, Baker, Montana

[32] Independent Order of Odd Fellows website, https://odd-fellows.org/

[36] State Historical Society of North Dakota website, https://www.history.nd.gov/

[38] "Notice to Contractors," August 14, 1914, *Golden Valley Chronicle*, Beach, North Dakota

[39] "Tales of the Town," August 21, 1914, *Golden Valley Chronicle*, Beach, North Dakota

Image of Odd Fellows emblem, Independent Order of Odd Fellows website, https://odd-fellows.org/

Photos and images property of the Bowen-Beach-Rustad-Lininger Family

Building a Legacy

[40] "4 Men Are Held in Jail for First Degree Murder," August 8, 1919, *Golden Valley Progress*, Beach, North Dakota

[41] "Locals," February 18, 1916, *Golden Valley Chronicle*, Beach, North Dakota

[42] "Locals," March 31, 1916, *Golden Valley Chronicle*, Beach, North Dakota

[43] Personal account by Maud Plummer Bowen, *O'Fallon Flashbacks*, 1975, O'Fallon Historical Society, Baker, Montana

[44] "Pastures Are Strewn with Cattle Bones," August 8, 1919, *Golden Valley Progress*, Beach, North Dakota

[45] "Locals," December 1, 1916, *Golden Valley Chronicle*, Beach, North Dakota

Photos and images property of the Bowen-Beach-Rustad-Lininger Family

Rise of the Nonpartisan League

[46 47 48 49 51 54 56 62] *The Story of the Nonpartisan League*, Russell, Charles Edward, May 1920, Harper & Brothers Publishers

[50 52 73 75] "A.C. Townley, Political Activist," Langemo, Cathy A., May 17, 2022, Prairie Public Newsroom, https://news.prairiepublic.org/

[53 55 58 65 67] The Bank of North Dakota Story website, https://thebndstory.nd.gov/

[57 63 76] "Remembering 'The Goat that Can't be Got' 'Insurgent Democracy' event examines the Nonpartisan League," interview with Michael J. Lansing, associate professor of history at Augsburg College and author, *Insurgent Democracy: The Nonpartisan League in North American Politics*; November 28, 2015, *High Plans Reader*, Fargo, North Dakota

[59] "Brinton Voters Arrested – Gang Voters Go Free," April 24, 1914, *Golden Valley Chronicle*, Beach, North Dakota

[60] "Locals," April 14, 1916, *Golden Valley Chronicle*, Beach, North Dakota

[61] "Largest Convention Held in State," April 7, 1916, *Golden Valley Chronicle*, Beach, North Dakota

[64 68 72 74] State Historical Society of North Dakota website, https://www.history.nd.gov/

[66] "Signing of Program Bills Is Big Event," August 8, 1919, *Golden Valley Progress*, Beach, North Dakota

[69] "Mob Ducks U. Nonpartisan," October 2, 1919, *The Bottineau Courant*, Bottineau, North Dakota

[70] Editorial Page, August 8, 1919, *Golden Valley Progress*, Beach, North Dakota

71 "North Dakota Kernels," May 8, 1918, *The Fargo Forum,* Fargo, North Dakota

Image of A. C. Townley, State Historical Society of North Dakota website, https://www.history.nd.gov/

Image of NPL Badge, Institute for Local Self-Reliance website, https://ilsr.org/

"The Farmer's Burden" cartoon, June 24, 1918, *The Nonpartisan Leader,* Fargo, North Dakota

Aggression at the Mallet Ranch

77 "Bowen Killed by E. W. Taylor," August 1, 1919, *The Beach Advance,* Beach, North Dakota

78 84 86 87 89 90 95 97 98 101 106 "Inside Facts Antedating Bowen Killing Show Futility of Boss' Campaign to Discredit Langer," August 6, 1919, *The Bismarck Tribune,* Bismarck, North Dakota

79 107 Written accounts by the Bowens' eldest daughter, Lois Bowen Beach; property of Bowen-Beach-Rustad-Lininger Family

80 "Coroner's Jury Finds Bowen Was Slain by Taylor," August 2, 1919, *The Bismarck Tribune,* Bismarck, North Dakota

81 "Seniors Into View," Dyke, Carol, May 19, 1994, *Fallon County Times,* Baker, Montana

82 "What the Organized Farmer Is Doing – North Dakota," September 22, 1919, *The Nonpartisan Leader,* Fargo, North Dakota

83 "Pastures Are Strewn with Cattle Bones," August 8, 1919, *Golden Valley Progress,* Beach, North Dakota

85 99 100 102 109 "4 Men Are Held in Jail for First Degree Murder," August 1, 1919, *Fargo Courier-News,* Fargo, North Dakota [reprinted in the *Golden Valley Progress*]

89 "Langer May Face Trial," August 7, 1919, *The Bottineau Courant,* Bottineau, North Dakota

88 "Cattle Thieves Busy in State," August 8, 1918, *The Weekly Times-Record,* Valley City, North Dakota

91 96 105 "Langer Office Not Blameless Fact Revealed," August 8, 1919, *Golden Valley Progress,* Beach, North Dakota

92 "Real Estate – Cattle Ranches," December 15, 1918, *Chicago Tribune,* Chicago, Illinois

93 "Murder of M. K. Bowen Is Reviewed," January 23, 1920, *Mandan Pioneer,* Mandan, North Dakota

94 "Conscription of Idle Lands for Flax Crop," May 24, 1918, *Grand Forks Herald,* Grand Forks, North Dakota

[103] "Ex-Law Partner of Langer's to Be Prosecutor," August 8, 1919, *The Bismarck Tribune*, Bismarck, North Dakota

[104] "Langer May Face Impeachment Trial," August 8, 1919, *The Producers News*, Plentywood, Montana *Progress*, Beach, North Dakota

[108] "4 Men Are Held in Jail for First Degree Murder," August 8, 1919, *Golden Valley*

[110 111 112] "Hearing at Beach to Remove State Attorney and Sheriff Is Closed Suddenly; Fireworks Are Missing," September 20, 1919, *The Bismarck Tribune*, Bismarck, North Dakota

[113] "Governor Suspends 2 Beach Officials," September 5, 1919, *The Bowbells Tribune*, Bowbells, North Dakota

Photos and images property of the Bowen-Beach-Rustad-Lininger Family

July 1919

[114 118 122 125 126 129 139 141 145] "4 Men Are Held in Jail for First Degree Murder," August 1, 1919, *Fargo Courier-News*, Fargo, North Dakota [reprinted in the *Golden Valley Progress*]

[115 136 140 146 148 149 152 160 162 166 169] "4 Men Are Held in Jail for First Degree Murder," August 8, 1919, *Golden Valley Progress*, Beach, North Dakota

[116] Handwritten note by the Bowens' youngest daughter, Ada Bowen Rustad, property of Bowen-Beach-Rustad-Lininger Family

[117 130 135 153] "Pastures Are Strewn with Cattle Bones," August 8, 1919, *Golden Valley Progress*, Beach, North Dakota

[119] "Writes Letter Blaming Langer and the County Authorities," August 1, 1919, *Fargo Courier-News*, Fargo, North Dakota [reprinted in the *Golden Valley Progress*]

[120] "Seniors Into View," Dyke, Carol, May 19, 1994, *Fallon County Times*, Baker, Montana

[121] "Bowen Writes That Canada Is Alright, But U. S. A. Is Good Enough for Him," undated, approximately July 1919, *Golden Valley Progress*, Beach, North Dakota

[123 124 127 128 131 134 137 168] "Langer Office Not Blameless Fact Revealed," August 8, 1919, *Golden Valley Progress*, Beach, North Dakota

[132] "Governor Suspends 2 Beach Officials," September 5, 1919, *The Bowbells Tribune*, Bowbells, North Dakota

[133] "Beach Rancher Is Shot from Ambush," August 7, 1919, *Jamestown Weekly Alert*, Jamestown, North Dakota

[138 151 157 159 161 163] "Coroner's Jury Charges Taylor with Murder in First Degree," August 8, 1919, *The Beach Advance*, Beach, North Dakota

142 "Beach Aroused Over Killing of League Farmer," August 1, 1919, *The Bismarck Tribune*, Bismarck, North Dakota

143 144 154 155 156 164 165 "Bowen Killed by E. W. Taylor," August 1, 1919, *The Beach Advance*, Beach, North Dakota

147 150 "Bitter Feud Is Developing in Beach District Over Shooting," August 2, 1919, *The Fargo Forum*, Fargo, North Dakota

158 "Widow Relates Bowen Killing at Hettinger," July 6, 1921, *The Bismarck Tribune*, Bismarck, North Dakota

167 "Trial at Beach of Sheriff and State's Attorney Drags Along; Mrs. Bowen Is Called to Stand," September 19, 1919, *The Bismarck Tribune*, Bismarck, North Dakota

Photos and images property of the Bowen-Beach-Rustad-Lininger Family

August 1919

170 188 "4 Men Are Held in Jail for First Degree Murder," August 1, 1919, *Fargo Courier-News*, Fargo, North Dakota [reprinted in the *Golden Valley Progress*]

171 "Beach Aroused Over Killing of League Farmer," August 1, 1919, *The Bismarck Tribune*, Bismarck, North Dakota

172 "Gang Editor Hounds Frantic Wife; Writes Scandalous Account," August 8, 1919, *Golden Valley Progress*, Beach, North Dakota

173 "Neighboring Town News – Webster," August 7, 1919, *Fallon County Times*, Baker, Montana

174 178 181 189 198 "Coroner's Jury Charges Taylor with Murder in First Degree," August 8, 1919, *The Beach Advance*, Beach, North Dakota

175 "Trial at Beach of Sheriff and State's Attorney Drags Along; Mrs. Bowen Is Called to Stand," September 19, 1919, *The Bismarck Tribune*, Bismarck, North Dakota

176 "Hearing at Beach to Remove State Attorney and Sheriff Is Closed Suddenly; Fireworks Are Missing," September 20, 1919, *The Bismarck Tribune*, Bismarck, North Dakota

177 184 189 191 192 193 197 215 217 "4 Men Are Held in Jail for First Degree Murder," August 8, 1919, *Golden Valley Progress*, Beach, North Dakota

179 "Coroner's Jury Finds Bowen Was Slain by Taylor," August 2, 1919, *The Bismarck Tribune*, Bismarck, North Dakota

180 185 194 "Langer Office Not Blameless Fact Revealed," August 8, 1919, *Golden Valley Progress*, Beach, North Dakota

182 190 "Cattle Feud of Long Standing Was Reason for Bowen Killing," August 4, 1919, *The Fargo Forum*, Fargo, North Dakota

[253] "From Golden Valley County," October 25, 1922, *The Bismarck Tribune*, Bismarck, North Dakota

[254] "What the Organized Farmer Is Doing – North Dakota," September 22, 1919, *The Nonpartisan Leader*, Fargo, North Dakota

[255] "National Federation of League Women," January 5, 1920, *The Nonpartisan Leader*, Fargo, North Dakota

[256] "Aid for Mrs. M. K. Bowen," October 2, 1919, *The Bottineau Courant*, Bottineau, North Dakota

[257] "Auxiliary Writes," January 23, 1920, *Golden Valley Progress*, Beach, North Dakota

[258] "Langer Office Not Blameless Fact Revealed," August 8, 1919, *Golden Valley Progress*, Beach, North Dakota

[259] "Pastures Are Strewn with Cattle Bones," August 8, 1919, *Golden Valley Progress*, Beach, North Dakota

[260] [262] "Two Officers Are Removed," September 12, 1919, *The Washburn Leader*, Washburn, North Dakota

[261] "League May Enter County Politics," August 7, 1919, *The Bottineau Courant*, Bottineau, North Dakota

[263] "Six Suits for $25,000 Each," September 12, 1919, *The Washburn Leader*, Washburn, North Dakota

[264] "Testimony in Removal Cases Favors the Accused Officials," September 19, 1919, *The Beach Advance*, Beach, North Dakota

[265] "Facts in the Case of Removing County Officers," September 5, 1919, *The Beach Advance*, Beach, North Dakota

[266] "Governor Suspends 2 Beach Officials," September 5, 1919, *The Bowbells Tribune*, Bowbells, North Dakota

[267] "Counter Suits Will Be Filed in Beach Mess," September 4, 1919, *The Bismarck Tribune*, Bismarck, North Dakota

[268] "Frazier Must Reinstate Men He Kicked Out," January 21, 1920, *The Bismarck Tribune*, Bismarck, North Dakota

[269] "Farmer Demands Action," August 4, 1919, *Fargo Courier-News*, Fargo, North Dakota [reprinted in the *Golden Valley Progress*]

[270] "Langer May Face Impeachment Trial," August 8, 1919, *The Producers News*, Plentywood, Montana

[271] "Langer Begins Speaking Tour in Cow Country," January 15, 1920, *The Bismarck Tribune*, Bismarck, North Dakota

[272] "Murder of M. K. Bowen Is Reviewed," January 23, 1920, *Mandan Pioneer*, Mandan, North Dakota

The (Eventual Trial)

273 "Asks Early Bowen Trial," November 27, 1919, *Sioux County Pioneer*, Fort Yates, North Dakota

274 Minutes of Trial, January 27, 1920, Golden Valley Courthouse

275 "Bowen Case Goes Over to June 1," undated, approximately January 1920, *The Beach Advance*, Beach, North Dakota

276 Judge Lembke Order, June 1, 1920, Golden Valley Courthouse

277 Maud Bowen Affidavit, June 1, 1920, Golden Valley Courthouse

278 H. A. Mackoff Affidavit, June 1, 1920, Golden Valley Courthouse

279 Maud Bowen, Martin Blank, S. A. Smith Affidavits, June 4, 1920; E. O. Johnston Affidavit, June 1, 1920, Golden Valley Courthouse

280 Change of Venue Proceedings, June 4, 1920, Golden Valley Courthouse

281 "Bowen Case Will Be Tried in Stark Co.," undated, approximately June 1920, *The Beach Advance*, Beach, North Dakota

282 Order for Change of Place of Trial, June 24, 1920, Golden Valley Courthouse

283 Notice of Appeal, June 24, 1920, Golden Valley Courthouse

284 North Dakota Supreme Court Appeal Decision, November 9, 1920, Golden Valley Courthouse

285 286 C. H. Starke Affidavit, January 5, 1921, Adams County Courthouse

287 "League Editor Admits Guilt in Libel Case - Charges Are Dropped," June 22, 1921, *The Devils Lake World*, Devils Lake, North Dakota

289 Ennis Walter Taylor Affidavit, June 14, 1921, Adams County Courthouse

290 Criminal Information, June 27, 1920, Adams County Courthouse

291 Notice of Planned Witnesses for the State, September 16, 1920, Adams County Courthouse

292 296 "Jury Incomplete in Murder Trial," June 23, 1921, *The Fargo Forum*, Fargo, North Dakota

293 "Defense Covers up Nothing in Murder Trial," July 9, 1921, *Grand Forks Herald*, Grand Forks, North Dakota

294 297 298 299 "State Is Dealt Blow by Court in Preliminary to Murder Trial," June 24, 1921, *The Fargo Forum*, Fargo, North Dakota

288 295 "Bowen Murder Trial Is Begun," June 23, 1921, *Adams County Record*, Hettinger, North Dakota

[300] "Attorney for State in Bowen Case Ousted," June 24, 1921, *Grand Forks Herald*, Grand Forks, North Dakota

[301] "Trial of Offley Progressing Slow," June 30, 1921, *Adams County Record*, Hettinger, North Dakota

[302 303 304 305] "Witness Says Expense Paid," June 27, 1921, *The Fargo Forum*, Fargo, North Dakota

[306 308 310] "Bowen Trial Drags Along Many Testify," June 29, 1921, *The Bismarck Tribune*, Bismarck, North Dakota

[307 309] "Bowen Girl and Hired Man on Stand Today," June 28, 1921, *Grand Forks Herald*, Grand Forks, North Dakota

[311 312 314] "Testimony Dull in Bowen Trial Case Drags Along," June 30, 1921, *The Bismarck Tribune*, Bismarck, North Dakota

[313] "Former Sheriff Is on Stand in Trial of Offley," July 1, 1921, *Grand Forks Herald*, Grand Forks, North Dakota

[315 317] "Threats to Kill Bowen Were Uttered," July 1, 1921, *The Bismarck Tribune*, Bismarck, North Dakota

[316 318] "No Surprises in Bowen Case," July 7, 1921, *Adams County Record*, Hettinger, North Dakota

[319 321] "Widow Relates Bowen Killing at Hettinger," July 6, 1921, *The Bismarck Tribune*, Bismarck, North Dakota

[320 323 325 326 328 330] "Judge Summons Two Witnesses in Bowen Case," July 7, 1921, *The Bismarck Tribune*, Bismarck, North Dakota

[322] "Dr. Stough of Beach Dies; Ill a Week," September 13, 1920, *The Bismarck Tribune*, Bismarck, North Dakota

[324 327] "Stories Told of Bowen Shooting Conflict, Judge Calls Doctors," July 7, 1921, *The Fargo Forum*, Fargo, North Dakota

[329 332 353 354 356] "Sensational Testimony Adduced in Offley Trial," July 15, 1921, *The Beach Advance*, Beach, North Dakota

[331 333] "Four Charged with Murder to Be Placed on Witness Stand in Murder Trial, Lawyer Says," July 9, 1921, *The Bismarck Tribune*, Bismarck, North Dakota

[334 336 337 339 341] "Bowen Murder Trial in Progress at Hettinger," July 14, 1921, *The Ward County Independent*, Minot, North Dakota

[335 338 340] "Witness Says Wife of Dead Man Had Rifle," July 11, 1921, *The Bismarck Tribune*, Bismarck, North Dakota

[342 343 345] "M. K. Bowen Was 'Dangerous Man' Witness States at Murder Trial," July 12, 1921, *The Fargo Forum*, Fargo, North Dakota

[344] "Character of Bowen Assailed," July 12, 1921, *The Bismarck Tribune*, Bismarck, North Dakota

[346 349 351] "Bowen 'Bad Man' Say Witnesses," July 13, 1921, *The Fargo Forum*, Fargo, North Dakota

[347 348 350 352 355] "Witnesses Assail Bowen's Character," July 14, 1921, *Adams County Record*, Hettinger, North Dakota

[357] "Offley Placed on Stand in Murder Trial," July 14, 1921, *Grand Forks Herald*, Grand Forks, North Dakota

[358] "'Not Guilty' Says Jury…," July 22, 1921, *The Beach Advance*, Beach, North Dakota

[359] "D. R. Offley 'Not Guilty' Is Verdict in Bowen Case," July 21, 1921, *Adams County Record*, Hettinger, North Dakota

[360 361 362 364] "New Startling Testimony in Murder Trial," July 16, 1921, *Grand Forks Herald*, Grand Forks, North Dakota

[363] "Bowen Murder Case Bobs Up," May 19, 1926, *Grand Forks Herald*, Grand Forks, North Dakota

[365 366] "Bowen Case May Go to Jury Today," July 19, 1921, *Grand Forks Herald*, Grand Forks, North Dakota

[367] Clerk Minutes of Trial, July 19, 1921, Adams County Courthouse

[368 369 371] "Jury in Session Eight Hours; Window Berates Men on Street," July 20, 1921, *The Fargo Forum*, Fargo, North Dakota

[370 372 373] "Some Facts on the Bowen Trial," July 26, 1921, *Fargo Courier-News*, Fargo, North Dakota

Image of Hettinger High School Building, April 7, 1913, *The Fargo Forum*, Fargo, North Dakota

Photos and images property of the Bowen-Beach-Rustad-Lininger Family

Orphaned, then Dismissed

[374] "Many Cases to Be Tried Here in Dist. Court," December 6, 1921, *The Bismarck Tribune*, Bismarck, North Dakota

[375] "Murder Case Will Not Be Tried in City," December 19, 1922, *The Bismarck Tribune*, Bismarck, North Dakota

[376] "Criminal Cases Put Over for Few Days When the Docket Is Called," December 4, 1923, *The Bismarck Tribune*, Bismarck, North Dakota

[377] "Bowen Murder Case Bobs Up," May 19, 1926, *Grand Forks Herald*, Grand Forks, North Dakota

[378] "Famous Bowen Murder Cases, Long in Court, Are Dropped," January 15, 1927, *The Fargo Forum*, Fargo, North Dakota

[379] WWI and WWII Draft Registration Cards, National Archives, via ancestry.com

[380] "Liquor store license," July 24, 1941, *The Oregonian*, Portland, Oregon

[381] United States Social Security Records, via ancestry.com

[382] "Ollie News," October 18, 1934, *The Fallon County Times*, Baker, Montana

[383] United States Federal Census, 1930, via ancestry.com

[384] "Taylor Rites Held at White Sulphur," February 10, 1962, *The Billings Gazette*, Billings, Montana

Looking Back, Looking Forward

[385] "Seniors Into View," Dyke, Carol, May 19, 1994, *Fallon County Times*, Baker, Montana

[386] Written accounts by the Bowens' eldest daughter, Lois Bowen Beach; property of Bowen-Beach-Rustad-Lininger Family

[387] Personal account by Maud Plummer Bowen, *O'Fallon Flashbacks*, 1975, O'Fallon Historical Society, Baker, Montana

Image of Maud's brand, Montana State Library website, https://www.mtmemory.org/

Photos and images property of the Bowen-Beach-Rustad-Lininger Family

Key Influencers

[388] [390] [395] [398] [401] [403] [411] [412] State Historical Society of North Dakota website, https://www.history.nd.gov/

[389] [392] [394] The Bank of North Dakota Story website, https://thebndstory.nd.gov/

[391] "North Dakota Council of Defense Opens Interesting Executive Session Today," June 14, 1918, *The Bismarck Tribune*, Bismarck, North Dakota

[393] *The Story of the Nonpartisan League*, Russell, Charles Edward, May 1920, Harper & Brothers Publishers

[396] [397] [399] [400] [409] "Who Was Gov. Lynn Joseph Frazier?," Hylton, J. Gordon, July 18, 2012, Marquette University Law School website

[402] "Wild Bill," United States Senate website, https://www.senate.gov/

[404] [407] [410] "'Wild Bill' Langer: Revered and Reviled, He Made Great Impact," November 1, 1988, *The Fargo Forum*, Fargo, North Dakota

[405] "Ghosts Walk Near Beach," October 16, 1919, *The Weekly Times-Record*, Valley City, North Dakota

[406][421] "Counter Suits Will Be Filed in Beach Mess," September 4, 1919, *The Ward County Independent*, Minot, North Dakota

[408][415] "Burleigh County Anti-Townley Club Formed Yesterday," April 7, 1920, *The Bismarck Tribune*, Bismarck, North Dakota

[413][414][416] "R. F. Gallagher, Mandan Attorney, Judge, Succumbs," February 12, 1952, *The Bismarck Tribune*, Bismarck, North Dakota

[417][423] "Two-State Deaths - John I. Pierzina," January 19, 1957, *The Winona Daily News*, Winona, Minnesota

[418] "Governor Suspends 2 Beach Officials," September 5, 1919, *The Bowbells Tribune*, Bowbells, North Dakota

[419][422] "Two Officers Are Removed," September 12, 1919, *The Washburn Leader*, Washburn, North Dakota

[420] "Stark County Sheriff Weds," September 25, 1920, *The Bismarck Tribune*, Bismarck, North Dakota

[424] "Lee & Rice," December 12, 1913, *Golden Valley Chronicle*, Beach, North Dakota

[425] "Trial at Beach of Sheriff and State's Attorney Drags Along; Mrs. Bowen Is Called to Stand," September 19, 1919, *The Bismarck Tribune*, Bismarck, North Dakota

[426] "Harry L. Berry," State of North Dakota Courts website, https://www.ndcourts.gov/

[427][429][431][433] "John F. Sullivan, Mandan Attorney, 65, Dies Thursday," June 8, 1950, *The Bismarck Tribune*, Bismarck, North Dakota

[428][430][432] "John F. Sullivan I (1884 - 1950)," Mandan Historical Society, http://www.mandanhistory.org/

[434][435] Mackoff Kellogg Law Firm website, https://mackoff.com/

[436] "Boxcar Robber Held at Chicago; Three Years Chase," May 26, 1921, *Jamestown Weekly Alert*, Jamestown, North Dakota

[437] "Dr. Stough of Beach Dies; Ill a Week," September 13, 1920, *The Bismarck Tribune*, Bismarck, North Dakota

[438] "Lost One of the Quartette," July 6, 1905, *Jamestown Weekly Alert*, Jamestown, North Dakota

[439] Application for License before the Wisconsin Board Medical Examiners, 1902, via ancestry.com

[440] WWI and WWII Draft Registration Cards, National Archives, via ancestry.com

[441][446] "Obituaries – Dr. Charles J. Maercklein," October 14, 1961, *The Sheboygan Press*, Sheboygan, Wisconsin

[442] United States Federal Census, 1910, via ancestry.com

[443] [445] "Arrested on a Serious Charge," May 2, 1918, *The Bowman County Pioneer*, Bowman, North Dakota

[444] "Dr. C. J. Maercklein is under arrest," May 8, 1918, *The Fargo Forum*, Fargo, North Dakota

Images of Lynn Frazier, William Langer, State Historical Society of North Dakota website, https://www.history.nd.gov/

Image of R. F. Gallagher, June 10, 1920, *The Bismarck Tribune*, Bismarck, North Dakota

Image of H. L. Rice, December 12, 1913, *Golden Valley Chronicle*, Beach, North Dakota

Image of H. L. Berry, State of North Dakota Courts website, https://www.ndcourts.gov/

Image of John Sullivan, June 8, 1950, *The Bismarck Tribune*, Bismarck, North Dakota

Image of L. A. Simpson, June 5, 1914, *Golden Valley Chronicle*, Beach, North Dakota

Role of the Press

[447] State Historical Society of North Dakota website, https://www.history.nd.gov/

[448] *The Story of the Nonpartisan League*, Russell, Charles Edward, May 1920, Harper & Brothers Publishers

[449] "How Farmers Are Freeing Their Press," June 24, 1918, *The Nonpartisan Leader*, Fargo, North Dakota

[450] [474] "To Our Readers and Patrons," November 20, 1914, *Golden Valley Chronicle*, Beach, North Dakota

[451] "Will Sell for a Song," May 16, 1913, *Golden Valley Chronicle*, Beach, North Dakota

[452] "Editor Brinton Weds Miss Helena Peek," September 18, 1909, *The Dickinson Press*, Dickinson, North Dakota

[453] "District Court in Billings Co. Grinds Merrily," March 13, 1910, *The Bismarck Tribune*, Bismarck, North Dakota

[454] "Editor Brinton 'Not Guilty'," June 2, 1911, *The Devils Lake World*, Devils Lake, North Dakota

[455] "Chronicle at Beach Blown Up," October 8, 1912, *The Fargo Forum*, Fargo, North Dakota

[456] "Statement from Publisher," December 13, 1912, *Golden Valley Chronicle*, Beach, North Dakota

[457] "What Is Justice?," August 8, 1919, *Golden Valley Progress*, Beach, North Dakota

[458] "Murdered! Chief of Police Shot and Killed Fred Blumsun," June 20, 1913, *Golden Valley Chronicle*, Beach, North Dakota

[459 460] "Chronicle Editor Assaulted by Wand and Police," August 8, 1913, *Golden Valley Chronicle*, Beach North Dakota

[461] "Factionalism Wins!," September 12, 1913, *Golden Valley Chronicle*, Beach, North Dakota

[462] "Who's the Troublemaker?," August 15, 1913, *Golden Valley Chronicle*, Beach, North Dakota

[463] "Chronicle Man Candidate for Mayor," March 13, 1914, *Golden Valley Chronicle*, Beach, North Dakota

[464 466] "J. W. Brinton Elected Mayor," April 10, 1914, *Golden Valley Chronicle*, Beach, North Dakota

[465] "Cold-Blooded Attempt on Life of R. O. Zollinger," April 6, 1914, *The Beach Advance*, Beach, North Dakota

[467 471] "Brinton Removes City Officials," April 24, 1914, *Golden Valley Chronicle*, Beach, North Dakota

[468 470] "S. A. Smith," October 9, 1914, *Golden Valley Chronicle*, Beach, North Dakota

[469 472] "Communication to Beach Advance," October 2, 1914, *Golden Valley Chronicle*, Beach, North Dakota

[473] "To the Voters," November 6, 1914, *Golden Valley Chronicle*, Beach, North Dakota

Cartoon, June 17, 1918, *The Nonpartisan Leader*, Fargo, North Dakota

Image of J. Wells Brinton, circa 1931, *Political Prairie Fire* collection, North Dakota State Library, https://digitalhorizonsonline.org

Reference Maps

Maps of North Central United States/South Central Canada and State of North Dakota created by Kari Lininger-Downs

Plat map of Bull Run Township, property of Bowen-Beach-Rustad-Lininger Family

Individual Index

[475] "Carlisle to Have 1st National Bank," December 1, 1916, *Golden Valley Chronicle*, Beach, North Dakota,

[476] "Sheriff, State's Attorney and Alderman Take Hand Against Mayor Brinton's Police Officers," July 31, 1914, *Golden Valley Chronicle*, Beach, North Dakota